THE FIELD
BOOK OF CRICKET

THE FIELD
BOOK OF
CRICKET

From 1853 to the Present

Edited by
DAVID RAYVERN ALLEN

PELHAM BOOKS

PELHAM BOOKS

Published by the Penguin Group
27 Wrights Lane, London W8 5TZ, England
Viking Penguin, a division of Penguin Books USA Inc
375 Hudson Street, New York, NY 10014, USA
Penguin Books Australia Ltd, Ringwood, Victoria, Australia
Penguin Books Canada Ltd, 2801 John Street, Markham, Ontario, Canada L3R 1B4
Penguin Books (NZ) Ltd, 182–190 Wairau Road, Auckland 10, New Zealand

Penguin Books Ltd, Registered Offices: Harmondsworth, Middlesex, England

First Published 1991
1 3 5 7 9 10 8 6 4 2

Typeset in 10½/12pt Old Style
Printed and bound in Great Britain by
Butler & Tanner Ltd, Frome and London

A CIP catalogue record for this book is available from the British Library.

ISBN 0 7207 1895 3

Note: David Rayvern Allen's editorial comments appear in italics. Ed. refers to the editor of
The Field.

CONTENTS

ACKNOWLEDGEMENTS

The compiler would like to record his gratitude to the following who have helped in many ways. There is no order of merit, as all qualify for a first prize:

Simon Baseley, Michèle Norton, Ruth Elliot, Ann and Simon James, John Pawsey, Bunty Ireland, Staff at *The Field* offices and Westminster Central Library, the British Newspaper Library personnel at Colindale, Hilary Folkes, Roger Houghton, Jessamy Johnson, John Beaton and Arianne Burnette.

Recognition is due also to Jeremy Alexander, Major-General Valentine Boucher, Colin Cowdrey, William Deedes, Andrew Fraser, Edward Hart, Robin Marlar, Roy McKelvie, John Parker, Sidney Rogerson, David Smith and E. W. 'Jim' Swanton. Their felicitous contributions form part of what is to follow.

If, inadvertently, any names have been omitted the author and publishers apologise and will be pleased to make appropriate acknowledgement in future editions.

INTRODUCTION

The Field was first opened to discerning country gentlemen for a pricey six penn'orth in 1853, courtesy of Robert Smith Surtees, creator of Jorrocks. Surtees came from Durham sporting stock and so, not unnaturally, one of his ambitions for the new paper was to appeal to the common interests of the landowning and farming fraternity. These interests obviously encompassed a wide variety of outdoor life and recreation and before very long cricket was making regular appearances in its pages.

The game was represented by excellent engravings of such giants as Caesar, Caffyn, Box, Mynn, Felix, Clarke, Lillywhite and Wisden; discursive comment on the merits of the All-England Eleven and rival combinations; and arguments for changes in the rules. As the century progressed, so did the coverage on cricket. The printer, 'taking the measure' of the galleys for the sports pieces in what was proudly proclaimed to be the largest paper in Europe, would call out 'cricket 30 columns, turf 20, angling 18,' and so on.

In 1922, *The Field* took an introspective look at its own cricketing ancestry.

In the early days of *The Field* the Cricket editor was Charles Box, who was also for some years the Cricket correspondent to the *Times*. His book, *The English Game of Cricket*, which was published by *The Field*, is still regarded as one of the classics of the game, although because of its large size it is not as widely read as it would have been if its bulk had been less. Possibly because of this very reason its contents have been extremely useful to many of the compilers of books since his time. Although in build and appearance Charles Box was so much like the famous Tom Box, the old Sussex wicket-keeper, that the two men were often taken to be brothers, they were not in any way related. Charles Box was regarded by his friends as a 'character', and his many quaint sayings were quoted with great glee. Once when he was at Canterbury during the 'Week' he was watching the batting of Mr C. I. Thornton, the great hitter. It so happened that Mr Thornton was in his very best form and made some astonishing hits. After a time he drove a ball far out of the ground, and when he was attempting another big drive the bat slipped out of his hands and went after the ball. Whereupon Box said sadly, 'And this is what they call cricket these days'.

The next Cricket editor was the late H.O. Moore, who was musical, a well-known athlete, a humorist, and a maker of many friends. In a short time it was necessary for him to divide his attention between racing and cricket, and the chief responsibility of the cricket department fell on the shoulders of another member of the staff who had assisted in several other departments, racing, coursing, athletics, and football, as well as cricket. When the acting Cricket editor became chief sub-editor of *The Field* his place was taken by the late E. T. Sachs, who was well known in the athletic world. A few years later Sachs was transferred to the racing department, his place as Cricket editor being taken by A. W. Browne, who had been editor of *Pastime* and *The Cricket Field* newspaper. Browne was one of the many good cricketers who only lacked opportunity to have been in the front rank. As a bowler he had the accuracy, the subtle changes in pace, the ability to make the ball break both ways a little, and the same peculiarity in flight as Alfred Shaw. He was, however, always diffident as to his skill and preferred to play in club cricket. It almost invariably happened that when he had to bowl to a first-class batsman of note he promptly got him out, but nine times out of ten he persuaded the batsman that he was merely the victim of hard luck. Browne was also a batsman who took a great deal of getting out. His solutions to the difficult problems which are always occurring in connection with the game were models of lucidity and sound reasoning, and no one was ever able to point out that one of his decisions was wrong. During Browne's period a drastic alteration was made in *The Field* cricket. Hitherto it had been practically confined to long and careful descriptions of all first-class matches and occasional articles by well-known authorities. But the increase in the number of first-class matches, the difficulties of finding new correspondents of the right kind, and the complaints of readers that the type was too small, brought about the curtailment of the reports and the introduction of the Notes, which from the first were the outcome of direct observation on the cricket field. Browne's sight unfortunately began to fail him in the year before the war, and when in 1915 he became totally blind he was succeeded by the present Cricket editor.

When *The Field* was in its infancy there were few first-class cricket matches, and it may frankly be stated that some of them were not very well described. Often when it has been necessary to refer back to a very early number of *The Field* for its account of an epoch-making event of the period, or a marvellous performance by a famous player, the result has been a little disconcerting. Thus there would be a detailed description of doings of little comparative importance, and the one thing which greatly mattered would be treated in the most cavalier manner. Thus almost every hit in Mr X's innings of 25 would be described, but of Mr Grace's famous innings in the same match there would be merely a remark that his innings was the theme of general admiration among the cognoscenti. Once when it was necessary to know what *The Field* had said about a particular much-discussed match between Oxford and Cambridge, no record of the game could be found in *The Field* of the date in which it ought to have appeared. Nor was there a word of reference to the match in the next week's issue. An experienced member of the staff said, 'Better look a little further,' and in the following week the score was given without the bowling analysis, but with an introduction stating that the game was played a week or two ago and was of more than ordinary interest. These lax methods quickly gave place to system, and it became, and has always been, a point of honour to avoid mistakes. Such, however, is the frailty of human nature that mistakes have occurred from time to time, one of the most vexatious being the publication some twenty years ago of the details of the great match, EATON v. HARROW. Cricket readers of *The Field* have always been very quick to discover a mistake, and at the same time have been most generous in letting us down very easily. Once or twice we have scored. For instance, after we had given a few figures in connection with the leg-before-wicket rule, a distinguished Professor of Mathematics wrote very nicely but firmly to point out that our figures were entirely wrong, and to prove this statement he enclosed figures of his own. With the modesty of injured innocence we were able to ask him whether he would still like his letter to be published, or whether perchance in compiling his figures he had for the moment forgotten that a cricket ball is not a point, but a globe with a considerable diameter. The Professor did not reply. One of our greatest and at the same time most interesting difficulties used to be in checking the figures of scores, which in past days we were able to give in multitudes. It is a curious point that the more distinguished or famous was the sender of a score the more likely it was to be wrongly added up.

W. A. Bettesworth, Ardingly College, Sussex, Gentlemen v. Players at Brighton in 1881, quick-footed batsman and finger spinner, was a schoolmaster who had joined the paper in 1904. Bettesworth was an assiduous recorder and commentator. It was he who drew the diagrams showing bowlers' approach to the wicket and strokes that the batsmen had made.

Another who wrote on cricket was A. C. M. Croome, the Gloucestershire middle order batsman, whose life had been saved by Dr W. G. Grace when he (Croome), in attempting to stop a boundary, had impaled his neck on railings at Old Trafford in 1887. Then there was Eric Parker, formerly of the St James Gazette. Parker became editor from 1931 to 1937. His books on game-rearing, English wildlife and the history of cricket showed how perfectly attuned he was to the life of countrymen. He used to enjoy recounting how, as a boy at Eton when walking through woods with birds' eggs perched precariously in his top hat, he had come across his headmaster taking a Sunday afternoon stroll. Parker knew that he would have to doff his hat and was terrified that the eggs would smash on the ground, revealing his illaudable action. Fortunately, he managed to perform the manoeuvre on the side furthest away from the 'venerable beak' and the eggs remained in place.

A. Wallis Myers, the *Daily Telegraph* lawn tennis correspondent and F. I. Watson, one-time assistant to Bettesworth, were among others who wrote on cricket for *The Field*. So too, of course, did the unsurpassable Neville Cardus in the 1930s, and that doyen of cricket writers E. W. 'Jim' Swanton, largely after the Second World War.

A prince of Edwardian raconteurs, Colonel Cyril Foley, claimed much space on the game. Foley pooh-poohed batsmen who complained of bodyline tactics and one day, looking at a photograph of fieldsmen tightly gathered around the wicket, exclaimed: 'My, shouldn't I have enjoyed torpedoing that lot!'

Over the years *The Field* has enjoyed an impressive mixed band of cricketing luminaries: their noble Lords Tennyson and Cobham, 'Shrimp' Leveson-Gower, 'Plum' Warner, Douglas Jardine, Arthur Gilligan, Humphrey Daniel, Leonard Crawley, Jeremy Alexander, Ivo Tennant, John Parker and Colin Cowdrey. Lustrous names – and the list far from complete as there are also many excellent anonymous contributions.

In the pages that follow, some of their words will reflect the cricket of their time and of an earlier age. They all wrote for a paper that has been around for longer than *Wisden's Almanack*, and which started life more or less at the same time as cricket became an institution.

I
HISTORICAL FEATURES

If one believes that 'the game of history is usually played by the best and the worst over the heads of the majority in the middle' then the history of the game, in this case cricket, should be surely exempt from such stricture. The telling of the tale should never fail to involve the reader, whether from the pen of an ebullient 'misplaced Regency Buck', Lord Tennyson, or from the frail 'Herodotus' of the game's highways and byways,

F. S. Ashley-Cooper.

SOME NOTES ON OLD-TIME CRICKET

BY F. S. ASHLEY-COOPER

IT is only a few seasons since a vigorous crusade was carried on against the use of bats exceeding the statute width. (In one match, at the Oval, a player was twice sent back from the wicket before he was allowed to commence his innings owing to the fact that the bats with which he appeared did not satisfy the requirements of the gauge.) Supervision has not been so strict recently as it was just about that time, yet if law 5 is to be respected every effort should be made to prevent it from being violated, for it is a well-known fact that many a bat which will pass the gauge before a long score has been obtained with it will not do so afterwards. In the oldest laws of cricket extant—those of 1744—nothing is said concerning the dimensions of the bat, a state of things which is not very surprising when it is recalled that in those far-off days the bat was shaped like a hockey stick, and that, as probably all the bowling was fast and along the ground, the batsman, finding 'a short life and a merry one' a good maxim, would not be likely to incumber himself with an unwieldy weapon. In the course of the game's development the length ball was discovered, and naturally batsmen found their old style of play rendered of little avail; hence to meet the innovation the bat with a straight pod was evolved, and it is of interest to note that the limitation in width to $4\frac{1}{4}$ in. was laid down in 1774 and has been adhered to ever since. The Hambledon Club possessed an iron gauge, by which all bats of suspected dimensions were tested, and this interesting relic could be seen in the village until about thirty years ago, when it was taken away by 'a gentleman who took a fancy to it'. In some of the eighteenth-century paintings and prints the width of the blade of the bat is to be found exaggerated to an extent which is nothing less than remarkable. Morland, if one-half of the paintings attributed to him were really his, was a great offender in this respect, but as, in order to save himself trouble, he was in the habit of making several copies from the pictures he liked best, or which he considered would prove the most remunerative, it was only natural that a mistake, once made and not detected immediately, should be repeated time after time. But much may be forgiven so great a genius, even by the historian, especially when it is remembered that a great deal of his work was accomplished at high pressure and under conditions which, to say the least, were not conducive to accuracy in detail. One of his representations of cricket was painted at the Cricketers' Inn, Chertsey, in interesting though characteristic circumstances. Being presented by the landlord with a

3

bill at a decidedly inopportune moment, he bolted himself in his bedroom and on one of the sheets painted a scene of a match in progress, and in this manner liquidated the debt. The introduction of the third stump was not long in following the change in shape of the bat. During a single-wicket match between Five of Hambledon and Five of England in the Artillery Ground, London, on May 22, 1775, John Small went in last man to get 14 runs, and obtained them. At the conclusion of the match the Duke of Dorset, being desirous of complimenting the batsman on his skill, made him a present of a fine violin. It was noticed, however, that Lumpy, the player who

> .... did allow,
> He ne'er could pitch but o'er a brow,

on three occasions bowled right through Small's wicket, and as this was considered very hard on the bowler the innovation mentioned was decided upon. In some quarters it was thought that the game would thereby be shortened, but it was rightly argued that the batsman, knowing the danger there would be in missing a straight ball with three stumps instead of two behind him, would redouble his care and his innings be better played. The introduction of this improvement was not effected at once, but the accounts which state that it was delayed until 1780 are certainly incorrect, for it was expressly recorded that in the match on the Laleham Burway ground, Chertsey, between Chertsey and Coulsdon, on Thursday, Sept. 6, 1776, the wicket consisted of three stumps and two bails. Furthermore, the *Hampshire Chronicle* of Sept. 7, 1776, announced that 'Another match of cricket will be played on Broad-Halfpenny Down, at Hambledon, on Monday, five of a-side, after a new plan, when they are to have three stumps instead of two, in order to shorten the game.' The score of the game has not been preserved, but the experiment evidently gave satisfaction, for in the following June a wicket of three stumps was used in the chief match of the year—Hambledon v. England, when James Aylward played his historic innings of 167 and Hambledon scored 403 and won by an innings and 168 runs. When the incident which caused the innovation occurred Small was beyond dispute the finest batsman in the country, and it is probable that had it involved any other player the alteration would not have been effected as soon as it was. It is a tribute to Small's skill that, although the shape of the bat was changed and the third stump added to the wicket whilst he was in his prime, and he was thereby compelled entirely to change his mode of play, he maintained his reputation. One can imagine the disappointment of Lumpy on that May afternoon 135 years ago, for Small was seldom clean bowled. In a report of the match between Hambledon and England at Bishopsbourne Paddock in August, 1772, it was stated that 'Lumpy had the honour of bowling out Small, which had not been done for some years.' In connection with his skill an amusing anecdote may be told. The great player was always accompanied to the important matches by his wife, who had a belief that if she did not attend the Hambledonians would suffer defeat. She always made her appearance with a green umbrella of enormous dimensions, which she would flourish excitedly in order to signal her husband's every hit, shouting the while, 'Run, man, run; you'll be out!'

It is not a little remarkable that, whereas much attention has been given to the dimensions of the bat and the wicket, the law makers have never considered it necessary or even advisable to deal with the question of the weight of the bails. In the early days of the game, when the wicket contained only two stumps, there was, of course, but a single bail, and for very many years following the introduction of the third stump the two bails to surmount each wicket were invariably supplied by the manufacturers in one piece, which the cricketers or umpires were left to divide. The operation was generally effected by means of a more or less haphazard snap, the consequence being that quite as often as not the two ends which rested on the middle stump were splintered. This circumstance, and the fact that the bails were generally lavishly coated in varnish, which would melt in the sun, often enabled a batsman to continue his innings when, having received from the bowler a ball which beat him, he had the satisfaction of seeing it strike the wicket without causing a bail to be dislodged. In order to guard against such an occurrence some old cricketers—the late Mr Fred Gale was of the number—made a point of diving the projecting ends of the bails into the ground, the intention being that they should, by possessing a light covering of earth, be made as impervious as possible to the sun's rays. Other persons overcame the difficulty by providing bails of indiarubber, which could be trusted to respond satisfactorily when one of the stumps was struck. Nowadays it seldom happens that the projecting ends are varnished, and therefore a difficulty—not a particularly serious one, it must be acknowledged—with which our fathers had to contend has been removed. On a few occasions the question has arisen, 'What course should be pursued when, owing to the force of the wind, the bails cannot be maintained in position?' The annals of first class cricket provide two solutions—the one, to dispense with them entirely; the other, to use iron bails. At Scarborough some of the latter are always held in readiness, and they have been requisitioned in more than one Festival.

It is probable that, so far as costume is concerned, present-day cricket compares as favourably with that of the past as in any other respect. The modern dress may not be so picturesque as the old, but that it is

appropriate to the requirements of the time probably none will be found
to question. From an artistic point of view there is much to be said in
favour of the light blue uniform affected by the M.C.C. in the eighteenth
century, and the Hambledon players, who were dressed in sky-blue
coats, with black velvet collars, and 'C.C.' (Cricketing Club) engraved
on their buttons, must have presented a pleasing sight in the field,
especially as their dress was completed with knee breeches, silk stockings, silver-buckled shoes, and velvet caps. It is not difficult to imagine
what a sensation would be caused if the Kent team entered the field at
Canterbury so attired; the novelty would in all probability cause such a
rush, especially of caricaturists, that the receipts would prove enormous
even for that particular side. (Perhaps the committees of those clubs
which have experienced a heavy loss recently will consider the advis-
ability of acting upon the suggestion.) The tall hat, the greatest mon-
strosity which was ever permitted to disfigure a cricket ground, was in
vogue for some decades during the first half of the nineteenth century,
but during that period sportsmen rowed, ran, shot, and perhaps even
slept in tall hats. 'Gentlemen,' the faithful chroniclers of cricket have
recorded, 'wore white hats', but, being ridiculed and called postboys,
discontinued the fashion. Then came the era, to recall which one need
not have reached the age of three score years and ten, of round hats,
still termed 'bowlers', with which one almost naturally associates
spotted and striped shirts. It was the last named which excited the
wrath of Mr Fred Gale. 'Do not be a zebra; it is low,' he wrote, and the
sight of a scratch twenty-two attired in all the colours of the rainbow
taking the field against the A.E.E. or another of the hydra-headed E.'s
was almost painful to the eyes. The spotted shirt enjoyed a long reign,
and had not disappeared from county cricket by so recent a date as
1880. For many seasons the Oxford and Cambridge teams wore shirts
of dark and light blue respectively. The former's colours originated
with Charles Wordsworth and Tom Garnier, afterwards Bishop of St
Andrews and Dean of Lincoln respectively. Both were in the Oxford
boat of 1829, and, discussing what uniform should be worn by the crew,
chose the Christ Church guernsey (four of the members belonging to
the House), only with a broader and darker stripe. Hence the origin of
'dark blue', which was almost immediately afterwards adopted for the
eleven. Cambridge obtained their colours, first pink and then light blue,
from the King's scholars and town boys respectively of Westminster.
Almost, if not quite, the last member of either University eleven to enter
the field at Lord's in a coloured—a Harlequin—shirt was Mr Russell
Walker; as he also wore a pot hat one can believe the report which
stated that his appearance created almost a sensation. Scarcely less
excitement was caused when, ten or a dozen years later, Mr H. M. Sims

fielded for Yorkshire at Bramall-lane attired in his Cambridge blazer. His appearance was by no means to the taste of the outspoken Sheffield crowd, which advised him in stentorian tones to 'Tak' off thi shirt!' The banter was thoroughly good natured, though disconcerting, and it was in all probability on the latter account that the fieldsman when at length a catch came to him dropped it. There was a death-like silence for a couple of seconds, and then the crowd bayed in unison, though not in so good humoured a way as before, '*Nah* will thee tak' off thi shirt?' Sims was then a stranger to the frequenters of Bramall-lane, but it was not long ere Yorkshire crowds, recognising his worth both as cricketer and as man, took him to their hearts, light blue blazer and all.

July 1934

TWO HUNDRED YEARS OF CRICKET

BY F. I. WATSON

Sevenoaks Re-Stages an Old-Time Match

LET us turn from the rigours of Test and County cricket of the present day and look back down 200 years of the game; for next week the Sevenoaks Vine Cricket Club is celebrating the bi-centenary of cricket at Sevenoaks with a series of matches and other special functions, culminating in a match to be played on Saturday, July 21st, in the costumes of 1734 and, as far as may be practicable, according to the rules and customs of that period.

The earliest record of cricket at Sevenoaks is a paragraph in the *London Evening Post* of September 10th–12th, 1734, reporting that 'We hear from Sevenoaks in Kent, that on Friday last an extraordinary Cricket Match was played there between the Gentlemen of Kent and Sussex. Lord Middlesex, Lord John Sackville, etcetera, played for Kent, and Sir William Gage, etcetera, for Sussex. The game ended to a very great Nicety in favour of the Kentish Gentlemen, but had so many diverting Turns in it, that the Lovers of that Diversion esteem it to be the best that has been played for many years.'

Here were names that were to live long in the history of Sevenoaks cricket. Lord Middlesex was Charles Sackville, eldest son of Lionel Cranfield Sackville, first Duke of Dorset, while Lord John Sackville was his second son. Lord Middlesex became second Duke in 1765, and was succeeded by his nephew, John Frederick Sackville, who ensured the continuity of Sevenoaks cricket by giving to the town the Vine ground by deed of trust 'to be a Cricket Ground for ever.' He was himself a great cricket enthusiast, playing for Kent and keeping in his employ at Knole many of the famous cricketers of the day. He afterwards became British Ambassador to the Court of France. Nyren describes him as a 'pretty player', excelling in the field at slip.

Kent played almost continuously on the Vine from 1771 till about 1829, and England played there in 1773 and 1777...

I know of no claim to dispute that of Sevenoaks Vine as having the longest *continuous* history in the country. [*The Hon. Artillery Ground in the City of London has had a comparably long existence, though perhaps not on as regular a basis.*] I am indebted to Lieut.-Colonel J. K. Dunlop, hon. secretary of the Bi-Centenary Week Committee, for some interesting particulars of the ground and the match, which is designed to reproduce the dress and methods of 200 years ago. The committee have expended a great deal of care and research to produce not only the correct costumes but also the bats, wickets and equipment of the period, and it is believed that this is the first time such a faithful reproduction has been attempted.

And lest we might repine with Andrew Lang:

> 'Ah, where be Beldham now and Brett,
> Barber, and Hogsflesh, where be they?'

we shall have actual names of that match of 200 years ago at Sevenoaks reproduced in the persons of Major-General the Lord Sackville, who will play with 'ten other Gentlemen of Kent', and Captain the Viscount Gage, who will lead 'ten other Gentlemen of Sussex'. Colonel Dunlop tells me, too, that Lord Sackville is bringing out the old family coach, and will arrive in it, with Viscount Gage and one or two other cricketers. So I shall hope to forget the world and go to Sevenoaks next Saturday.

July 1934

ROUND THE WICKETS

The Old-time Spirit of Sevenoaks

WHEN Lord Sackville drove on to the Vine cricket ground at Sevenoaks last Saturday in the old family coach and the players, umpires and scorers assembled for the old-time match in celebration of the bi-centenary of cricket at Sevenoaks, you could picture through the mists of time the scene and the spirit of the early players who pitched their wickets on the Vine 200 years ago. It was a wonderfully realistic effort on the part of the Vine Club. The players, in their knee breeches and stockings, buckle shoes and wigs, might have stepped straight out of one of the old prints of early cricket, and they played as their forerunners of 200 years ago played—with two forked sticks and a six-inch bail as a wicket, with bats, if not 200 years old, at least as ancient looking, and without pads or gloves. There were, too, the umpires in snuff-coloured breeches and coats, the scorers seated on three-legged stools some 40 yds. from the wickets busily cutting notches on cherry-wood sticks as runs were made—though one fears that they never could quite keep up with the actual rate of scoring and round the ground strolled ladies in crinolines—were they just as pretty 200 years ago? (the ladies, I mean, of course)—and gallant gentlemen in the elegant dress of the same period.

The Vine ground itself bears the real stamp of antiquity in the game. It might still be the village green. Bounded on two sides by a road and enclosed by a single wooden rail, it is surrounded by trees. From one side you look, over the roof of a cottage, to the wooded slopes of the North Downs. On other sides ivy-covered houses seem to nod pleasantly to the pretty little pavilion. There is a distinct slope on the ground, of which we may be sure the old bowlers took full advantage in choosing their wickets, as would the 'batters' who ran out all their hits. In Saturday's match, between 'Major-General the Lord Sackville and ten other Gentlemen of Kent', and 'Captain the Viscount Gage and ten other Gentlemen of Sussex', the rules of 1744, the earliest known rules, were observed. The bowling was all under-hand and the batting was all hitting—as, indeed, Old Nyren says it used to be. And the players were able to show how well the old-shaped bats could drive.

The bowling was nearly all along the ground—true again to history— and once or twice the ball passed between the stumps without removing the bail, as it used sometimes to do to the joy of the batsman, who was not out unless the bail was struck off. In the end Viscount Gage's team scored 123 and Lord Sackville's team 197 for seven wickets, and so the match ended 'to a very great Nicety in favour of the Kentish Gentlemen,' as the *London Evening Post* said of the match played in 1734. What is more, a very large number of spectators had as enjoyable and entertaining an afternoon's cricket as they could wish for.

April 1949

SIDELIGHTS ON CRICKET HISTORY
BY F. I. WATSON

Unpublished recollections of Alfred Mynn and Fuller Pilch

CRICKET history resounds with the names of Alfred Mynn and Fuller Pilch, for they were unquestionably two of the greatest and most popular players of their time. They were contemporaries in a glorious period of Kentish cricket, when the county team met and beat the rest of England more than once. A hundred or so years ago they were in their heyday—days when cricket still retained much of its nativity [*sic*], before overarm bowling had been born, when pads and gloves for the batsmen were novelties scorned by many players.

We are indebted mainly to a few old cricket chroniclers like Charles Box, William Denison and the Rev. James Pycroft for what little is known about them. Recently I discovered some unpublished recollections of both players among old private papers and letters that have lain neglected for many years. In faded writing, these old papers record incidents in the lives of the two great players in a way that kindles the imagination.

Among them were four foolscap pages written in a large hand and headed 'Reminiscences of N. Pilch'. There were three brothers Pilch, of whom N. [*Nathaniel*] Pilch and W. [*William*] Pilch were first-rate cricketers but attained nothing like the fame of Fuller, the youngest, whom Denison described as 'one of the brightest luminaries of the cricket world.' They were Norfolk born, tailors by trade, and all three played for the Holt Club, then one of the strongest in the country.

The three brothers were together in the Holt team against the M.C.C. in the historic match at Lord's in 1820, when W. Ward, for the M.C.C., made the astonishing score of 278, which remained for 105 years the highest individual score made at Lord's. Fuller Pilch, then a lad of 17, made his first appearance at Lord's in this match and at once impressed good judges by his promise.

The reminiscences of N. Pilch were apparently written by someone from Pilch's dictation when he was a very old man (as far as I know there is no record of his age when he died). He says: 'I am afraid I cannot tell you much, for it is a long time ago and my memory, especially for names, isn't good for much. Brother Fuller was the youngest of us three. We was all born at Brinton, you know. The Holt Club was fit to play with any club in the Kingdom. We used to play up there on the heath. It was all heath then, and Lor' bless me, how quick brother Fuller was in making his runs.

'Fuller's first match at Lord's I remember well, and Squire Ward's great score. He gave a chance back to brother William when he had made but twenty. William used to twist the ball a good deal—came in from leg—and Mr Ward he drove one back with a great deal of spin on it, and William he thought it was coming this side, but the work on it made it come here you see, and he dropped it. Then there was another chance I thought I was going to get to, but I couldn't manage it. However, in a long innings there's always something.'

It is noteworthy that N. Pilch says the three brothers were born at Brinton, whereas the old chroniclers say that Fuller Pilch was born at Horningtoft. The two villages are actually some miles apart, but Brinton is only about three miles from Holt, whereas Horningtoft lies about 15 miles away.

N. Pilch goes on to refer to the famous single-wicket matches between Fuller and Tom Marsden, of Sheffield, a left hander who had put out a challenge to play any man in England. He was no match for Fuller, who in two innings scored 77 to Marsden's 7 and in the return match scored 190 to Marsden's 62. The only comment N. Pilch makes is: 'How pleased we were when Fuller beat him.'

Pilch mentions incidents connected with matches against York, which always aroused great interest, for Yorkshire teams were among the most enthusiastic in the country. Pilch says: 'I remember the 1836 match against York as if it were yesterday. I said I never would take a team down again without a gentleman would undertake it with me; the expense, you know, sir, in those days was so great. And then one day I came across Squire Bagge in the street and he says, Pilch, you may count on me for Yorkshire, you know; and then I knew I was right. It was a good match, too. I remember catching Dearman at long leg. I placed myself just right for Dearman, but I could only just reach it. We ought to have won that match if there had been anyone to stay with Fuller.'

Squire Bagge was a well-known amateur cricketer of Norfolk who did much to foster the game. Dearman was one of the leading Yorkshire players, an all-rounder from Sheffield. Pilch voices a wistful memory of another Yorkshire match: 'Aye, and that '34 match, too, when Fuller made his 153 not out. It was drawn on the Friday owing to rain. Fuller was well in and he'd have soon pulled them off if the others had kept their wickets up. Squire Rippingall was mad that we stopped, but what could we do? Just think of the expense of stopping over the Sunday. Fuller was in fine-form that year. He made 87 not out and 73, as well as his 153 not out, against York, and 105 for England against Sussex. We used to have good matches at Blickling in old days. Squire Mott was a fine player at that time, and so was Squire Upcher, a fine off-hitter. Norfolk was a famous cricketing county in those days, equal to any in England.' Pilch adds a final tribute to his brother William as 'the first man I've heard who ever kept averages.'

The Squires Rippingall, Mott and Upcher, mentioned by Pilch, were all enthusiastic amateur players of Norfolk, and the Rippingalls were well-known as a cricketing family. It is one of the curiosities of cricket that Norfolk should never again have been able to equal the deeds of those days and, indeed, has never since risen to the status of a first-class county in championship cricket.

A bundle of letters which I unearthed were written by N. Felix, who was contemporary with Alfred Mynn and one of his closest friends. Felix (whose real name was Nicholas Wanostrocht), was not only a very fine cricketer, but wrote thoughtfully on the game. A Surrey man by birth, he played with Alfred Mynn in Kent and England teams on many occasions.

The letters were written some years after Felix had ceased to play in first-class cricket, about 1852. He writes with a simple grace about himself and his life in retirement as well as about the game that he loved. The first of the letters was written in 1861, on hearing of the death of Alfred Mynn, 'one of the noblest specimens of manliness and courage combined with all that was becoming in a man.'

He continues: 'From the first moment of our introduction we chimed in together and every time we met only cemented our friendship. I fought by his side—and I have been enlisted to oppose him—but the same spirit of kindness ever prevailed. Many a time he has bowled me a ball that, as he said, "would have bowled six men out", and instead of feeling annoyed with me for stopping it (although at that moment against him) he would pat me with his dear old hand and say "Well done, my little man." As you have truly said, he had, he could have had, no enemies. This same high-minded sentiment prevailed throughout his character.'

Felix then refers to the time when Mynn came near to losing his leg as a result of blows from a cricket ball; he was in fact kept out of the game for two years by his injuries. Felix says: 'In the days of Redgate (a fast bowler), Alfred Mynn played at Leicester (for South against North). He obtained over 100 runs (125 not out). During the innings he received on the inside of his right knee (in those days no pads were worn) numberless blows from the ball. Inflammation set up in his leg and he was obliged to lay up at an inn in St Martin's Lane. I called in one day after the surgeons had been, and I shall never forget the smile which played upon his fine handsome face as he told me that the surgeons had agreed not to take his leg off. I have seen him under almost every circumstance of trial and trouble, and his bearing was in strict accordance with all that has been written upon the subject of "tribulation working patience." With the gigantic stature unequalled in symmetry there was combined the docility of a child.'

Alfred Mynn could have had no better tribute to his memory. All his contemporaries agreed in extolling his great skill as a player and his kindliness and high temperament as a man.

Felix was famous for his cutting, and lost no opportunity of advocating a stance at the wicket similar to that of the *en garde* position in fencing. In 1872, some years after he had been stricken with paralysis, he wrote: 'I read the remarks of that wonderful batsman, Grace, and although I honour him for his great perseverance in practising, as he must have done, yet with all this vast accumulation of acknowledged superiority as a batsman, I am as obstinate as ever in adhering to the opinions with which I worried the cricketing world some years ago, touching the position of *en garde* at the wicket, with the knees slightly bent.

'Grace has objected to my opinion with all due delicacy, and somewhat shelters himself under the banner of the Rev. J. Pycroft—who, *mirabile dictu*, suffers a diagram of this attitude to appear in the "Register", with the toe of the right foot overlapping the line supposed to pass to the opposite wicket—and therefore and thereby endangering his position, even with a good and honest umpire. When I read my manuscript over to that wonderfully clever man and excellent cricketer, the late W. Ward, he gave his hearty consent to what I had written on that point.'

It is not clear whether the Grace referred to by Felix was W. G. or E. M. W. G. would then be a man of 24, in the flood of his fame, and he would certainly have disagreed with the *en garde* position at the wicket; there was never a suggestion of bent knee in his stance.

In another letter of 1872, Felix writes about tie matches. He says: 'I have often been in tie matches, when every poor fellow was in a state of delirium tremens. Old Lillywhite, at Marylebone, once lost a match which should have been a tie by drawing in most of the field close up to the wickets, to intimidate or otherwise. Whereas, had he left the field alone, Walter Mynn, the last man in, would have been caught easily at the point. Caffyn, at Newark, lost us a three days' match by violently throwing at and missing the wicket, causing an overthrow, when by giving the ball to Box (wicket-keeper) the tie would have saved dishonour.'

In an undated letter, Felix comments on what was evidently one of the earlier attempts to devise a rule of qualification for players in county matches. Referring to the practice of his day, he says: 'My dear old friend, Alfred Mynn, was anxious to meet the views of one Houghton, the then proprietor of the Oval, in getting up a match Surrey v. Kent. For some time it was a matter of dispute as to the side I was to play upon. At last Surrey allowed me to play for Kent, and as fortune would have it, I was very instrumental in gaining the match against my native county. The cricketing world thought and spoke against me; but the words "mutual consent" protected me from further annoyance.

'In older days we always used to say "county first", and this held good in the selection of a batsman or bowler. Of course, excepting by "mutual consent" you would not suffer your best bowler or batsman to be employed against you.'

Qualification by 'mutual consent' was a typical instance of the simple understandings, rather than rules, which then governed the movements of players. It strikes a notable contrast with the present rigid rules of qualification, which have sometimes kept a player out of first-class cricket for a whole two years while he qualified for a county by residence.

March 1948

FIFTY YEARS OF CRICKET

BY H. D. G. LEVESON-GOWER

The game past and present, some questions and answers

BY a strange coincidence, and at the same time a very happy one, this year brings three jubilee anniversaries in my cricketing life. In February, 1898, I received an invitation to serve on the M.C.C. Committee; in the following May I was elected a member of the Surrey County Cricket Club; and next September I shall have been identified with the Scarborough Cricket Festival for fifty years.

To be asked to become a member of the M.C.C. Committee is naturally a singular compliment. It came as a great surprise to me, for at the time I had not yet attained my twenty-fifth birthday. I was, therefore, very fortunate, for membership of the Committee brought me in contact with many famous cricketers of fifty years ago, and gave me an insight into the administration of the game and the problems which such an important cricket body has to deal with, experience which has been of much value to me. I think I can claim the distinction of being the only member of the M.C.C. alive to-day who has served on this Committee with four secretaries; Henry Perkins, Sir Francis Lacey, W. Findlay and the present secretary, Colonel Rait-Kerr. Perkins was just about to retire when I joined, but I am glad to have had the opportunity of meeting him in his official position, if only for a few months. M.C.C. have always shown ripe judgment in their choice of secretaries and assistant secretaries. In his admirable book on Lord's Sir Pelham Warner has laid full stress on this point.

I have been asked a number of questions that no doubt have been put to many who have been associated with cricket over a long period. How does the game to-day compare with that of fifty years ago? Were the cricketers of that era more skilful than those of 1948? Were the wickets more difficult then, than they are at the present time? Does cricket still maintain its popularity? To all these questions I will attempt to give a general answer.

With regard to the 'game' itself there is really no change. It is still 'cricket' with the same definition. It is staged with the same keenness at the schools, on the village greens, at the Universities, in County cricket, in Test matches and in club games. Its popularity is as great as, and probably greater than, at any time in its history. Interest is more widespread, due in no small measure to the fact that there are more frequent visits of teams from overseas and that more tours are made overseas by our own players. It will be remembered that, as far as Test cricket is concerned, Australia may be said to have been the sole challenger until the early years of this century. Then came South Africa and, at intervals, India, New Zealand and the West Indies, with the result that to-day we have touring sides in this country practically every summer, and every winter M.C.C. is responsible for sending teams abroad.

No one can deny that these interchanges must do a great deal of good in more ways than one, but I ask myself, 'Is there a danger that this continuous cricket, for this is what it amounts to, is too great a strain on players in this country?' It may be argued that there are so many first-class cricketers here that it may not be necessary to send the same teams. Test matches, however, abroad as well as here, are considered of such importance that only the best are looked upon as essential, both from the spectators' point of view and, it cannot be denied, from a financial consideration as well. A problem that the M.C.C. and the Counties may have to face in the near future is whether there should not be longer intervals between visits overseas.

When it comes to comparing batsmen of the past and present, my answer is that you cannot make a comparison. One star differs from another in glory, and you must take players during the time that they played. Could any one have excelled W. G. in his day? Could anyone have been better than Hobbs in his time? Can there be any more prolific run getter than Bradman to-day? And the same arguments apply to so many other famous batsmen in their day.

One writer summed up attempts to compare W. G. and Bradman as follows: 'Comparison between great players of different generations are unsatisfactory and often futile, but it may be said that in a *regular profusion of runs* Bradman has never been excelled.' This able opinion will be generally accepted.

For length of service, however, I must put W. G. higher than the rest. Two examples of his skill come to my mind. The first when, at the age of forty-seven, in 1895, he made a thousand runs in May! The second, when he played for the Gentlemen against the Players in his fifty-eighth year—an interval of forty-one years since he had played for the Gentlemen in 1865. I was selecting the sides at the Oval and asked him

15

to play. He scored 74 runs! Next July we shall be celebrating the 100th Birthday of this 'Agamemnon' of Cricket—and it is good to know that M.C.C. and Gloucestershire at Lord's and at Bristol have arranged matches to mark this historical event round about July 18th, the date of his birthday.

I was very fortunate in having two conversations with Dr Grace shortly before he died, at his home in Kent. During my first visit I asked him 'Who do you consider the best batsman next to yourself that you have played with?' It took him a little time to reply, but his answer was 'Arthur Shrewsbury'—the famous Nottingham player. 'And after Shrewsbury,' said I, 'who next?' 'Well,' said W. G., 'there are three or four that come together, amongst them, that "conjuror" Ranjitsinhji and that cricketer of "pranks", Timothy O'Brien'—superb batsman fifty years ago.

My second visit, and the last time I saw him, was during the period Zeppelins were coming near his home at Eltham, possibly with Wool-wich as their target. W. G. was not very well and I asked him what was the matter with him. His answer was characteristic. 'I don't like these Zeppelins.' I said to him, 'You afraid of Zeppelins! You who played all the fastest bowlers of the day and many of them on rough wickets, and on one occasion had a fast one through your beard!' 'Yes,' said W. G., 'quite true. I could see the fast balls, but I *can't* see these Zeppelins.'

I have written at some length on W. G. because in this year—the centenary of his birth—it is nice to be able to keep alive the memory of the Greatest Cricketer of All Times.

When considering the bowling of to-day and yesterday and the wickets at the present time and the wickets of fifty years ago, there does seem to me to be a difference. I think it will be generally conceded that we do not now, as a whole, possess the bowlers of class. There is a lack of fast bowlers. It was quite usual at the beginning of this century for every county to produce a fast bowler and in some instances two or more. To-day there is a scarcity.

Is this to be attributed to the 'wickets'? It may be, at any rate. I have observed one important feature of present day wickets. After heavy rain and when dried by a hot sun the difficulties from the batsman's point of view do not exist in anything like the same way as formerly. Under such conditions a side that reached 100 runs would be said to have done well against bowlers like Richardson, Lockwood, Hirst, Rhodes, J. T. Hearne, Peel and Hugh Trumble, to mention only a few. On occasions, a first-class county match has been finished in one day. This seldom happens now.

When three days were allotted to Test matches more often than not there was a definite result. I have in mind the three Test matches of 1902 in England. It is, I know, very difficult to lay down a hard and fast rule for the preparation of wickets, different turf may need different treatment. But evidence, I think, goes to prove that the over-preparation of wickets tends to take from them that 'life' which is essentially an asset for the pace and spin of a bowler. A bowler's length nowadays seems to be sacrificed for the in-swinger and googly, but if the bowler could obtain more assistance on fast and slow wickets when the weather is in his favour it might be the means of improving the standard which at the present time seems to have been lowered.

The team from Australia will shortly be arriving and are assured of a hearty welcome. In Bradman they will have a captain who will see that the great traditions of 'cricket' are jealously upheld; that it is a *game* and that Test matches are *tests* of friendship and goodwill.

As I look back on the fifty years of my anniversaries they bring memories of days that time can never obliterate, memories which stand out as happy milestones on the road of the late autumn of one's life.

April 1948

AN ILLUSTRIOUS ELEVEN

BY E. W. SWANTON

Players who have made and are making cricket history

W. G. GRACE enjoyed honour and fame enough while he lived. Was it not said that he was the best-known man in England, and did not the station-master at Paddington, none less, open his carriage door when he set off home to the West? But there is perhaps no more remarkable indication of his powerful influence on the game of cricket than the interest shown in the great man this centenary summer of his birth by the generations to whom he is a legendary figure, and nothing more.

For myself I feel I have come to know 'W. G.' quite intimately from the reading and re-reading of Bernard Darwin's delightful picture of him in the Great Lives series, and the likeness of him that seems the most expressive is not the famous Wortley portrait in Lord's Long Room, or the resplendent bust that commands the corresponding position at the Oval, but the photograph, often reproduced, showing him in mufti with Stanley Jackson.

There is affection as well as appreciation in the expression of 'the Old Man', in mufti, with the thick, silver-banded blackthorn stick, the watch-chain, the stout boots, the long cut-away coat, and the 'Churchill' hat, as he looks down on the flannelled figure of the man who was his most distinguished successor as captain of England, and of the Gentlemen. Thus he smiles out on all members of M.C.C. who climb the last flight leading to the top of the pavilion, giving perhaps a spring to the stride of the elderly.

There was one champion, and one only, and the tyro among cricket historians knows why there can never be another, for he 'made' cricket, brought it from the amusement of rustics and the business of the shrewd colony at Trent Bridge to the status of an English institution. But great figures have followed the greatest, and the present perhaps is an appropriate time to recall some of them. By the time W. G. clumped up the Oval steps on his fifty-eighth birthday in July, 1906, and flung down his bat for the last time after hitting the Players for 74, a young man named Hobbs was firmly established among the coming cricketers, his play, as *Wisden's* tells, more than bearing out the promise of the previous summer.

In modern times three batsmen have been transcendent in turn, and it is a tidy arrangement of providence by which W. G. was just overlapped by Hobbs (they played against one another on the Oval in bleak April weather in 1905), while Hobbs had the two Test rubbers of 1928–29 and 1930 in company with Bradman.

The Edwardian Age was full of excellent cricketers, and it is not in any equivocal spirit that, among the portrait-gallery accompanying these notes, I have picked out Sir Stanley Jackson to represent the Englishmen. It was reasonable surely to choose an amateur, for, so far as batsmanship was concerned, it was predominantly an amateur age; and if there were others who, playing more regularly, scored more runs and took more wickets over the years his achievements in the great matches were second to none. It is pleasant at the moment, too, to ponder on the deeds of a cricketer who saved up his most shattering performances for the confusion of the Australians. As for Victor Trumper, he has a place as prince of Australian batsmen that none of his countrymen will ever dispute. When has the batting art been more brilliantly shown than by Trumper, with his 11 centuries, in the wet summer of 1902? It is, incidentally, a paradox worthy of some analysis, that the Australians, so often pictured as 'hard-boiled' practitioners whose yard-sticks are averages and analyses, in retrospect venerate their stylists beyond all record-holders.

This is not the place for an essay on Hobbs, who spanned the old cricket and the new, fusing in his own batsmanship the best of both. As he gradually declined Hammond's star rose, so that the classic method was perpetuated in the England XI. Hammond's play, while firmly subordinated to the stern purpose of winning Test Matches which now, in the late twenties, had become so weighty a national question, had about it a fine natural poise and dignity.

Undeniably great was he, and equally so in his own sphere was Maurice Tate, whose bowling for England in Australia in the middle twenties first revived hopes that the old enemy might be beaten again. Tate, the cartoonist's delight, with the broad grin and the impossible boots, was the stout back-bone of our attack during the climb to equality and finally supremacy that began in 1924 and ended with the ripening of Bradman's powers in 1930.

The name of Ponsford does not perhaps strike quite so clear a note to-day as that of some other more spectacular Australians, but if that is so it is because Bradman put all other record-makers out of business. Time was when Ponsford was a scourge beyond equal, with a strong predilection for going on, if he could, to make two hundred, or three, or four. Ponsford indeed bears a heavy responsibility, for Bradman (who knows?) might not have thought in terms of such indecent totals if Ponsford had not set up the figures for him to beat.

O'Reilly needs no other claim to fame than that Bradman considers him the finest bowler he ever played against. All the virtues were there, the wonderful control of length, with the co-ordination of brain and muscle which generate 'flight', the strength of finger-spin and the affectation of stark hostility.

And so to Bradman, greatest of modern batsmen, and each country's heroes of the new generation, Compton and Miller. The time will be soon upon us when a final appreciation of Australia's captain comes due, and his praises will wait until then. Compton is our champion, and it is true that if he were to be out of the England XI, this would hardly be a Test rubber at all. And it is enough to say of Miller that if he were on the other side England might well be the favourites.

July 1934

THE BEST INNINGS I EVER PLAYED

BY LORD TENNYSON

One-Handed at Leeds

JOY, desperation, gloom, tragedy—such was the greatest hour of my cricketing life! Thirteen years have since elapsed; it is as it were but yesterday! And as I write I am made to revel in the memory of it all. For it may never be forgotten! It was at Leeds in the third Test match of the 1921 series against Australia, whose skipper was the mountainous and immovable Warwick Armstrong, that I was made captain of my country, an honour, need I say, of which I was enormously and pardonably proud.

England was already two down; we had lost the first Test at Nottingham and also again, when I had been lucky enough to play at Lord's. The critics were excusably rampant! Much vitriol had indeed flowed from their pens! I found comfort and solace in philosophy—when the sky is darkest there is light! I reckoned without the gods and their devilry!

Armstrong won the toss, and the wicket was fast and true. It was a batsman's day, but with no more than 22 runs on the board Johnny Douglas, fighter to the last ditch, bowled Warren Bardsley. Warren was in his heyday a giant left-hander, unruffled, cold, logical and majestic, and when Frank Woolley caught Andrews off J. W. H. T. Douglas, with the total at 45, we had the highest hopes, though the 'Governor-General' Charlie Macartney remained at the wicket in all his glory. Two wickets were down for 45, and on a really run-getting Paradise!

Not an hour had gone when, whilst fielding, my left hand was split between the thumb and first finger and perforce I had to give myself over to the surgeon and had four stitches put in it.

'No more cricket for thee, lad.' 'Damn bad luck and aw that, but there it is.' 'Why the 'ell didn't tha teck thi hand owt o' t' road?' 'But never mind, war's war, tha knows.'

So I was reminded and twitted as, with my sadly damaged hand, I strolled around and commiserated with myself! However, I was not for packing up, and though I almost despaired of taking further part in the match I determined to do so. Far worse than my own physical disability was to happen. Late in the afternoon appendicitis seized and left Jack Hobbs helpless, and on the morrow an imperative operation robbed England of her master batsman, the greatest at that time in all the world.

No words of mind can describe my feelings! In this, which I decided was the hour of my triumph, I was as a man accursed. No Hobbs, myself a cripple! A captain indeed! Cecil Parkin, however, ran amok, for in three overs he bowled Gregory and Hendry, and got that wonderful Macartney out leg before. This did much to lift me out of the doldrums! Then came Armstrong to show that he, at least of his country's rearguard, was no wobbler. He remained for 90 minutes to score 77, and with Carter and McDonald far from being 'rabbits', the Australians were not got rid of until the total had been raised to 407.

With Hobbs absent it was almost a nightmare, and I shuddered at my own helplessness. The weather the second day was grey, cold and dismal, and even the jaws of the good old Yorkshiremen dropped when the news was broadcast that Hobbs and myself were out of the match for good and all; but still they then did not even know what I knew! Douglas had been telegraphed that his wife had been stricken with appendicitis.

Johnny, whose tragic death we all so much deplored, never wore his heart on his sleeve. 'Lionel,' he whispered, 'this is too bad. But it might have been a sight worse. I shall carry on. Say nothing. There's a job of work for us both.' How like Johnny! In grit and determination he was many normal men rolled into one. But Frank Woolley, who with Hardinge had opened our innings in a failing light on the Saturday, had been quickly bowled, and Hearne, too, had gone for a mere bagatelle. Ducat did little more than break his duck when, with his bat splintered by one of McDonald's fastest, he presented Gregory with the tamest of catches in the slips. Laborious toil brought an additional 17, and then Hardinge, who had hoped to stem the onrushing tide, was given out leg before, when he would have it that he had played the ball good and hard. Noon had come on the second day, and five men were out for a paltry 67, when Douglas and Brown (the Hampshire stumper) were together. They held on like leeches. Armstrong, rare captain, like a man with a bludgeon, hammered at the stone wall as represented by Douglas and Brown, and tried all the bowling at his command. The partnership was not broken until the score had been taken from 67 to 165, then Brown was fatally wrong in his treatment of a long hop. White was bowled neck and crop, and England, with Hobbs in hospital, and myself with one hand, had either to get 92 or follow on. And there were but two wickets (counting myself) to fall. I had already decided that though the heavens might collapse I could take a chance, rotten reed that I was! Out I went to join up with Douglas.

The huge crowd had taken it for granted that they had seen the last of Lionel Tennyson! I emerged, my hand heavily bandaged, to such applause that I was almost scared. However, when I saw a smile upon the sunburned face of Douglas, who had already scored 51, maybe a smile of pity, as if to say, 'Lionel, my boy, if you survive a single round you'll be a marvel,' I summoned up courage. Douglas, you must know, as an amateur boxer, and at his particular poundage was, like his father in his day, beyond compare, and whenever we were in a tight corner (and in our many exploits together we were often in many) I was given to appraising his values in terms of the Ring.

'So, Lionel,' says I, 'stick out your left straight!' (that I had no sort of left owing to my accident did not occur to me!); and I nodded to Johnny. Precisely how and what I did I cannot and never will be able to tell. I would leave the story to my good friend Neville Cardus, cricketer-writer of the *Manchester Guardian*—who wrote about me in his book of the Leeds 1921 Test as follows:

> '... Tennyson, in a ruinous hour, for his side, to the accompaniment of stabs of pain from his wounded hand, played the happy wayfarer, and again he blazoned the news to the land that a big heart will take one a long way against these Australians.... He drove to the off and glided through the slips to such tune that he made 62 while Douglas made 24. He put Gregory and McDonald to flight by hitting eight fours from their fast bowling ... in all he batted eighty minutes and scored 63 out of 106.... With all its gusto there was yet plenty of the marks of culture in Tennyson's batsmanship. He showed us that a man can drive one-handed if he will get quickly into the right position for driving. His footwork had quickness always, and the classical left leg motion showed in every hit to the off side, the forward foot pointing in the way of the ball's direction. He rose high on his toes to the fast bowler's bumpers and played them down with a left elbow beautifully up. Tennyson returned to the pavilion at the end of his fine adventure to the wildest cheering one has heard on a cricket ground for many a long day.'

But England lost, and so it was that my joy was eclipsed by my country's tragedy.

January 1974

THE FAMILY OF FOSTERS

BY LEONARD CRAWLEY

The sporting achievements of nine of the eleven children

THERE have been a number of great games-playing families ever since sporting events were first recorded. Of these it strikes me that pride of place must be given to the Foster family. I shall always think of them as the first 11 and it is therefore appropriate that the Rev. Henry Foster and his wife, Sophia (née Harper) had seven sons and four daughters in the days when such families were possible.

All but Maud the eldest, who died as a child aged two, were blessed with good brains, flashing good looks, good physique and that co-ordination of mind, hand and balance that enables a human being to play all manner of games and excel in first-class company.

Monkey's instinct
I deliberately omit 'eye' since I believe that the ability to play games

well depends far more on the monkey's instinct to copy from another the best and easiest way to play, than it does on an eye that is supposed to see a ball quicker or better than another.

It also occurs to me that the village parson and his consort, by reason of their calling and the careful upbringing of a family, have been successful in raising many of our most distinguished citizens over the years. Much in life depends on a good beginning.

At the age of 14 Henry Foster had been awarded his cricket colours at Winchester but, when he went up to Clare College, Cambridge, he was unable to afford to play games and had to content himself stroking the college boat.

After taking Holy Orders he was appointed to the Malvern College staff where presently with Sophia they ran a most successful house and began to raise their remarkable family. Here I think it best to set down the order of batting, if not of merit, in some detail as to their achievements.

Their ability for games was inherited from their impecunious father and there is no evidence that grandfather Foster was a good games player. The same applies to Sophia, their mother.

After poor little Maud came Harry Foster of imperishable memory, without question the greatest racquets player of his time, a grand batsman who made a century in the University match, played for the Gentlemen against the Players and made countless runs for Worcestershire. He was also a strong and tireless full back and played for Corinthians and Oxford at soccer.

He described racquets—not to be mistaken with squash—as the most difficult game and the best in the world, since if one could ever learn to hit the ball with confidence no other moving ball would ever present any difficulty. He must have derived great pleasure from playing games with his brother Bill (W. L.), a soldier—in the opinion of many the best of them all. Cricket, football, racquets, and the rest all came alike to him and as a batsman he had so solid a defence that he seldom failed.

Legendary figure

Mabel, who married Charles Bullock, came next and was good enough to play racquets with her brothers and to bowl to them in nets. Then there was R. E.–the immortal Tip—a legendary figure in his short life, said to be the best batsman in the world at the turn of the century, who captained England against South Africa at cricket, England at soccer against Scotland, Ireland and Wales with 10 professionals under him, and won the doubles championship at racquets with his brother Bill.

For years his 171 against Cambridge at Lord's was the highest score ever hit in the University match, and the following week on the same ground he scored a hundred in each innings of the Gentleman and Players match. In 1899 he enjoyed the immense pleasure of scoring 141 and 106 for Worcestershire v Hampshire, while his brother, W. L., was making 140 and 172 not out at the other end—a unique achievement in the annals of the game, let alone for two brothers. When in 1903 he made 287 for England v Australia at Sydney the Australians wondered what had hit them. He was a stroke player with dazzling ability and the terror of all the bowlers of his time. Then came two more girls, Jessie and Cecily, each blessed with the same talent for games. Both played golf for Worcestershire before marriage.

Smaller mould

If Basil the actor was not of quite the same calibre as some of his brothers, he played cricket for Worcestershire, football for Corinthians and won the doubles racquets championship with his brother Harry. Geoffrey was rather smaller than the rest but cast in the same classical Foster mould. Apart from brother Tip he is reputed to have been the best footballer of them all and won an amateur international cap.

He was a beautiful batsman and after playing for Oxford and Worcestershire (which by his time had become known as Fostershire) he played with success for Kent from time to time. I did not see him in the middle until after his fiftieth birthday when, against a hostile school attack at Winchester, he made an impudent 100 on an unfriendly pitch. He was a beautiful racquets player and also won the doubles championship.

I had the joy of playing cricket under Maurice for Worcestershire as a boy and for one year as an undergraduate. He was suffering from diabetes at the time after living in the East, and was never 100 per cent fit. And yet he was among the most gifted batsmen I ever watched. He came back into county cricket in the 1920s as though he had never been out of it. All games came alike to him as with his elder brothers.

Lone survivor

Last of all came Johnnie, the youngest of the family and the only one alive; he is 83 and is living in Hove. Though twelfth man for Malvern, he played with success for Worcestershire, was a fine soccer player and, with his elder brother, Maurice, won the amateur doubles racquets championships.

When hearing about their deeds, the first thing people want to know is how many of them played for Worcestershire at one and the same time. The answer is four, though all seven played at one time or another.

I suggest they had all been superbly taught by their father and mother technically and mentally and in such a large and devoted family it is natural that the younger members received a big hand from the elder. Physically they were well made and beautifully balanced. It is hard to believe anyone of them ever made a shot in a hurry or looked unnatural. Mentally they were tough, playing all games according to the rules.

All scratch
Their batting was a joy to watch, full of confidence and with every shot in the game they played like the best West Indian batsmen of today. While his family were growing up, Parson Foster frequently won golf competitions from scratch, a handicap with which all his sons were credited before leaving Malvern.

May 1949

NEW ZEALAND AT THE WICKETS

IN matters of cricket, New Zealand has suffered from the vast prestige built up by Australia in the last seventy years. Some of her greatest players have emigrated to that country—Grimmett is a notable example—and English touring teams have been liable to treat New Zealand as merely a pleasant place to visit after the grilling ordeal of Australian Tests. Moreover, the English counties have previously drawn off such valuable talent as C. S. Dempster, C. C. Dacre, W. E. Merritt, and K. C. James; and it is significant that our present visitors count M. P. Donnelly, of Warwickshire, as one of their most powerful batsmen.

No doubt the balance will be adjusted in time, since Australia could once tell much the same story in this respect; but cricket in New Zealand dates back at least as far as 1842, when our own Canterbury Week was just being inaugurated, and it was in December, 1848, that *The Otago News* published the terms of a challenge issued by Dunedin to the Cricket Club at Wellington

'to a trial of skill at any point equidistant between the Port of Otago and Port Nicholson.'

Evidently the difficulties of travel were too great, for the challenge was not accepted, and the first inter-provincial match was played between Wellington and Auckland in 1860.

Parr's team of 1863–4 visited New Zealand, after which there was an interlude of two Maori wars before the formidable Australians of 1878 toured there prior to their historic achievements in England. This was followed almost immediately by a team from Canterbury visiting Victoria, and cricketing enthusiasm became widespread.

New Zealand entertained cricketers from the Fiji Islands, and it is related that King George Tubow II, of Tonga, the last independent sovereign (who died in 1918), having learnt the game at school in Auckland, introduced it into his realm with devastating effect. In the end he had to ban it throughout the working week, since his subjects were deserting the plantations for the cricket field, and famine was threatened.

The formation of the New Zealand Cricket Council in 1895 and the institution of the Plunket Shield Competition in 1906 mark the progress of cricket in the two islands; but the initiative of a pioneering people is best illustrated by the story of a New Zealand club which played on matting: there had been heavy rain preceding an important fixture, and, though the sun was shining, the hard surface of the pitch was under water. The groundsman accordingly poured petrol over the flooded area, and set it on fire. After a short conflagration, the matting was relaid, and the match took place.

It is with the memory of such ardent enterprise in our minds that we should measure the cricketing prospects of New Zealand and consider how far we are justified in limiting the approaching Tests to four, of three days each. How the fourth touring team (believed to be the best New Zealand has sent here) will fare this summer is a matter for agreeable exercise in conjecture, as seasonable as the new May flowers. A pleasant air of expectation and traditional uncertainty hangs over the new-mown grass, as we welcome W. A. Hadlee and his fellow-guests, wishing them the happiest of tours.

April 1950

WEST INDIAN CRICKET

THIS year brings us the jubilee visit of the West Indians. Fifty years ago, they were led by Aucher Warner, Sir Pelham's brother, which reminds us of the latter's early days in the West Indies, where his famous nickname was acquired. Another member of that team was L. Constantine, father of the man we know for the vigour of his cricket, his pen, and his political excursions. Their matches were not then accounted first-class—so far off is that Mafeking Spring of 1900.

Cricket in the West Indies, however, goes back further than is generally supposed. When the 59th Foot, whose Club was formed at Antigua on New Year's Day, 1842, won 50 dollars by defeating Trinidad that summer on the Grand Savanna, it was stated to be the first time Trinidad had lost a match. The Club was already of 'very long standing'. Ten years later, we hear of 3,000 people watching the match between Club and Garrison, among them the Governor, Lord Harris, father of the famous Kent cricketer.

In the Barbados, again, we find the regiments of the garrison providing the principal rivalry in 1845. The West Indian Tournament dates from 1865, when Barbados opposed British Guiana at Bridgetown—two seasons after the formation of the Kingston Cricket Club in Jamaica.

The introduction of cricket did not please everybody in the West Indies. There were even some who regarded it with alarm. When the strange cult spread to the Windward Islands, a French lady of St Lucia was moved to write a letter of protest:

> 'On introduit dans ce pays une espèce de bataille meutrière qu'on nomme, par une étrange perversité morale, un jeu. Il est vrai, grâce à Dieu, que ceux qui se tiennent à l'écart courent relativement moins de risques, mais même ceux-là sont loin d'être â l'abri du danger.'

The most remarkable West Indian cricket match recorded in literature is the single-wicket contest, described in *Pickwick Papers*, between Mr Jingle and Colonel Blazo. The following facts emerge from the well-known telegraphic style of that narrative:

Mr Jingle, having won the toss, opened his innings at 7 a.m. to the bowling of Colonel Blazo, who was supported, sometimes literally, by relays of native fieldsmen. The Colonel eventually retired, overcome by the heat, whereupon his attendant, Quanko Samba, was permitted to bowl, dismissed Mr Jingle, and expired soon afterwards. Mr Jingle, who had scored 570, then went to dinner. As there is no record of Colonel Blazo resuming the game, Mr Jingle is presumed to have been the victor.

To return from this pleasant digression into the apocryphal, it is noticeable that all who watch cricket in the West Indies bear testimony to the ardour of players and spectators alike. E. V. Lucas has given a significant example. At an important cricket-match in Jamaica, he saw onlookers filling the trees overlooking the ground. Suddenly there was a terrifying crack, as the burden proved too much for one of them, and an avalanche of yelling darkies went plunging earthwards. Horrified, he hastened to the scene of disaster—just in time to see all the victims scrambling into another tree.

This is the kind of mettle we now welcome to our pastures, hoping that England's best may prove a match for it. While we wish our guests a happy tour, we may be sure that, whatever sunshine our summer allows, their cricket will never lack that warmth which keeps an old game young.

December 1950

TEST MATCH NEWS

THOSE days are now with us to which the devoted cricketer has been looking forward, with unbroken fervour, since the last storms of summer. The average Englishman thinks only spasmodically of his national game after September: he is aware that a team is on its way to Australia, but, having delivered himself of a few dark prognostications concerning its probable fate, he diverts his enthusiasm, vigorously or vicariously, to football.

It is true that occasional newspaper paragraphs, dealing with the voyage, announce that somebody has injured himself at deck tennis, or won a prize for fancy dress; but our progressively contracting newsprint ensures that these items will be so limited as to escape the notice of most people who are not exclusively cricket-minded.

The general reader may give a passing glance at the reports of matches against States, but his attention is not seriously engaged until a Test Match is imminent, and he then tunes in with something like a sense of unreality; for no amount of education in the Solar System quite reconciles him to the notion of people playing cricket in December. In our insular eyes, there is something freakish about it, like the midnight sun, by whose rays British sailors have, indeed, been known to play cricket, and we cannot get used to scores coming over the air on a dark winter morning, even though it is 77 years since news of W. G. Grace's 'honeymoon tour' was first flashed home by 'electric telegraph'.

Messages were then expressed laconically, not only by reason of there being neither broadcast commentaries or cinema newsreels to record the 'cooees' of Boyle's Bendigo supporters when he hit The Champion's leg-stump at Melbourne, but because cricket-reporting had not yet developed that eloquence which has become such a mixed blessing today. Where there is a literary touch, devoid of that 'controversial' stimulus sought by writers proud of 'not pulling their punches', we may be grateful for this brightening of our December gloom, whatever the close-of-play score; and it is a matter for retrospective regret that there was no Robertson-Glasgow to accompany James Lillywhite's team to Adelaide, where the authorities dared not use the roller for fear of damaging the grass, to Ararat, where the only roller was made of wood, and to Goulburn, where the outfielders were reinforced by two young kangaroos.

This was the tour on which news of the first Test Match between the two countries was cabled home. Australia, opposed by a team which had only just returned from exhausting adventures in New Zealand, won at Melbourne by 45 runs, and their Bradman of the day was a Bannerman, who retired hurt for 165, the next highest score on his side being 20.

It is a far cry from those days to a morning, some 25 years ago, when a total stranger snatched Mr Neville Cardus's paper from his hands, read what had happened at Adelaide, cried 'Oh, my God!' and vanished into the fog; father still from those early commentaries, sufficiently remote from the present, which were relayed commercially over Radio Paris. These were timed to coincide with the matutinal shave—a perilous proceeding with the razor held in trembling fingers while an exultant Australian voice brought added chill to the atmosphere with his greeting—'Hullo, England! I'm afraid I haven't got very good news for you this morning!'

2

PERIOD
PROSE

The *longeurs* of Victorian prose style give a
clear reflection of the leisured existence of
country gentlemen and, moreover, of what
they expected from their newspaper. We can
laugh inwardly at the pompous sentiments
and quaint humour and yet, at the same time,
relish the opportunity to study journalistic
fashions of another era in reports of doughty
battles on the sward . . .

THE CAVALRY v. THE INFANTRY

MUSIC and cricket are becoming like twin brothers; it is now no uncommon thing to see a band of men expert with bat and ball accompanied by another band skilful in the mysticisms which bring out the most enchanting strains from wood and brass. Two warlike contending parties met at Lord's on Thursday for a day's play; the band of the Horse Guards Blue, under the direction of Mr Tutton, and that of the Coldstream, under Mr Godfrey, accompanied the combatants with such popular *morceaux*, that Lord's ground had the appearance of a day in England's history worthy of special remembrance. The Infantry went first to the wickets, and as every man scored, the gross amount at the close of the innings came to 181. The Cavalry were less successful; they fell 102 short, and as a consequence followed their innings. Captain Heneage's attack on the Cavalry was of so determined a character that eight warriors and one civilian fell to it. At the close of the day the score stood as follows:—

INFANTRY

Cpt. Parnell, c Bateson, b Johnson 23	Major Lord Bingham, b Baillie. 11
H. Willet, Esq., b Denne 4	Capt. Tower, b Denne......... 17
A. Dalzell, Esq., b Muttlebury . 21	Capt. Heneage, run out........ 9
W. Kempson, Esq., b Hill 6	R. Buller, Esq., b Johnson..... 7
W. Walton, Esq., not out...... 44	Byes 9, l b 2, w 8........... 19
Major Goodlake, b Hill........ 5	
E. Tremlett, Esq., b Muttlebury 15	Total.................. 181

CAVALRY

	1st inn.		2nd inn.
A. Stewart, Esq., b Heneage...........	0	b Heneage...........	0
P. Du Cane, Esq., b Parnell...........	5	b Goodlake...........	3
Capt. Denne, b Heneage	7	not out	11
F. Marshall, Esq., b Heneage..........	35	b Heneage...........	9
Capt. Bateson, b Heneage.............	5	not out	0
Capt. Johnson, b Heneage.............	2		
Capt. Gunter, l b w, b Goodlake	0		
Col. Thomas, not out	1	b Goodlake............	2
G. A. Muttlebury, Esq., b Heneage	0		
Hon. G. Hill, b Heneage	1		
Capt. Thornton, b Heneage............	0		
Byes 12, l b 2, w b 3, n b 6.........	23	Byes 7, l b 1, w 7, n b 1..............	15
Total	−79	Total	−41

CRICKET AT ETON COLLEGE

SIR,—We old Etonians are vexed at seeing our boys again beaten hollow by the Harrow boys, and we ask each other how to account for the confessed weakness of our side. It may be worth while to suggest that there are some remediable causes.

(1.) Eton College has a very pretty pleasure-ground, of which it gives up a very good piece to its own scholars, seventy in number; of these seventy about ten or twelve never touch a bat, ten or twelve more play in Upper Club with the Oppidans, the remaining four dozen keep up two clubs with considerable spirit. So far, so good. An assistant master, at his own expense, keeps in good order a very nice ground for the hundred little fellows of the lower school, and they play freely and briskly as if they were at a good private school in the country. This also is satisfactory. There remain about six hundred, or, say five hundred and fifty, boys to be provided with playground. About half the really available ground in the College park is reserved for 'Upper Club'. How many boys play in Upper Club in games? Perhaps in the early part of the season forty (I speak under correction). But as soon as the 'eleven' or an 'eleven' has been chosen to play a match with visitors, you may say roughly, that about fifteen boys play in Upper Club the double wicket game sufficiently often to give them practice. There is hardly more than one double wicket game a week in June and July. The ground is used as much by men as by boys. It is a pleasant place. It is a sign of good wholesome taste in young guardsmen and roving cricketers that they like to picnic at Eton, and get up their averages off the boys' bowling. The boys in the eleven like to see them, like getting leave out of church, like the dinner in the tent, or the hungry tea in Poet's Walk. It is all very agreeable; and for the eleven it is generally good practice, though some say that good days are given up to gentlemen who bring down rather inferior teams. But, meanwhile, what becomes of the young rising players? What practice do they get whilst their playground is occupied by grown-up people? They are either looking on or killing time in tubs on the river, or playing stump and ball. Why are they not playing matches of their own in Lower Club? Why, they have no leaders to get up matches. Lower Club is officered by players who after the first few weeks have no further interest in their duties; and, indeed, you cannot expect the second-best players to go back to Lower Club, whilst the boys just a little better than themselves are enjoying all the sweets and glories in Upper Club. What, then, is proposed? Simply that there should be, as in the football system, a succession of *school* matches all through the season; fewer matches with strangers; in particular, fewer 'scratch' matches. Is it not hard that an industrious young player, who gives up all the gaiety of the 'boats', and sticks to cricket from year to year in the hope of some day being in the eleven, should, when he is perhaps the seventeenth or twentieth best player in the school, find his place in Upper Club filled by some undergraduate just released from Oxford or Cambridge, or some parasitical hanger-on dropping down from London or Windsor? It is impossible for the captain of the eleven to decline a challenge from the Household Brigade, or King's College, Cambridge, or University College, Oxford. It is almost as difficult for the Provost and Head Master to refuse permission to their good-natured and honoured visitors to use the ground. But is it not to be wished that these gentlemen should refrain from bringing down elevens so often? Are they not killing Eton cricket with kindness?

(2) I have said that, one hundred Lower School and seventy Collegers being deducted, there remain between five and six hundred boys to be provided with cricket ground, and perhaps it will be granted that not more than thirty or forty are provided for in Upper Club. What is left for the five hundred? My critics will at once say, half of them are on the river. I know they are; but the question is whether there would not be many more young cricketers if there were more opportunities for distinguishing themselves in games and matches? Suppose these five hundred boys were broken up into five private schools. Each school could maintain with spirit at least one club, even if it were on the banks of the Thames. What have we? Only two clubs—Lower Club and 'Sixpenny'. For 'aquatics' you would hardly reckon. The amateur free-and-easies take up a good large piece of the playing fields, and such practice as they give in their three hours a week is, I believe, rather more mischievous than advantageous to real cricket. What then is proposed? That there should be more clubs for the Oppidans, four instead of two, each club with a good piece of ground (there is level meadow enough in the parish for as many clubs as you like), each club having a regular series of matches in itself, and with other school clubs, the houses playing against each other, as at football, with a similar register of precedence year by year. Make it easy, and give some chance of honour, and you will draw to cricket many of the boys who now waste their time on the rafts or in their stupid skiffs. Make cricket as universal as football is at Eton, and you will have a higher standard of play, and a far larger number of aspirants to choose an eleven from.

W.

HILLYER'S BENEFIT

ON the 6th proximo, 'Eighteen Veterans of England' are to play All-England, at Kennington Oval, for the benefit of the above celebrated bowler. As most of our readers are well acquainted with the name and character of the man, remark on this score is totally unnecessary. Hillyer's cricketing race is run; the once elastic limb has grown rigid, the quick eye become dim, and the firm step less willing than of yore to obey the impulses of the mind. Hillyer has been one of the bright cricketing ornaments in the Kentish diadem, but although its lustre has faded the man yet remains. The sunshine of popularity is at the best mutable and of short-lived date. It ought always to be borne in mind that it is one thing to please others, and quite another thing to taste of pleasure oneself. A day may come in which skill and prowess is little else than a wreck, and talent merely a memento of what has been, but of what cannot by possibility exist any more. As chroniclers of public men, especially of the deserving, we feel that we should be lax in the discharge of duty if we were to overlook a coming match fraught with such especial interest.

August 1858

THE GRAND WEEK AT CANTERBURY

AS the earth in her annual journey round the sun is presented with variable points of attraction in the spangled fields of the firmament, so in the world of cricket, as time runs its unresting race, the bright objects change and move with it; sometimes they are here and anon there. East Kent, in its turn, has become again a brilliant constellation, and Canterbury, as in ancient days, the cynosure, *id est* if the 'Itinerary of Antoninus' and others be built on something more substantial than fable. What the early British King, Vortigern, would have thought of the feats on St. Lawrence ground and in the old city, could he have been called up from his dusty bed, it is impossible to imagine; with what the subjects of Queen Victoria said about them during the past week's tourney we are somewhat familiar. Canterbury has been a 'gay and festive scene' for five days. On Monday Kent met All England for the seventeenth time on the same tented field, and in the evening the old stagers appeared at the old theatre in *Old Faces and New Pieces*. Tuesday was devoted again to the match in hand, and in the evening 'amateur theatricals' were repeated at the Theatre Royal. Wednesday found the Gentlemen of Kent in opposition to I Zingari, after which a grand 'cricket ball' took place at the New Music-hall, St Margaret's. The next day brought the Gentlemen of Kent together again to do battle with the Gentlemen of England, and at the close of their match on Friday another 'light fantastic' at St George's Hall. If this is not doing the thing 'slap', we should just like to know in what sense the expressive monosyllable is to be understood. As the chief cricketing army was encamped out of town, we gladly seized the opportunity of bidding a short adieu to mountains of brick and mortar, miles of hard and blistering pavement, the endless din of revolving carriage wheels, and 'the busy hum of men', for a short gaze on green broad acres, fruitful orchards, fertile hop gardens, crowded stack-yards, and a whole land laughing with abundance; but, ere the thoughts suggested by such glowing pictures had time to be assorted, the rich journey was ended, and in less than no time we were on the floor of action, where two excellent wickets were pitched—the men of Kent aided, as on the 5th of July at Lord's, by Caffyn Jackson, and Parr, ready to commence the first contest in the programme . . .

September 1858

UNITED ELEVEN OF ENGLAND v. EIGHTEEN OF ENGLAND (WITH CAFFYN AND LOCKYER)

IN proportion as the strings of matches played by the great rival Elevens of England dwindle into fine and yet finer degrees, the activity of their exponents increases. Rest with them is known only in name. The All-England team have their wickets pitched for three days not far from a good view of the Irish Sea; they are struck, and so repitched within five days as to get a glimpse of the German Ocean; but during the journey a halt has been made for another three days' encounter in the heart of Yorkshire, and, *mirabile dictu*, they are found a few hours later in the land of 'tin', 250 miles S.-W. of London. The United, equally erratic, are discovered at Southgate on Wednesday, busy as bees at Croydon on the two following days, and then clear a dozen counties at a leap so as to be at Nottingham on Monday. If this is not keeping the game alive we confess ignorance in knowing what is. Quidnuncs themselves express astonishment at the rapid strides of cricket; but the seeming mystery is of simple solution. Not a day passes at this season of the year without the managers of papers, provincial as well as metropolitan, finding something for their cricketing corner. Was it so twenty years ago? Assuredly not. This shows the growth of the game in the public mind; people are anxious to know what has been, is, and is to be. So long as this interest in the game is on the stretch, just so long will these peripatetic teachers be found going circuit—aye, and be much more welcome visitors than the javelin-man and trumpeter, because, whether conquest or defeat follow, there is no sting behind...

October 1858

SUMMARY OF THE SEASON

JUNE 10, at Eastwell.—*All-England v. Twenty-two of Eastwell and District*. England, 214; Eastwell, 226 and 7, with one wicket down. Drawn. Two days were occupied in playing an innings each. On the third day a violent storm arose, which turned the booths, tents, &c., topsy-turvy, burying for a short time their merry occupants. In the midst of the confusion, however, no one sustained any serious personal injury.

July 8, at Leeds.—*England v. Twenty-two of Leeds.*—England 57 and 170—total, 227; Leeds, 129 and 37—total, 166. Drawn. Leeds had five wickets to fall. This was one of the many matches confirmatory of the wisdom of the admonition, 'Don't halloe before you are out of the wood.' Cricket is a ticklish and uncertain game; results never can be depended on while the contest lasts. The issue of the first innings of Leeds was announced 'a victory without honour, as 16 of the Leeds players were able to play England.' The summing up put a very different face on the matter. Alfred Clarke scored the highest number, 40, on the part of England; G. Atkinson, who stood in the Leeds ranks, put 20 on the sheet.

August 1859

MATCHES TO COME

THE long-talked of visit by the chief cricketing sons of Mr John Bull to Cousin Jonathan has at length been finally agreed upon. Instead, however, of the 'United' having the exclusive honour of representing 'Old England', as at first mooted, we find that the brilliant constellation embodies Julius Caesar, Caffyn, Carpenter, Daft, Diver, Grundy, Hayward, Jackson, Lillywhite, Lockyer, Parr, and Wisden. The twelfth man goes out as umpire. According to arrangement they sail from Liverpool on Wednesday, the 7th of September next. Four matches are already fixed on. These will most probably be played at Toronto, Quebec, Montreal, and New York. A very liberal sum has been subscribed by our friends 't'other side of the Atlantic,' in order to perfect this novel enterprise—one that we feel fully confident will be carried out with a generous spirit, and a right appreciation of the merits of the men, from whom such great and valuable lessons may be learned in the noble art to which the prime of their youth and of health is devoted.

THE UNITED ELEVEN OF ALL-ENGLAND v. TWENTY GENTLEMEN OF SUSSEX WITH TWO BOWLERS

MANY a timid but thorough lover of cricket in the neighbourhood of St Leonard's might well have been excused on Thursday for pausing at the ugly and dangerous approach to the East Sussex ground, seeing that it was marked out by flags over a proscribed 'iron way', along a narrow and irregular patch abounding with sharp and slippery declivities, and beyond which a ravine crossed by an isthmus not quite so wide that 'two might go abreast'. Once landed, however, all previous disagreeables were at once a blank in memory's waste. To those unacquainted with the drawing-room cricket-ground belonging to the East Sussex Club we would just observe that it is a remnant of the old Hastings racecourse, beautifully embosomed with hills, and, when viewed from the railway which skirts it, a picture of cricket is presented that mocks alike the effort of the artist and the imagination of the poet. In a playing sense the ground, though a little hard for want of rain, was level as a billiard-table. Soon after eleven a strange tinkling was heard—some said it was a sheep-bell, while others less happy in determining the question imagined it to be no bell at all; be this as it may, the ground was soon cleared of groups of practice-bowlers and hitters in obedience to the tinkling summons, and Messrs Hale and King went forward to receive the first balls put down by Grundy and Caffyn. In two of the earliest overs three runs were scored, but Mr Hale, from too anxious a desire to go ahead, found himself in the abhorrent quandary of not knowing whether to return or proceed. This incident precluded any figuring beyond four. Mr Napper exercised more caution, and stuck to his text of slow and sure. Grundy, however, was not to be resisted for ever, and as Mr Napper's wicket appeared to be unassailable by direct attacks, Grundy tried the other plan, and succeeded in catching his own ball. Mr King had retired previous to this event for two, and Mr Fawcett was taken by the wicket-keeper for a similar number, so that 15 runs only were subscribed by the four leading members. Stubberfield, however, put a better face on the affair. The Brighton player (one of the given men) made two brilliant forward hits for four, two to the leg for three, and sundry others equally well meant, but checked by the efficiency of the field. The amateur performance of Mr Beecham was not less meritorious than that of the professional who spurred him on to take every advantage that time and circumstance would admit of. When the two latter retired, six wickets were declared vacant for 43. Mr Stent was caught off the first ball by Grundy, and Hood's off stump assumed an angle by no means in keeping with the mid and leg, at the third ball presented by Carpenter. Mr Curteis, another great patron of cricket, now assumed an attitude of defence. He got first a single, then two more, when his companion, Mr Hume,—ran out. The attempt for the second run, that cost him his wicket, was a cruelly ill-timed one. Mr Beasley was caught by Caffyn off his first ball. A change of bowling was now adopted; Wisden went on at Grundy's end, and wicket after wicket fell for inconsiderable numbers. Mr Curteis went out for five, and the sixteenth wicket had the figures 76 attached to it. Mr Watts gave a temporary check to the rampant triumphs of the Eleven, and by two threes forward, a cut for three, and four little goes equally well worth the encomiums paid to hits of a more extended length, placed a dozen on the record, and thus helped to bring up the seventeenth wicket to 84. Saving a score of seven by Mr Day, all the rest were of exceedingly humble proportions. In casting up the sheet, the figures 93 appeared to be the irrefutable result of the Two-and-twenty Gentlemen of East Sussex.

It was drawing on for six before Hearne and Mortlock, fully caparisoned for a sharp contest, presented themselves. On looking at the Two-and-twenty out, it did seem to be almost impossible to squeeze a ball through the doubly-guarded passes. Hearne, renowned as a stiff wicket, could not get the ball away, and in less than a quarter of an hour he was seen returning to the tent from which he had recently emerged, Hooker, the other given man, being successful in catching him off his own ball. Mortlock was also doomed to a very short existence; Stubberfield bowled him, and the two leading celebrities were disposed of for runs that might be counted on the fingers of the left hand. Lillywhite and Wells were next in together, scoring slowly, when the business of the first day was announced as brought to a finish.

In order to accommodate the public to the greatest extent possible, the South-Eastern Company, through their manager, Mr Eborall, allowed the trains to pull up both going to and coming from the St Leonard's station. This was a matter of especial convenience to many, who in all probability would not have been able to witness a match so full of interest to the cricketing world in general and to the county of Sussex in particular.

November 1859

THE CRICKETER'S SONG

Written for the dinner at the close of a first season's play

Air—'A wet sheet and a flowing sea'

I.

A smooth sward and a balmy sky,
    A bowler swift and true,
Whose 'shooters' all our courage try,
    As we wield the 'willow and yew'.
As we wield the willow and yew, brave boys,
    And 'drive' from the shoulder free,
And the 'leather-hunters' pant and blow,
    And the 'ins' are in utmost glee!
    And the 'ins' are in their glee,
    The 'ins' are in their glee,
As the 'leather-hunters' pant and blow,
    At a 'drive' from the shoulder-free!

II.

Oh! for a full pitch, straight and slow,
    I hear some novice cry!
But the cricketer loves the volleying 'twist'.
    That will all his science try.
For his 'bails' will surely fly, brave boys,
    If he 'swipe' with graceful swing;
Better to 'block' with watchful eye,
    For it twists like a living thing.
    It twists like a living thing.
    It twists like a living thing;—
The wisest will fall to a dangerous ball,
    That twists like a living thing

III.

'Tis the king of Anglo-Saxon games,—
    The type of our strength confessed;
Where the charm of perils bravely dared
    Inspires each manly breast!
Inspires each manly breast, brave boys,
    As we scorn the pain and the toil,

And meet each chance of bat or ball
  With an ever-cheerful smile!
  With ever-cheerful smile,
  With ever-cheerful smile,—
We meet each chance of bat and ball
  With ever-cheerful smile;

J. H. G.

'CRICKET', A NEW GAME WITH CARDS

SIR,—Should you think it worth while to insert the following account of a new game with playing cards in the columns of *The Field*, which in my leisure time I have invented, I write it for your approval. I entitle it, as it is a sort of parody on that game,

'CRICKET'.

Cast out all cards out of the pack above the sixes, with the exception of king and queen and knave of hearts, the king, queen, and knave of diamonds, the ten of hearts, and the ten of diamonds. You then turn the cards with their faces downwards, and the players (two only can play, one on each side) cut for innings, which the lowest obtains; the one who is 'out' then shuffles the cards about on the table, while the one who has 'innings' draws from the pack. The number of pips on the cards drawn count as runs; so, if a 3 is turned up it counts three runs, or a 6, six runs. If the ten of hearts is turned up it counts a bye; if the ten of diamonds, a wide; if a king, the man is bowled out; if a queen, he is caught; if the knave of hearts, run out; if the knave of diamonds, stumped. You therefore write down eleven men on each side on a piece of paper, and mark the runs as they are obtained; when the whole eleven men have been got out, the other side goes in. It is best to have a third person, to act as scorer. As soon as a card is drawn it must be replaced in the pack, the man who is 'out' meanwhile shuffling the cards about, so that the man who is in may not draw the same card twice running.

In writing down the elevens on the paper, you may either write down any persons' names you like, or write the numbers 1, 2, 3, &c., up to eleven.

POPE JOAN

HIGHGATE SCHOOL v. THE BRITISH MUSEUM

PLAYED on the School ground, Highgate, on Wednesday, June 28, and resulted in the total discomfiture of 'the Mummies'. The highest score of the School side was made by A. Lake, whose steady play was much admired. Messrs Knight and Hannan also scored thirty and twenty respectively in very good style. On the other side Mr Greenfell is especially worthy of notice for 'general proficiency', his underhand bowling being most effective.

ALL-ENGLAND ELEVEN v. TWENTY-TWO OF SWALLOWFIELD AND DISTRICT

SWALLOWFIELD, the seat of Sir Charles Russell, situate about six miles from Reading, is a spot both picturesque and lovely. The cricket ground in front of the mansion was prepared expressly for the above match, which began on Monday and terminated on the Wednesday following. During the three days mentioned upwards of 3000 persons visited the scene of action. Among this large number were many of the aristocracy of the neighbourhood. In order to their accommodation, tents, booth and marquees, were erected at different portions of the ground. Two bands were provided, who performed alternately from the beginning to the end of the match. Play began on Monday, at 12.30, by Oscroft and Rowbotham appearing at the wickets, on the part of England. The ground, though recently prepared, stood the wear and tear well pretty. The bowlers at the outset were Slinn and James Lillywhite; Rowbotham ran out when his score had reached five only, and Carpenter went to the assistance of Oscroft; the stay of Carpenter was unexpectedly brief— he got two singles and a two, and was then clean bowled by Lillywhite. (Two wickets, 25 runs.) Hayward appeared, got nine singles in succession and subsequently a two; Mr Wright caught him almost immediately after at point. (Three wickets, 34.) Smith was clean bowled by Slinn for three. (Four wickets, 38.) Parr came next, but his stay was also a very brief one)—Mr Wright caught him at point off Lillywhite. (Five wickets, 46.) Tarrant then appeared, and was quickly sent to the right about. (Six wickets, 51, in which Oscroft was included.) No. 8 was E. Stephenson, who batted superbly. Bignall did nothing, but Jackson, who went in late, made the longest score, and brought out his bat. At the close of the innings 87 runs were chronicled as the result of it. Slinn bowled 50 overs (26 maiden), 5 wickets, 26 runs; Lillywhite, 43 overs

(28 maiden), 32 runs, 2 wickets, 1 wide ball; Maitland, 9 overs (3 maiden), 19 runs, 1 wicket.

The Twenty-two began the batting with Messrs Davenport and Palmer; opposed to them as bowlers were Tarrant and Jackson. Runs at first came sparingly—only ten were recorded for three wickets. Mr Balfour—a name well-known in the upper circle of cricketers—played a good innings of 24, and during the time he occupied the wicket he saw seven companions come and go. He was the only member of the Twenty-two who soared into the region of double figures. The innings was completed on Tuesday, about two o'clock, for 65.

Nothing of note occurred during the second innings of the Eleven, although many of the spectators were not a little surprised at the hitting of Tarrant, and also at the easy way in which Stephenson, Bignall, and Jackson were disposed of. The first wicket fell for 0; second, 3; third, 10; fourth, 16; fifth, 17; sixth and seventh, 33; eighth, 36; ninth, 38; tenth, 41. The Twenty-two began their second innings shortly before six o'clock, and several wickets were lost before the time for drawing stumps. On Wednesday there was an unusually large attendance for a third day and the 'fag end' of a match. To account for this, an opinion was almost generally entertained that the 'home-dwellers' would become masters of the field, and such proved to be almost the case, but not quite. The eighteenth wicket had reached 46, and the amateurs were thus within 17 runs of the other side. At the fall of the nineteenth they only wanted five runs to win; a single resulted from the twentieth; but, alas! here the scoring came to a dead lock, and the All-England Eleven were proclaimed victors by three runs. The match created a great sensation in the neighbourhood, and it is by no means improbable that the seat of Sir Charles Russell will on a future occasion be the scene of some similar festivity.

CRICKET IN PARIS

THE Paris correspondent of the *Daily News*, writing on the 28th ult., says: 'The Paris Cricket Club never saw such a great day as this. Between five and six in the afternoon, just as the 73rd Regiment was completing the easy victory which, owing to its own prowess and the absence of some of the leading players on the other side, it was enabled to achieve over the club, the Emperor and Empress, attended by M. Drouyn de l'Huys, appeared upon the ground. Alighting from their carriage, their Majesties sat down in a small tent, and, while watching the game, accepted a simple luncheon, of which Mr T. H. Sparks, the secretary of the club, did the honours. The Empress asked a great many questions about the game both of Mr Sparks and of M. Drouyn de l'Huys, who, in his character of successor to the Duke de Morny, as president of the club, she seemed to take it for granted must be familiar with the sport. The Minister of Foreign Affairs, however, confessed that cricket was foreign to his studies, and he continually applied to other people for information to enable him to satisfy her Majesty's curiosity. Mr Sparks, although a most efficient secretary, and in fact the life and soul of the club, is not manually a cricketer, and therefore, perhaps, was not so ready at answering a sudden call for a lecture on the game as Professor Wanostrocht, cricketer and schoolmaster, would have been. However, in one way or another the Empress heard a great deal about wickets, stumps, bails, long stops, wide balls, bye runs, catches and "overs", and at the end of all the explanations, the Emperor, who had been conversing apart with a captain of the 73rd, exclaimed in French, "Je n'y comprends rien du tout" (I can make nothing of it). The Empress rejoined in English, "I understand a great deal, and I hope that next year the little prince will have learned this interesting game." Mr Sparks pointed out to the Empress a piece of copse wood too near the ground, and which was a frequent cause of "lost ball". The Emperor appeared to bow assent to the Empress's request that this wood should be grubbed. Their Majesties, on returning to their carriage, were escorted without ceremony by several Englishmen on the ground and loudly cheered. Their visit will no doubt give a great fillip to the club, though I do not think it will have the effect of making Frenchmen take to the game.'

August 1865

MORNINGTON v. WOOD GREEN—JULY 29th, 1865

[COMMUNICATED]
From Mr Peep hys Diary

ON Saturday to ye Eton and Middlesex cricket green to see ye game of Paile-Maile or hurly burly cricket between some gentlemen from Wood Green and ye Mornington Club, which was mighty fine. Mr Nash did throw ye ball very straight so that ye Wood Green men could not stop it with their bats, and ye wickets did rattle cheerfully, but one little gentleman did get a fierce blow from ye ball upon hys shins which made him to caper and dance, whereat I did laugh much. When ye Wood Green gentlemen had scored forty-one notches, ye Mornington men did take their place, and did hit ye ball and ran to and fro until they were profusely hot and must drink much beer. I also did drink with them and did find it very pleasant. But ye Morningtons were too strong for ye Wood Green men and claimed a victory with much rejoicing, after which I did visit ye refreshment rooms where was playing of pool and more beer, which I did much admire, until I did get sleepy and so home and to bed.

THE JOYS OF THE CRICKET FIELD

FEW men in their whole lives are so fortunate as to feel a moment of keener joy than a successful boy-cricketer in such an hour of triumph; it is without alloy; the only Nemesis he need fear is 'a pair of spectacles' in his next match, and to avert that he need not now crawl on his knees up the pavilion steps. Nor will the severest philosophy blame his exultation. He has done best what all his schoolfellows are eager to do well, and for doing which well even his masters, who have not forgotten that they too have been boys and cricketers, are proud of, and even grateful to him. The whole scene is English; the public schools are English; the game is English; the feelings it excites and the demonstrations of them which it prompts are English; and in the energy with which victory is sought, in the elation of those who achieve it, in the patient good humour of the defeated party, and in the sympathy of the spectators with both, we see a fair sample of the manly, good-tempered, honest character which pervades the whole of our nation, and is the parent of success in more important fields of action.—*The Shilling Magazine*

KNICKERBOCKERS v. WESTMEATH

RESPECTING this, a contributor remarks 'Day, Aug. 8; place, Phœnix Park; time, eleven a.m. Ten Knickerbockers present. Where is the other? Promised to play—never wrote—odd, very; however, got a substitute. Won the toss—went in. Poor Westmeath! Such leather hunting—ball knocked to pieces; park worn like a road—so much running, feet in blisters. Jolly game, very! Total, 217. Other side much disheartened; all disposed of for 96. Pleasant match, very! Hope the Knickerbockers will soon meet again; jolly good fellows, very.'

October 1868

LORD HOLMESDALE'S HOUSEHOLD v. SIR E. FILMERS'S HOUSEHOLD

PLAYED at Linton Park on Thursday, the 5th, and, according to an enthusiastic spectator, 'was one of the happiest days that it is possible to spend in a cricket field.' Lord Holmesdale's party scored 52 and 57—total 109; Sir E. Filmer's 76 and 15—total 91. Another (unkind) informant says the fielding was 'dickey' on both sides. We leave the adjective to be thought out by the general public.

January 1890

YORKSHIRE COUNTY CRICKET CLUB—PROFESSIONALS AND DRINK

THE annual general meeting of the Yorkshire County Club was held at Bramall-lane on Tuesday evening, when the following report was presented: 'Your committee regret that now, for the first time, they should have to report an actual loss upon the working of the year 1889. Commencing with a balance in hand of £139. 16s. 9d., the accounts for the year show that this has been reduced to £7. 9s. 10d. For this result the experimental colts' matches are responsible, the loss upon them being £203. 15s. 11d. The matches arranged for the season of 1890 are more numerous than usual, and should, with favourable weather, contribute largely to bring about a better state of things.'

In moving the adoption of the report, the Chairman (Mr M. J. Ellison) referred to the position which the county had occupied during the last season. They embarked upon it with full expectations that they would be at the top of the tree at the end. He did not know whether all present knew the cause of their failure. For that cause a very large number of people who called themselves supporters of cricket were responsible. The great difficulty with which they had to contend was what he would call the demon drink. The committee had had to put out of their team one upon whom they had looked to be of use, and for a good number of years a tower of strength, and at a critical time they had to suspend another. In a great measure this state of things had to be attributed to those people who, calling themselves friends and supporters of cricket, could not when they reached the ground see a professional cricketer without wanting to give him drink. If the grateful professional accepted one offer he had to accept others, or friends were offended. The worst thing they could do was to offer a cricketer drink, as it not only imperilled his immediate advantage, but told against him when he applied for a benefit. He appealed to all true friends of the game to abandon the practice of treating professionals.

November 1872

The deeply rooted love for the game, taken in conjunction with its gradual development among all classes of society, may be considered a sterling testimony to its value, not merely when regarded from a physical and hygienic point of view. Creeds, whether political or religious, no matter how extreme, melt away surprisingly under the sunshine and genial surroundings of a cricket match, and the descendants of Abraham are quite familiar friends for the time being with the followers of George Fox. What ground then is there for alarm that the incursions of Jonathan with his bustling base ball will hurl cricket from its throne, or that Polo with its pageantry can to any appreciable extent dim its attractions, or affect its popularity? None whatever. During the past season, that is from May to October, more than a thousand matches have received attention in the columns of this journal alone. In so large a number, it is obvious that the distinctions of merit must be various, seeing that England is now the centre of a great circumference, in many parts of which the game is but imperfectly developed. Hence we frequently receive intelligence of its progress from Bermuda, Bombay, Callao, Coquimbo, Ceylon, Candia, Gibraltar, Geneva, Galatz, Kustendjie, Poonah, Shanghai, and other stations less written about than the foregoing, and but recently brought into notice at all.

3
A GIRDLE
AROUND
THE GLOBE

A glance at practically any cricket coverage
in an issue of *The Field* during the late nineteenth century would reveal instantly the
extraordinarily wide catchment area for the
game when performed by service teams and
other expatriate outfits. As will be seen,
many times little detail accompanied the
bald statement of a match.

The concentration in this chapter is on
some of those more unlikely venues as
opposed to the front-line cricket-playing
nations.

CRICKET AT SPEZIA
H.M.S. Victoria v H.M.S. Gibraltar

CRICKET AT HALIFAX, NOVA SCOTIA
Officers 101st Fusiliers v Non-Commissioned Officers and Men
Played on the Garrison Cricket Ground at Halifax, N.S., on July 19
and 20, and resulted in a somewhat easy victory for the Officers.

CRICKET IN CEYLON
Uda Puxlawa v Kandapolla
Played on Aug. 13 and 14, on U.P. ground, and resulted in favour of
Kandapolla by five wickets.

SICILY
Gun Room Officers v Ship's Company H.M.S. Alexandra
Played at Port Gravosa (Ragusa) on Sept. 22.

ASCENSION
H.M.S. Charybdis v The Island
During the few days' stay at the Island of H.M.S. Charybdis, homeward
bound from China, a match as above was played on Sept. 4, resulting
in a very easy victory for the Island, who were doubtless more at home
on the clinker than their adversaries.

NAVY (H.M. SHIPS 'EURYALUS' AND 'ECLIPSE') v GARRISON AT TRINCOMALEE
Played on May 15, 22 and 29

NEUCHATEL v LAUSANNE

Played at Lausanne on Thursday, June 24. Neuchatel won by 117 runs.

Neuchatel	1st inn.		2nd inn.
Total	44	Total	149
Lausanne	1st inn.		2nd inn.
Total	31	Total	45

CRICKET IN AFGHANISTAN
Veterans (Over Ten Years' Service) v The Rest

January 1885

EGYPT
Cairo v Alexandria
Played on the Ramleh ground, Dec. 29 and 30, and ended in a victory for Alexandria by 89 runs.

February 1885

CHINA
H.M.S. Merlin v Swatow
The above clubs played a one day's match on Jan. 10. Lieut. Brenton's bowling contributed in no small degree to the unexpected success of the naval team.

June 1885

AFRICA
The 2nd West India Regt. v The Royal Navy
Played at Sierra Leone, West Africa, June 2.

July 1888

CRICKET IN SWITZERLAND
Geneva v Lyons
Played at Geneva, July 14, resulting in a win for the former by 26 runs. Scores: Geneva 72 and 48; Lyons 69 and 25.

H.M.S. SYLVIA v PERIM ISLAND

Played on Saturday, June 16, and resulted in a win for the Perimites by 60 runs. Scores: Perim Island, 100 (Mr A. W. Prosser 41 not out); H.M.S. Sylvia, 40.

August 1888

NAVY v ST. JOHN'S (NEWFOUNDLAND)
Played at Qui di Vidi.

September 1888

THASO ISLAND
H.M.S. Agamemnon v H.M.S. Temeraire
Played at Thaso on Sept. 10.

QUETTA
Yorkshire L.I. (105th) v Worcestershire Regt. (29th)
Played at Quetta, Oct. 3 and 4.

NOVA SCOTIA
Navy v Bankers of Halifax
Played at Halifax, Saturday, Aug. 18. Navy won by an innings and 29 runs.

MEDITERRANEAN SQUADRON v CONSTANTINOPLE

Played on the Beicos cricket ground at Constantinople on Aug. 31, an eleven from the Mediterranean Squadron, then anchored at Tenedos, having been previously brought up in H.M.S. Surprise, by the kind permission of H.R.H. the Duke of Edinburgh. The naval team obtained an easy victory by seven wickets.

December 1888

HONGKONG
Hongkong v The Garrison
Played on Oct. 19 and 20. Won by The Garrison by forty-six runs.

BURMA
The Station (Mandalay) v 2nd Batt. Royal Munster Fusiliers
Played at Mandalay on Oct. 11 and 13. The Fusiliers won by eight
wickets.

April 1890

MALTA
Wardroom v Gunroom Officers
Played at Malta on March 22, the Gunrooms winning by 58 runs.

EGYPT
2nd Batt. Suffolk Regt. v Royal Irish Rifles
Played at Cairo, March 14, on the Gezireh cricket ground. Owing to
heavy rain, the match did not begin till after 2 p.m. Capt. Withington
played a fine innings of 110 not out, and he and Mr Stothered put on
86 runs for the sixth wicket. Corp. Moir played well for the Rifles. The
light was not good during the latter part of the day, the sun being in
the batsmen's eyes.

July 1895

BELGIUM
English College, Bruges v Capt. L. Silvester's Eleven
Played on the College ground on June 27.

NORWAY
H.M.S. Ruby v Rest of Training Squadron
Played at Trondhjem, Norway, on July 5.

YOUGHAL v SPIKE ISLAND
Played at Youghal on July 13. Scores: Spike Island, 269 for six wickets
(C. Phillips 25, Capt. Norris 83, St J. Killery 46, Sergt. Reilly 51, Corp.
Nicholls not out 37); Youghal, 81 (B. W. Wise not out 28) and 71 for
seven wickets (F. Rouayne 29).

H.M.S. ROYAL ARTHUR AND NYMPHE v VANCOUVER CITY
Played at Vancouver on July 1.

CHINA
Navy v Chefoo
Played at Chefoo on June 6.

August 1895

JAPAN
Royal Navy v Kobé
Played at Kobé on June 20.

September 1895

MAURITIUS
Officers of Garrison v Warrant and Non-Commissioned Officers
Played at Port Louis on July 18.

October 1895

SALONICA
Salonica v S.S. Liffey and S.S. Bedford
Played at Salonica on Sept. 7, and resulted in a win for the former by
177 runs.

JAPAN
H.M.S. Peacock v H.M.S. Caroline
Played at Yokohama on May 23.

BRITISH HONDURAS
H.M.S. Tartar v Mr Young's Eleven
Played at Belize on Saturday, Sept. 28.

PARAGUAY
New Australians v Englishmen of Paraguay
Played at Loma Riyua on Oct. 11 and 12. Score:

NEW AUSTRALIANS	1st inn.		2nd inn.
Thomas c and b Smead	8	c and b Keen	4
Marsden b Smead	6	b Keen	2
H. King run out	24	c and b Keen	7
T. King c Spence b Smead	9	c Fairburn b Smead	0
Birks b Smead	3	b Smead	6
Bond not out	11	run out	5
Weidenhofer b Brown	0	c Fairburn b Keen	0
Jenkins lbw b Brown	0	b Smead	14
Butterworth c Smead b Keen	0	not out	0
A. King b Smead	2	c Stanley b Smead	1
Cummings b Smead	0	c Stanley (sen.) b Smead	2
Walker c and b Smead	0	b Keen	0
Byes etc.	11	Byes etc.	6
Total	74	Total	47

ENGLISHMEN OF PARAGUAY	1st inn.		2nd inn.
Scratton b Jenkins	6	hit wicket	9
Stanley (jun.) run out	4	b Jenkins	1
Fairburn b T. King	2	c H. b T. King	1
Keen c Jenkins b T. King	10	b T. King	1
Gomm b Jenkins	0	c A. King b Jenkins	0
Blackmore c Jenkins b King	3	c and b T. King	0
Smead b Jenkins	10	c Birks b King	11
Stanley (sen.) b T. King	0	c and b Jenkins	14
Goodacre b Jenkins	2	hit wicket	0
Spence run out	0	not out	0
Hawes c Weidenhofer b Jenkins	0	b Jenkins	0
Brown not out	0	b Jenkins	10
Byes etc.	5	Bye	1
Total	42	Total	48

BAGHDAD
Mr F. Pickard's Eleven v Mr H. J. Andrewes's Eleven
The first game of the Baghdad season was played on Oct. 29, near the Mounds, and resulted in favour of the latter by 46 runs on the first innings.

MADEIRA
H.M.S. Cordelia v Excelsior Club
Played at Sao Martinho on Dec. 9, and ended in favour of the home team by eleven runs.

August 1905

BRAZIL
Banks (Past and Present) v The World
Played at the Bosque Municipal, Manaos, June 25.

December 1910

108th INFANTRY v MAHOMEDAN C.C.
Played at Aden, Nov. 12. Score:

108th INFANTRY		MAHOMEDAN C.C.	
Major E. Saulez		Abdul Ahmed c Saulez	
b Abdul Ahmed	68	b Narayan	2
Bhuru lbw Abdul Khan	0	Shaik Mahomed c Masters	
E. G. Ford not out	101	b Narayan	27
P. I. R. Sandilands b Hari	10	Ahmed Hussain b Ford	10
Gopal b Shaik Mahomed	15	Abdulla Khan c Saulez	
E. Masters b Sayid Jaffer	4	b Parasnak	7
Narayan not out	7	Haji Gannu c Bhuru	
F. W. Jacomb did not bat		b Parasnak	2
Arjun did not bat		Hari b Narayan	10
Bhiwa did not bat		Yasayaen b Ford	6
Parasnak did not bat		Sayid Jaffer c Bhuru	
		b Narayan	2
		Ahej Suttar c Gopal b Ford	2
		Channoo not out	2
		Sultan Ali b Ford	0
Byes etc.	9	Byes	15
Total	214	Total	85

August 1924

CRICKET IN SWITZERLAND
Zuoz College v Mr Gannon's Golfers' Eleven
Played at Zuoz College on July 24th.

August 1865

CRICKET IN ST PETERSBURG

THE St Petersburg Cricket Club played their first match this season on Thursday, July 20, the contest being the annual match of Island v. the Town, or the Left v. the Right banks of the Neva. The interest of the match was somewhat marred by an accident which happened to the captain of the Town eleven, Mr C. Gwyer, who wrenched his leg so severely from a fall at the commencement of his innings as to be incapacitated from taking any further part in the game. The heat was intense, the consumption of liquids alarming—the play, owing to the heat, not very brilliant. Mr B. Gibson played a careful innings of nineteen, not out, for the Island; Messrs F. Bennett and R. Anderson reaching double figures for the Town. The match not being played out, was decided in favour of the Island by the first innings.

CRICKET ON THE CONTINENT

GREAT preparations are being made at Homburg this season in the cricketing way. It will be remembered that last year the Paris Club sent over an Eleven to Homburg to play against the visitors and German clubs, which proved a success for them in every sense. This year will see not only a Paris Eleven, but also an All-England Eleven (gentlemen) at Homburg, and arrangements are made for two matches, which will come off on the 15th, 16th, 17th, and 18th inst. In one, the Paris Club will play against the German clubs and visitors, and in the other, an eleven drawn from the Marylebone and other clubs will play on behalf of England against the rest of Europe. This character of nationality will, doubtless, add a further interest to the events, and induce our foreign friends to make themselves acquainted with this (to them) ferocious sport. Balls and other festivities are projected by the Homburgians for the entertainment of their visitors, so that not only capital cricket, but also a most delightful trip may be anticipated by the elevens and their friends.

September 1865

CRICKET ON THE CONTINENT

GERMANY v. THE PARIS CLUB

FOR some time past notice has been given, in the way of talk, of a grand week on the Continent, and among the proposed matches Germany were to play the Paris Club. The city of Homburg, near Frankfort-on-the-Maine, was the appointed place of meeting, and on the 15th ult. the first match of the proposed three took place, . . . and . . . which . . . France won by six wickets.

***

Civil Service Cricket Club v. Paris

On Monday, the 28th, a civil service team, rather short in numbers, but with no lack of pluck, found their way to the Pelouse de Madrid, in the Bois de Boulogne, and prepared to do battle with the representatives of the Paris Club. The sun was shining its brightest, and the heat was quite enough even for cricket. Thanks to the untiring exertions of the honorary secretary to the Paris Club a capital wicket had been prepared, and though the fielding was not such a certainty as might be expected on the Oval, and though the ball was occasionally lost in the surrounding forest, the game was cricket all over, and it was difficult to realise the fact that it was being played close to Paris. The visitors were of many different nations, including, among others, Prince Demidoff and the Marquis of Hertford. Some of the more inquisitive natives were for examining the game closer than prudence suggested, but scampered away at a good pace when the ball came near. The game was continued on Tuesday, but the weather was very unfavourable. Eventually the Civil Service won, but it would not be fair to omit the fact that several of the best of the Paris men were unavoidably absent. The Civil Service were most sumptuously entertained at dinner after the match by their hospitable opponents, and the *garçons* of the Café Mongrolle, had the pleasure of hearing English songs and English cheering till a very late hour of the evening.

***

French Opinion of Cricket

The Gallic mind is really most obtuse as regards our great national pastime—cricket. They can see no delight at being bowled over at twenty-two yards, or at getting in the way of the 'leather' at a much longer range. The report of the Greenwich Pensioner match was read in France with astonishment, not unmingled with feelings of compassion for the maimed veterans who took the field. Surprise reached its climax when it was seen that on the 'One Arm' having terminated their innings the stumps (*moignons*) were drawn. The error on the part of the translators led to the belief that the drawing of the stumps was a punishment inflicted on the 'One Arm' for having lost the match.—*Army and Navy Gazette.*

A. TO K. V. L. TO Z. (DINAN)

AT length, after the scare of 1870, visitors and residents are returning to their habitual haunts in Brittany and Normandy. Cricket, for which Dinan is pre-eminent amongst French towns, was slack at the beginning of the season, but has now taken a turn for the better, which nothing but 'horrida bella' will interfere with. Several good cricketers, including some public school performers, being in the place, an alphabetical match was arranged on Wednesday the 4th inst., and the old ground looked something like itself again. The drought made the ground cracky, hence scoring uncertain.

SUAKIM

R.A. v. GRENADIER GUARDS

A CORRESPONDENT, writing on the 12th ult., sends us the following: Yesterday saw the opening of the Suakim cricket season, on the ground of the Royal Artillery, which was prepared with great skill by the Rocket Troop, assisted by a Bengalese sweeper, whose services with the besom, in removing superfluous stones, sand, &c., from the cocoa-nut matting, were very frequently called into play during the game. Taking advantage of a comparative day's rest from moving camp—an instructive, if somewhat arduous pastime, with which the whole of the troops have lately been regaled—a match was arranged between the R.A. and the 3rd Battalion Grenadier Guards, and was to have commenced at two p.m. sharp, but as the Grenadiers were competing at the game of 'shift-camp', they were thereby delayed for upwards of an hour. However, they arrived full of go, and, winning the toss, went in on an excellent 'cocoa-nut' wicket, with a good light, and put together a fine score of 89. The Gunners followed, but failed to overhaul the Guards, their last wicket falling for 46, one minute before time. The Guards lost the services of Mildmay, who was drilling his mounted men a short distance off, and of others who were completing the arrangements of the new camp, while the Gunners were short of three of their best men, Capt. Fox, and Lieuts. Allsopp and Herbert, who were otherwise engaged. The thermometer was 96° Fahr. in the shade, and the sand heavy. Tea and iced drinks were provided by the R.A. for the ladies, Osman Digna, and parties, who, however, failed to put in an appearance;

but we understand, on the authority of the Intelligence Department, that they were watching the match with lively interest through Ross's best glasses from the top of the Hasheen Hill.

July 1888

CRICKET IN SPAIN

Vigo v. Training Squadron

THIS match, which is the first played by Spaniards, was played on June 21 on the ground of the club. The club was formed only three months ago by Spanish gentlemen who have been to school in England for two or three years, and so got a taste for the game which they are sporting enough to start in their own country. Thousands of people assembled in the afternoon to witness the, to them, very novel sight. A very good military band played at intervals during the day. The Governor and his staff arrived on the ground about five o'clock and remained until the conclusion of the match. The Squadron Eleven were most hospitably entertained at luncheon by the Vigo Cricket and Sporting Club. Score:

TRAINING SQUADRON	1st inn.		2nd inn.
Lieut. Booth, b F. Yañez	0	b F. Yañez	0
Mr Shelford, b F. Yañez	0	b Chambers	9
Mr Vivian, b Sherlock	7	b F. Yañez	1
Lieut. Stileman, b Chambers	45	not out	8
Lieut. Wellings, c Sherlock, b F. Yañez	1	c and b Sherlock	9
Mr Johnson, c Hempsted, b P. Yañez	18	b Chambers	3
Capt. Hayes (R.M.L.I.), b Chambers	18	b F. Yañez	3
Lieut. Gibbons, b Chambers	5	b Sherlock	16
Mr Grant, b Chambers	3	b P. Yañez	0
Mr Bradshaw, not out	1	c and b F. Yañez	2
Lieut. Boothby, b P. Yañez	1	b P. Yañez	2
Byes 4, w 1	5	Byes 2, l-b 1, w 1	4
Total	104	Total	57

Vigo	1st inn.		2nd inn.
Mr Sherlock, b Stileman	0	b Grant	5
Mr F. Yañez, b Stileman	0	c Wellings, b Gibbons	0
Mr Chambers, b Stileman	1	c Wellings, b Gibbons	5
Mr P. Yañez, b Stileman	8	run out	1
Mr J. Conde, b Stileman	2	b Grant	3
Mr F. Conde, c and b Shelford	1	c Wellings, b Gibbons	0
Mr Hemsted, run out	1	c Johnson, b Grant	0
Mr A. Conde, b Shelford	4	run out	0
Mr A. Fernandez, h w, b Shelford	2	l b w, b Gibbons	0
Mr Santas, b Shelford	1	b Gibbons	4
Mr J. Cubera, not out	1	not out	2
Byes	3		—
Total	24	Total	20

September 1888

CYPRUS

Officers 1st Batt. P.W.O. Yorkshire Regt. v. Officers H.M.S. Carysfort

Played on Mount Trodoos on Tuesday, July 31. Some allowance must be made for the Naval team, as they had to ride a distance of forty miles on mules, and only arrived the morning of the day on which the match was played.

Officers P.W.O. Yorkshire Regt.	Officers H.M.S. Carysfort
Total 126	Total 34

CRICKET AT GIBRALTAR

R.A. and R.E. v. The Rest of Garrison

Played Sept. 4. An interesting match, it being the first appearance of Capt. Renny-Tailyour, R.E., abroad, and also on matting. Major Cummings's analysis of eight wickets for 48 runs with 'lobs' is about the best record on the Rock.

August 1895

SPITZBERGEN

H.M.S. ACTIVE AND CALYPSO V. H.M.S. VOLAGE AND RUBY

PLAYED on Aug. 2 on the shores of Recherche Bay, Spitzbergen. The ground was a most picturesque one, being surrounded by glaciers. These latter are continually breaking up as they work down into the sea, and the bay was thus studded with floating masses of ice, which added to the scenic effect. Play commenced late in the evening, and was continued till past midnight. In this latitude (77° 30′ N.) cricket might be played all night through at this time of the year, the climate being warm enough (except when the wind is from the north). The match resulted in a win for H.M.S. Active and Calypso.

September 1895

MOROCCO

DAR-AL-BAIDA V. H.M. SHIPS ARETHUSA AND FEARLESS

PLAYED at Dar-al-Baida, Casablanca, on Aug. 15, on the occasion of a visit from H.M. Ships Arethusa and Fearless. It is noteworthy as being the first match played in Morocco south of Tangier [*possibly*]. Score:

DAR-AL-BAIDA		H.M. SHIPS ARETHUSA AND FEARLESS	
Smith b Taylor	41	Taylor b Grieve	0
Capt. C. F. Cromie b Taylor	39	Saunders c Smith b Grieve	15
Dr Grieve b Johnson-Stewart	1	St John b Grieve	0
T. Spinney b Johnson-Stewart	1	Johnson-Stewart b Spinney	4
A. Maclean b Taylor	4	Baker c and b Cromie	10
Griffin b Johnson-Stewart	2	Pasley b Grieve	1
Armour b Johnson-Stewart	0	Fox b Grieve	4
G. H. Fernan c Fox		Sergt.-Major Burgis	
b Johnson-Stewart	0	c Armour, b Cromie	5
Novella not out	0	Bissett b Cromie	12
A. Karam c Taylor		Wells st Smith b Cromie	0
b Johnson-Stewart	0	Holmes not out	1
Byes &c	19	Byes &c	5
Total	107	Total	57

THE ENGLISH CRICKETERS IN AMERICA

Third Match v. Pennsylvania University

A TEAM representing the past and present of Pennsylvania University met Mr Mitchell's Eleven on the Wissahickon ground, at Philadelphia, on Friday last, in the presence of about 4000 spectators. The visitors opened the batting, and so excellent was their defence that the last wicket did not fall until 284 appeared on the board. Mr Mitchell contributed 58, and during his stay did not give a single chance. Four of the Pennsylvanian wickets fell for 38 runs, when stumps were drawn for the day. On Saturday, the over-night score of the home team was only taken to 138, in consequence of which they had to follow on. Much better form was displayed in the second innings, and at the close eight wickets were responsible for 283 runs, Patterson, Noble, and Coates, jun., each claiming over 60. The match was brought to a conclusion on Monday, when, contrary to anticipations, Mr Mitchell's team suffered defeat by 100 runs. The last two wickets of the home players added 24, which brought the total to 307. The English men required 162 runs to win, but they collapsed in a remarkable manner, the whole side compiling 61 runs. Messrs Robinson, Hill, and Hemingway were the only batsmen to reach double figures.

July 1910

NIGERIA

IN the very middle of the cricket season in England the season in Southern Nigeria came to an end. Necessarily the number of matches is limited, and a series of four is played between Europeans and natives. This year's matches in this series ended in a couple of wins to each side. In the last of them, the closing game of the season, the Europeans were victorious by nine wickets, F. E. G. Johnson taking six wickets for 19 and W. E. B. Copeland-Crawford, who went on with lobs towards the end of the innings, bowled ten balls for four wickets and two runs. In the averages Copeland-Crawford comes out first with 49·7 for nine completed innings, and a highest score of 102, while C. W. Taylor is second with an average of 47·3 for five innings and a highest score of 116. In bowling F. E. G. Johnson is easily first with 69 wickets in 17 innings. As showing the difficulties with which cricketers in the colonies have to contend, it may be added that in the part of the season which fell in 1909 only three matches could be played, because the cricket ground was required for an agricultural show.

July 1949

GOLD COAST CRICKET

ONE of the few stable things in a changing Empire is cricket. Some of the more active elements that clamour for self-expression and self-government are to be found in the Gold Coast; yet the claims of cricket have recently engaged the attention of African chiefs in conference. They are anxious, it seems, that interest in the game should be stimulated, but their anxiety is tempered with financial discretion. At the Western Province Council of Chiefs it was unanimously decided that each Chief should contribute ten shillings to the Gold Coast African Cricket Association.

It is perhaps fortunate that African cricketers are content to do without some of the more expensive appurtenances; but the hope is expressed that the Chiefs' example will be followed by other social, economic and political bodies in the Territory.

August 1922

GERMANY

A NEW version of an old story is always welcome, and the following, from the *Cologne Post*, seems particularly good: 'At a cricket match the other day a batsman went in with only one pad on. Noticing it adorned the right leg, the fielders assumed he was a left-hander and altered their positions accordingly. But he turned out to be right-handed after all, so the wicket-keeper pointed out to him that he had the pad on the wrong leg. "Nothing of the sort," was the reply. "You see, I thought I was going in at the other end." '

September 1922

M.C.C. TOUR IN DENMARK

CRICKET has been played in Denmark since the eighties. It was actually played by some English engineers employed in laying down a railway in Jutland. From time to time English club sides (generally from the Midlands or the North) have gone over and played matches with the Danes, and as recently as last year a team from the Leicester and County Cricket Association played a draw in Copenhagen, the scores being: Leicester, 285 and 123 for eight (declared); Copenhagen, 263 and 101 for five. The M.C.C. team, which was playing in Denmark in the latter part of August, was not only the first the club had ever sent to that country, but (according to the Danish papers) distinctly the strongest combination yet seen there.

In its original conception the tour was to include a couple of matches in Jutland – one at Aalborg and another at Aarhus or Fredericia. This would have added greatly to the interest and value of the tour, and it was a thousand pities that the project had to be abandoned. The difficulty arose from the lateness of the season. Danish cricket – more cursed even than our own by the encroachment of football – ceases at the end of August, and the sole remaining week-end, at which the principal M.C.C. v. Jutland match would have taken place (mid-week 'gates' being small), was already earmarked for the final of the Jutland (inter-town) Championship, and, although an attempt was made to re-arrange this date, it fell through. The English team therefore remained on in Copenhagen, and a third match was played against a combined Copenhagen team. Apart from the Copenhagen clubs, there are said to be a great many clubs all over Denmark – in Zealand, Funen, and, above all, Jutland. Every town of any size has its cricket team, and inter-town feeling gives great keenness to the matches.

Everywhere in Denmark cricket is played on a matting pitch, but little or no attention seems to be paid to the fielding surface, which is left unrolled and, to a large extent, uncut. This applies not only to the outfield, beyond the cover-point distance, but right up to the matting itself. Ground-fielding is therefore of the most speculative, not to say dangerous, description, and players and spectators alike are robbed of one of the most attractive features of the game. Moreover, when the ball has been struck by the batsman, it has so little run on it that the value of hitting along the ground is severely discounted, and so a wrong style of batsmanship is encouraged. . .

After repairing, both outside and in, the ravages of the journey, the side went up to the ground for a little practice. This was just as well, for some had never before played on matting, and even those who had found the conditions very difficult to assimilate. Batsmen were clean bowled every other ball when they first went in, a very pronounced glare and a tendency for the balls to shoot giving the player a sort of 'nightmare' feeling (as one described it whose wicket was bowled down three balls in succession). Heavy rain at lunch-time made the ground very heavy, and when play began at 2.20 – the Englishmen having lost the toss – sawdust had to be freely used. C. Buchwald, who opened the innings with Boertmann, is generally regarded as the premier Danish batsman; he has many centuries to his credit. He certainly showed extraordinarily sound defence, but even with him there was a certain stiffness, or absence of proper wrist work, which is the most general flaw in Danish batsmanship. It was a wretched afternoon. There were no fewer than five intervals for rain – and this, in spite of the fact that the Englishmen several times continued fielding until the rain was really coming down quite hard. It was not a case of dodging in at the first drop. Clay, who at the start was bowling very fast and extremely well, soon found himself unable to get a foothold; in his second spell of bowling he reverted to the slow leg-breaks of his Winchester days. Homan found the sodden ball quite useless for in-swinging. The best stand of the innings was made by Stavnsbjerg and Saabye, who added 60 for the eighth wicket. Both hit hard and with a fair amount of wrist, but Stavnsbjerg (who used to play with Englishmen in St Petersburg before the war) is much the better batsman. On the showing of this tour he is the best all-round cricketer the Danes have got; 128 was not a bad total considering the dead slowness of the outfield, and was perhaps worth 250 on a normal ground. . . .

The M.C.C. had lost two wickets for 24 overnight, and on resuming next morning (at 10.15!) they had quite a bad time. Saabye (fastish) and Noergaard (medium), both right-handers, were bowling an extremely good length and bowling it straight. Moreover, the ball was repeatedly shooting dead, so that batsmen, even if they were not clean bowled, were forced out of their usual game through looking for 'the one that creeps'. One unfortunate was bowled by a ball that broke 3 in. and shot as well. Six wickets were down for 57, but on Clay joining V. T. Hill (who made a hundred in the University match as far back as 1892) some resistance was offered, left-handed batting once more demonstrating its usefulness in throwing successful bowlers out of their stride. Hill actually found the boundary four times, but many of his singles would have been fours in England; his shots through the covers were as crisp and delightful as ever. Still, the side were all out for 105, or 23 behind. Saabye and Noergaard both bowled well, but might perhaps have been rested earlier; they bowled 43 overs between them before a change was made. Then Leopold and Brysting seized their belated chance to the tune of two for 5 and two for 2 respectively. The Copenhagen second innings was, to a large extent, a repetition of the first, although this time the weather was beautiful. They lost four for 21 before lunch, Homan securing three of these, while the ball was new, for 12 runs; but afterwards there was some stout hitting, Noergaard, promoted to No. 7, being 'top scorer' (to use a word beloved of Danish journalists) with 28. The M.C.C. had thus 124 to get to win. In half an hour they lost V. T. Hill, Bonham-Carter, and Durlacher for 21 runs, Noergaard taking all three wickets at a cost of only two runs. The score was taken to 38, but Leopold, relieving Saabye, clean bowled Clay with his second ball. At this gloomy moment, when over two thousand Danish onlookers were beginning to work themselves up to the idea of victory, the M.C.C.'s batting at last asserted itself. Robinson and Keigwin added 33 before the former was caught at the wicket, and then Kent stayed with his captain until only nine runs were required. Kent was then yorked by Stavnsbjerg, who, after keeping wicket for nine-tenths of the match, doffed his pads and bowled half a dozen overs as well as anyone. With Mathias in, Keigwin hit Noergaard to the boundary, and the match was over. The margin of four wickets by which the M.C.C. won was not a convincing one, especially when one considers that the three batsmen to come in had only aggregated one between them in the first innings, and great credit is due to the Danes for what was a very fine performance. Noergaard had a particularly good match, for, besides scoring 30 for once out, he took six of the 16 M.C.C. wickets that fell, and bowled as many as 37 overs for only 59 runs. Even allowing for the difficulty of getting the ball to travel, this was a notable feat.

This was undoubtedly the most interesting match of the tour. To begin with, there was all the interest of seeing Danish cricket for the first time, and, secondly, from a sporting point of view, it was so much better fun as a contest. The two matches that followed were runaway victories, which confirmed, but gave no new impressions of Danish cricket. . . .

The thanks of the M.C.C. are especially due to Hr. Heiberg, who acted throughout as scorer for the club, and never was the job more thoroughly done. He managed to keep on the score-sheet a neatly pencilled chronology of the whole of each match, together with other notes most useful to anyone subsequently attempting to reconstruct the story of the game. The team was most cordially entertained at dinner after both the first and last matches, the president of the Dansk Boldspil Union being in the chair on each occasion, and at all times the Danes did everything imaginable to make things pleasant for their visitors. Englishmen resident in Copenhagen were also very hearty in their welcome. Lord Granville (the British Minister) and Lady Granville very kindly had several of the team to lunch at the Legation, and on another non-cricketing day the team were entertained by members of the British community at the Hotel Phoenix. Parties were also organised for viewing farms, castles, and what not.

The newspapers were very lavish in the columns and the headlines they devoted to the 'Engelske cricketspillere' (the word has a butter-finger look about it!), and the photographs that were taken – it has been estimated by a careful statistician that one exposure was made for every six and a half runs scored. Above all, they adored snapping this wonderful wicket-keeper who stood right up almost touching the stumps. Perhaps they secretly hoped they might catch him nudging the bail off as the ball was bowled! How they all came off unscathed, goodness only knows. They were just as dauntless when Clay was swiping. It certainly was a relief to finish the tour without having killed a photographer.

First Match

M.C.C. won by four wickets. Clay took eight wickets for 67 runs, and Noergaard six for 59.

Second Match (12-aside)

M.C.C. won by an innings and 212 runs. Homan took 11 wickets for 38, and Clay seven for 44.

Third Match

M.C.C. won by an innings and 65 runs. Saabye took four wickets for 55 and Noergaard three for 31. For M.C.C. Homan obtained eight for 60, Clay six for 32, and Kent six for 36.

March 1923

A PORTUGUESE VIEW OF CRICKET

IN an old *Lillywhite's Guide,* Mr A. L. Ford has found a newspaper cutting and has sent it to us. There is no clue as to the date, but from the appearance of the cutting it must be pretty old, and the printing on the back shows clearly that the extract appeared in a Devon newspaper. There is no indication whether the quotation from the Lisbon paper is a translation, but its first sentence is charming. The complete extract is as follows: 'Englishmen to whatever part of the world they wander, carry with them their national habits and customs, and even their games and sports. The active and athletic character of these last seems to puzzle the natives of the South, in whose minds great muscular exertion is by no means associated with the idea of pleasure. The English residents at Lisbon and Oporto have each of them a cricket club, and the rival clubs have lately had a match at Lisbon. The fact that a number of English gentlemen residing at Oporto were to make a journey to Lisbon, for the purpose of contending for the palm of victory in the national pastime with their countrymen there, excited some interest in the Portuguese capital; and a Lisbon journal gives the following picture of the noble game of cricket, which, as being taken from a Portuguese point of view, will amuse our readers.'

'*Cricket Match.*—To-morrow there was to have come off an interesting game of cricket between the cricket clubs of Lisbon and Oporto. The object of the formation of these societies is the playing of the game of cricket-match, an active, running, driving, jumping game, which only can be played by a person having a good pair of legs, and in a climate where warm punch is found insufficient to keep up the animal heat. Does the reader know how to play a game at cricket-match? Two posts are placed at a great distance from one another. The player close to one of the posts throws a large ball towards the other party, who awaits the ball to send it far with a small stick with which he is armed. The other players then run to look after the ball, and while this search is going on the party who struck it with the stick runs incessantly from post to post, marking one for each run. It is plain, then, that it is to the advantage of the party who strikes the ball to make it jump very far. Sometimes it tumbles into a thicket, and the players take hours before they can get hold of it, and all this time the player does not cease running from post to post, and marking points. Then those who find the ball arrive, exhausted, at the field of battle, and the one who has been running falls down half dead. At other times the projectile, sent with a vigorous arm, cannot be stopped and breaks the legs of the party who awaits it. The arrangements for the cricket-match include a sumptuous dinner in the marquee for fifty persons—an indispensable accompaniment to every cricket-match. We may, perhaps, assist at this great battle, and hope the committee will place us at a safe distance from the combatants, where the principles of the game can be seen with the help of an opera glass.'

July 1924

CRICKET IN SAMOA

MANY times during the last few years references to cricket as played in Samoa have cropped up, but there has always been a difficulty in arriving at actual facts. Some months ago a correspondent suggested that the Bishop of Bunbury, Australia, who, when he played for Kent as Mr Cecil Wilson, was one of the greatest batsmen of his day, might be able to give us the facts, as he had lived there. The Bishop has very kindly sent us the following letter, but does not refer to his own experiences in Samoa:

'In reply to your letter about stories of cricket in Samoa, I refer you to A. W. Mahaffy's article in *Imperial Cricket*, edited by P. F. Warner. He describes a match he had seen in Samoa in which the teams were 75 a side, and says that this was considered a "very moderate" number. The game opened with speech-making followed by a feast. There were four or five umpires at each end. Seventy men fielded in a ring round the ground and under the trees beyond it. There were four long-stops behind the bare-handed and unpadded wicket-keeper. Each batsman had three men to run for him by turns, to avoid exhaustion and to save time. The ball was not bowled, but thrown. A man with a long whip chased anyone who dropped a catch. In another match there were 150 aside. A fieldsman standing in the sea in 3 ft. or 4 ft. of water made a fine catch. So much time and money were spent in cricket that a paternal Government stepped in and limited the duration of the game. A match was not allowed to go on for more than a week, and chiefs were restrained from ruining themselves in providing hospitality for visiting teams. Mr Mahaffy came from Samoa to the Solomon Islands to be our Deputy-Commissioner, and he told me there of what he afterwards described in *Imperial Cricket*.

'About the same time (it was in 1897) I brought an eleven of Solomon Islanders to play against H.M.S. Pylades at Gavutu. In that match I managed to drop a skier into the crown of a coconut tree just over mid-off's head. We ran six whilst mid-off, an officer in white ducks, tried to climb the tree. This hit won the match, as "last man" succumbed to the next ball. The scores were 56 and 55. Cecil Wilson, Bishop of Bunbury.'

CRICKET IN SAMOA

Sir,—In your issue of April 10th you have some reference to cricket in Samoa, from which I gather that the game has altered somewhat since I played it there ten years ago. We invariably played with three stumps, but the bat used by the natives was a sort of cross between a hockey stick and a cricket bat—thicker at one end and tapering off to a handle—there is only one possible stroke with it, the blind swipe! As all their bowling was very fast, and often, in my opinion, a deliberate throw, whatever it may be now, the natives scored freely in a sort of tip-and-run fashion; but when they came up against some real slow bowling they were unable to score—invariably hitting at the ball far too soon. The batsmen used to run their own runs in those days—perhaps they are fatter now under our administration! I can bear out what Capt. Bell says about champion villages being reduced to poverty from having to entertain some 200 visiting players for a week or more for each match.

I remember soon after we had taken possession of Samoa in September, 1914, Jamasese's village challenged my regiment to a match. We went over to play, and were considerably handicapped by various trees at one end of the pitch—one just behind the wicket-keeper, another in the slips, and a third close to square leg. We got beaten, chiefly because we all tried to bowl fast, and also, I regret to say, because we had to play their umpire as well.

After the game the chief asked me if we would play again, and I replied yes, but not on this ground, because the trees get in the way. Next morning he invited me to come over and look at the pitch, when I found that not only had he cut down the trees before mentioned, but also several others which had been too close; as this represented the sacrifice of considerable food supplies—one, if not two of them, being bread fruit trees—I consider we ill repaid his generosity by giving them a thorough beating by means of a wily slow bowler the next time we played them.

My liveliest recollection is one of nearly killing a small naked urchin of about four years old, who was standing just in front of one of the huts. I had lifted the ball over cover's head, and I stood horror-struck when I saw it was going to hit the child on the head. Luckily it missed him by an inch, hit a post and bounced off at an angle, and was caught by one of the numerous odd fielders—I am not sure he was not a spectator who was sitting down close by—anyhow, I was given out—caught! The doctor and I put on about 80 runs that day, and we spent the next hour under the shower-bath!

E.E.M.

August 1935

SWITZERLAND

ZUOZ COLLEGE, in Switzerland, has for long been a very live outpost of cricket on the Continent and the standard of play there is commendably high. It is interesting to note, therefore, that a team of Zuoz Old Boys and Corinthians has recently made a week's tour in Holland—the fifth annual tour—with matches at Utrecht, Bilthoven, Laren, Amsterdam and Haarlem.

F.I.W.

December 1910

CONTINENTAL JOURNEY

BY F. S. ASHLEY-COOPER

THE holding of an international exhibition at Brussels this year afforded Belgian cricketers an opportunity of which they were not slow to avail themselves, of arranging a series of matches in which teams from England, Holland, and France could take part. The English side, which was captained by Mr R. H. Fox, was sent out by the M.C.C. Owing largely to the interest taken in the matter by Comte Joseph d'Oultremont, who had prepared a good ground and put down a matting wicket, the tournament proved a pronounced success in every way. The results of the matches may be summarised briefly. Belgium beat France, but lost to Holland, who in turn were beaten by France, but the M.C.C. won both their games—that with Belgium by an innings and 209 runs and the one against Holland by two wickets. Mr R. E. More scored 151 off the Belgian bowling, 14 sixes and 11 fours being included in his hits, and the English total amounted to 494. Cricket on the Continent, though not of a very high standard, is undoubtedly improving, whilst the number of players is growing, and it cannot be denied that the matches of an international character which were contested there this year are likely to cause an increase in the popularity of the game. The tournament mentioned was held in June, and in the following month a French team visited Brussels again and were beaten by the Belgians by ten wickets. This match was the fifth which has been played between the two countries, each of which has now two wins to its credit. Holland, where the game has been in favour for many years, still have a tower of strength in Mr C. J. Posthuma, whose bowling contributed to his country's success by 33 runs when Belgium were met on the Haarlem ground in August. Perhaps the strongest club on the Continent at the present time is the Stade Français of Paris, which dismissed the Standard Athletic Club for two runs at Suresnes on July 3, and thereby established a record for France and in all probability for a much larger area. Their chief player is M. Kellerman, brother of the well-known Australian lady swimmer. Several good scores have come from his bat at various times, the highest being 207 not out at the expense of Albion at St. Cloud on July 10. Not many three-figure innings have been recorded in connection with French cricket, and some prominence, therefore, deserves to be given to that mentioned, although it falls short of the 239 played by Capt. J. G. Greig in a match between visitors and residents at Dinard some years ago.

October 1939

JERUSALEM CRICKET

BY S.C.M.

A One-Day Match on Mount Scopus

'JERUSALEM crickets!' was a phrase much used by my grandfather as a harmless expletive. I was never quite sure whether he referred to the insects or to the game, but my young mind was left with the impression that a Jerusalem cricket was something fabulous, unlike the artichokes similarly entitled.

Yet Jerusalem cricket is, as they say, a living force. There are three grounds in the Holy City, one at the Sports Club, one at the Y.M.C.A. and one on Mount Scopus. Mount Scopus lies some little way from the centre of the city; it is away to the north. The depot of the Palestine Police is there, and to-day the Police are entertaining the Army to a one-day match.

Affairs are still unsettled in the land, and there are last-minute absentees from both elevens, owing to an expedition against a gang of bandits. While substitutes are sought a grim little ceremony takes place, viz., the careful searching of the pavilion for time-bombs. A patrol goes rummaging about the foundations of the building. It reminds one of the way in which the vaults of the Houses of Parliament are searched for the successors of Guy Fawkes.

On this occasion the pavilion is declared free from infernal machines, and the spectators—a handful of officers and their wives—take their seats. By this time it is nearly noon. Substitutes have been found for the unlucky soldiers and policemen who are by now scaling distant hills, and the Police win the toss and take the field.

'Field' in this case is a courtesy title for an arid expanse of dust with a few stones protruding. Only one patch of green refreshes the eye; that is the new strip of matting laid over concrete to form the pitch. On one side of the ground lies the Nablus Road, where armoured cars and military trucks hum along, camels amble, and donkeys trot past. Behind them is the British War Cemetery, and behind that again the Mount of Olives. There are trees on the Mount as a result of recent planting, but few of them are olives.

Occasionally, the passing traffic pauses and forms a gallery. There is something in the expression of a camel that makes it appear a critical, if supercilious spectator.

Something goes wrong with the opening batsman of the Police. Perhaps it is the row of meditative camels that he finds unnerving;

perhaps it is the Army fast bowler. At all events his wicket falls with the score at 0. After this early set-back there is a gallant stand, yielding 80 runs and lasting until lunch-time.

Lunch is taken in the Police depot, in a light and airy room that keeps comparatively cool. Even here there is a reminder of the state of affairs in the country, for shields are hanging up, and they bear the names of police officers and constables 'killed in the gallant execution of their duty.' It is a long list, and some of the dates are very recent.

A fierce sun in a clear sky makes the task of the Army fielders a strenuous one as they hunt leather in the early afternoon over the burning desert of the outfield. But the attack does not weaken. Another policeman is dismissed, though not until he has made a nice 62, and then comes a bad patch for the batsmen.

Then a constable knocks up a welcome 55, and the Police declare at 183 for 6. They are lucky in having no batting 'tail'. Their last man in is as likely to score his half-century as any of his mates.

Their fast bowler has his eye in, too, on this occasion. He takes five wickets at small cost in runs; only two of the batsmen can do much against him. At last one of them goes, though not until he has put on 41.

The sun is sinking now and the shadow of the pavilion creeps stealthily across the ground. When it reaches the pitch stumps must be drawn, and the question is whether the Army will play out time and make a draw of it. They do not. With the shadow on the very edge of the matting the last wicket falls. 109 all out.

Then the matting is rolled up, and thirsty players stroll up to the bar of the Sergeants' Mess, where cool drinks are waiting. From the road a measured ting, ting of camel bells sounds faintly across this cricket field.

October 1949

FREE FORESTERS IN B.A.O.R.

SIR,—In August the Free Foresters paid their fourth visit to Germany since the end of Hitler's war. The tour was sponsored by the R.A.F. in B.A.O.R., and from the moment of arrival at the Hook of Holland until the side sailed for England eleven days later, every care was taken to ensure their comfort. The weather, too, was kind and apart from the second day of the match against Rhine Army it was warm and sunny.

A great deal of cricket is being played by the Services in Germany, the standard of play is high and much time and care has obviously been spent in making grounds as good and attractive as possible. The wickets are matting on concrete or shale as suitable turf cannot be grown. Shale wickets are better in that they more nearly resemble conditions in England, being slower than concrete.

The tour began with a match against the British Air Force of Occupation XI and resulted in a win for the Free Foresters by an innings and 50 runs, thanks to good bowling by T. Frazer and J. M. Mills and a century by K. Stubbs. The ground is near the Bückeburg airfield with a concrete wicket and a very fine pavilion surrounded by a magnificent display of flowers which would do any professional gardener credit.

A high-scoring match against a Combined Service XI was drawn. The Berlin ground is part of the Olympic Stadium, built by Hitler for the Olympic Games. It has a shale wicket, but the straight boundaries are a little short.

The next match against Rhine Army brought the one defeat of the tour by eight wickets, in spite of a century by Mills in the second innings.

The tour ended with a win by seven wickets against C.C.G. in spite of two very fine innings by Burley, who made 119 not out and 38 not out, out of totals of 264 and 82.

M. H. LEE
London

October 1955

OUT, TOVARICH

The Russians are credited with a desire to play cricket

'I AM in mourning for my life—my charmed life that was thrice given back to me by the bourgeois-imperialist-capitalist-assassin fielding in the slips for the Wall-street dominated profiteers and war-mongers who are now known as M.C.C. comrades.'

'But you are out, comrade. The little father of the white coat raised his finger.'

'True, comrade. And I am in mourning for my life because my runs-tally falls below the norm demanded by the Marxist-Leninist conception of opening-batsmen comrades of the Stakhanov class.'

'Batsmen-comrades who under-produce their norm may be shot. All the Selector-Commissars shall certainly be shot. As for you comrade. . . .'

'I go to the state shop to buy corpse-candles for the Selector-Commissars. As for me. I must prepare for an invitation to a fraternal discussion with the inner-cell of the Supreme Soviet Cricket Co-operative. It will, I fear, be Adieu.'

'The way ahead is dark, comrade. But perchance it shall be revealed.'

'The wicket had softened, comrade. Perchance the wicket had been watered by night by an agent of the unscrupulous British intelligence secretly introduced among the groundsmen-comrades of the motherland.'

'The nights are long comrade. They are also cold. Let us buy corpse candles.'

'But the wicket, comrade. The little fathers of the Kremlin must be warned of the sabotage by the collective groundsmen. I shall, of course, confess my failure, but I shall declare in mitigation that the wicket was soft ... the previous wicket was soft ... all the wickets are soft ... the next wickets....'

'They will be hard enough in Siberia, comrade.'

4

CURIOUSER
AND
CURIOUSER

Cricket can be a game where the impossible
becomes probable and the probable becomes
impossible . . .

BOWLING EXTRAORDINARY

IN the match Godmanchester v. Willingham, Cambridgeshire, on Tuesday, Mr Charles Brawn, of Godmanchester, Huntingdon, bowled six wickets in six successive balls. The two first Willingham bats had scored twenty when Mr Brawn got Elwood 'leg before', and with the next two balls he bowled Askew and Thoddy, and the umpire called 'over'. With the first ball of his next over Brawn bowled a crack batsman, Mr Few, with the second Frohock, and the third Gleaves, making six good wickets with six consecutive balls. Such a performance would not be likely to pass unrecognised by those who were fielding, and presents in the form of cricket necessaries were suggested on the ground. Mr Brawn's bowling had not been overlooked by the county captain; the victory obtained by Sixteen Colts of the County against the County Eleven, last May, was partly credited to this same fast, good bowler.

THE MOST MARVELLOUS INNINGS ON RECORD

IN cricket, as in the universe of mind and matter, all things are measured and estimated by comparison. Historians of the true stamp have frequently meted out with careful exactness the merits of this and that player, and lifted him to the pedestal of honour after 'what flourishes their nature will.' It is reserved, however, for the columns of this journal to speak of a performance and a performer which eclipse all that has been said or anticipated. Now, as figures of arithmetic are usually more convincing that figures of speech, it may be as well at once to say that a match between the Freshwater and Northwood Clubs was played at Bowes on the 27th of August last, in which Mr Collins—formerly captain of the Radleigh Eleven—scored 338 runs in little more than three hours! Those who live in 'Doubting Castle' may be eased by a statement of the way in which this gigantic 'not out' innings was compounded, viz., one nine, two sevens, six sixes, 12 fives, 25 fours, 17 threes, 18 twos, and 33 singles.

July 1877

EXTRAORDINARY SCORING

ON the 21st, the Castleton Club and Ground played Rusholme Club and Ground, at Castleton. The residents went in first, and lost a wicket when 35 runs were scored; the second reached 208. All the remaining portion of the day was occupied in trying to get the third, but without success. 484 runs were obtained in five hours and a quarter on a dead wicket against good bowling and fielding. Mr Chadwick, who went in first and brought out his bat, made 213, by two fives, eight fours, 25 threes, 28 twos, and 40 singles. The other not out was Mr Leach, with 92. Mr Taylor was stumped with a score of 125, and Mr Brierly caught at 20.

August 1888

Though not by any means the largest innings ever played, the score of the M.C.C. and Ground against Wiltshire on Monday and Tuesday has never been equalled on Lord's ground. On July 24 and 25 Norfolk scored 695 against the club bowling, and this stood until Tuesday last as the record for Lord's, but on the days previously mentioned this number was exceeded by exactly 40 runs. Mr E. Sainsbury, of Somersetshire, was the chief contributor to this huge total, and went very near to the completion of his second hundred. Mr H. Brougham, Mr F.G.J. Ford, and Flowers also added large sums, while Messrs J. S. Russell and D. D. Pontifex rendered much assistance in amassing the total of 735. The innings lasted about nine hours, so that the pace of the run-getting averaged just over 80 per hour.

July 1895

REMARKABLE SCORING IN IRELAND

IN a match between Leinster Cricket Club and Fitzwilliam Lawn Tennis Club, played at Dublin on Wednesday, Mr R. H. Lambert, of the former club, did a very remarkable all-round performance. The Fitzwilliam eleven, which included the two old Oxonians, Messrs T. B. Case and W. S. Case, were got out for 60, Mr Lambert capturing seven wickets for 23 runs. Leinster, in three hours, knocked up 413 for four wickets. Mr Lambert was batting two hours and five minutes, and made 218 (not out), including seven sixes, one five, 36 fours, four threes, 13 twos, and 19 singles, and he scored his first hundred in 40 minutes.

October 1895

AN IRISH RECORD

DURING the season which has just closed, Mr R. H. Lambert, of the Leinster Cricket Club, Dublin, achieved an all-round performance which, as far as Ireland is concerned, has never been equalled. With the bat he scored 2040 runs in 47 innings, average 51; and he took 200 wickets at an average cost of seven runs per wicket. It may be mentioned that the only previous instance of a player getting 2000 runs in one season in Ireland was when the ex-Harrovian, the late Lieut. Dunn, who went down with the Bokharn in the China seas a few years ago, accomplished the feat. Col. F. W. Rhodes (brother of Mr Cecil Rhodes), when quartered in Dublin with the Royal Dragoons early in the eighties, scored close on 2000 runs. Mr Lambert, who is not yet twenty-one years of age learned his cricket at St John's College, Preston.

January 1898

BOWLING FEAT IN SOUTH AFRICA

ADDITIONAL particulars have been received of a match reported in our last issue as having been played on Dec. 11 between the Navy and Simonstown. It was decided on the first innings. The Navy having made 64 runs, their opponents' score stood at 55 with five wickets down when Mr Straubenzee, midshipman of H.M.S. St George, went on to bowl. With the last four balls of his first over he took four wickets, and with the first ball of the next over dismissed the last of his opponents, three runs having in the meantime been made from the other end. The Navy thus won by six runs. Mr Straubenzee, we are informed, is in his seventeenth year.

September 1905

ADLESTROP v. STOW ON WOLD

PLAYED at Adlestrop on Sept. 2. W. Timms accomplished a good performance for Adlestrop, taking the first eight wickets for one run, and his average was nine for nine, while he caught the tenth man off F. Goddard's bowling. Score: Adlestrop, 65; Stow on Wold, 27.

Writing from Satara, India, a correspondent, 'A. R. B.', mentions a curious incident which occurred there a month ago: 'A fast ball struck the top of the off stump without dislodging a bail, though the stump was moved out of the perpendicular to an extent clearly visible in the pavilion and the click of the impact was audible all over the ground. Further, the batsman had just touched the ball, and the wicket-keeper, catching it, appealed. But the umpire, intent only on the undislodged bail, or not having observed the touch, gave the batsman in, and the appeal was not repeated. This was hard on the bowler, who, however, spread-eagled the wicket two balls later.'

One of the most remarkable incidents ever seen in a Test match occurred at Manchester on Monday. A ball from Barnes had nearly proved fatal to Macartney who, happy in the consciousness that he still survived, did not notice what had become of it, or that his partner, Armstrong, was not only frantically beckoning him to run, but was even now close upon him. A little late in the day Lilley realised that something was wrong, and, running to the ball, which lay a few yards in front of the wicket on the on side, picked it up. At this moment Armstrong, in desperation, was about to return, but hesitated. Lilley also seemed in doubt whether he should run with the ball to the wicket or throw it, but eventually tossed it to Barnes at the same moment that Macartney, suddenly awakening to the fact that his partner was in danger, offered himself as a sacrifice and ran past him. Unhappily for England the ball came inconveniently to Barnes, who had not placed himself in the best position to receive it, and the result was that it was not stopped, and Macartney got home without hurrying. If Lilley had seen from the first what was happening, Armstrong would have been run out while Macartney was still standing in his ground oblivious of his partner's movements. Perhaps the most curious point about the whole occurrence was that neither of the slips nor mid-on made any effort to get to the ball, or even seemed to be aware of the occurrence.

Having taken ten wickets in an innings for Sidmouth v. Incogniti, C. Wells was disappointed of the eleventh wicket by the batsman most inconsiderately falling to another bowler. The exploit was the more remarkable as the match, played at Sidmouth on Monday and Tuesday last, was anything but a bowler's harvest, and the innings in question nearly reached the 300th run.

As a curiosity of military cricket—which is fertile in such occurrences—it is worthy of note that A. Carton de Wiart, playing at Brighton for the officers of the 4th Dragoon Guards against the Sergeants' Mess, took seven wickets for no runs in 11 balls, having just retired after making a score of 102.

A well-known umpire in one of last week's matches at Lord's, after signalling a boundary, continued from force of habit to watch the batsmen, and to the amusement of the scorers and spectators automatically shouted 'One short.'

July 1910

One of the most remarkable catches of the season was made at Hastings on Monday. Vincett, who had been hit very hard on the hand by a bumping ball from Fielder, seemed to become restive. He tried to hit the two following balls and missed them, but putting all his power into the stroke, he sent the third in the direction of cover point. Unfortunately, he failed to time the ball, which went so slowly that Fairservice seemed to have the easiest of chances. To the general surprise Fairservice, evidently expecting that from the force which had been put into the stroke the ball was coming to him at a great pace, stood still instead of running forward. When he discovered his mistake, he made a sharp dash, hesitated, and seemed to give up all idea of getting to the ball. He continued, however, to move slowly, almost at a walking pace, and suddenly, as one waking from a dream, stretched out his right hand as far as it would go, with the result that the ball dropped into it almost as if by magic.

August 1910

Commander Sidney Olivier writes: 'On Aug. 11 we had a curious incident on the Mount Wise ground (Devonport). In a match—Navy v. Leinster Regiment—Lieut. Allenby, R.N., hit a ball hard and straight to Capt. Borrett, his partner at the wickets. Capt. Borrett jumped out of the way, but the ball hit his bat and soared, giving mid-on an easy catch. I have never seen this happen before, and thought it might interest your readers.' The occurrence is not unprecedented, but we believe very rare. It has happened comparatively frequently that a striker has been caught through the ball glancing from some part of his partner's person.

September 1910

With reference to a note in last week's *Field* about Spring, the Surrey cricketer who batted with one hand with some success against Leicestershire, Mr Charles Armstrong, a Huntingdonshire cricketer, states that in a minor county match in the sixties between Bedfordshire and Huntingdonshire Mr Stileman-Gibbard went in first for the former, as usual, although unable to use his left hand, and made over forty runs, including a few fours. Many old Surrey and Sussex cricketers will remember the large scores and the powerful drives made by Mr Casswell, a one-armed master at Cranleigh School, and more than once Lord Harris batted with the left hand only.

July 1914

When King was run out by M. Howell in the first innings of the M.C.C. against Oxford at Lord's on Monday, Parliament met at the pavilion end to pass a vote of thanks to the fieldsman. King's innocent partner, A. C. Wilkinson, came from the Nursery end to assist at the proceedings. The next man in, C. B. Ponsonby, not unnaturally walked to the vacant crease. Wilkinson, fortunately for himself, did not dispute possession of it with him, and Mellé immediately sent down the unplayable ball which shattered Ponsonby's stumps. No one noticed until it was too late, that Ponsonby had no business to be where he was, and consequently no appeal was made to the umpires.

Recently in an ordinary club match when a wicket fell the batsman at the other end retired to the pavilion with his defeated colleague. The incomer had taken guard and been yorked first ball before it was discovered that his partner had not returned. In this case the man who had been bowled was, rightly or wrongly, permitted to continue his innings on the ground that if he had made a stroke worth one or more runs off the ball which defeated him he would have had no partner to help him in running them. But it is highly probable that this incident should not be regarded as a binding precedent, for the next straight

The English XI of **1847**, 'selected to contend in the great cricket matches of the north'. *Left to right:* Guy, Parr, Martingell, Mr A. Mynn, Mr W. Denison, Dean, Clarke, Mr N. Felix, Mr O. C. Pelt, Hillyer, Lillywhite, Derrinton, Pilch, Sewell.

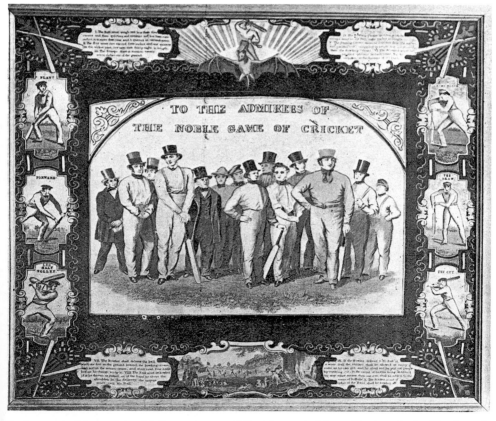

A decorated handkerchief once owned by the notable collector A. L. Ford and illustrated in *The Field* to accompany F. S. Ashley-Cooper's article 'Some Notes on Old-Time Cricket'. (See p. **3**.)

A blue and white fish strainer from the collection of A. L. Ford.

This bowl was made by Wedgewood for John Durand, of Woodcote Lodg
Surrey, in 1790 and was known as the Carshalton Bowl after its purchase b
the residents of that borough. The depiction of the game appears inside th
bowl.

'Lillywhite at Home'. 'The Nonpareil', William Lillywhite, pictured in a lithograph by John Corbet Anderson, bowling to an aspiring youngster outside the family cottage at Westhampnett, Sussex.

A political caricature from an engraving in the collection of A. L. Ford.

Many think that the preparatory pose is a modern invention. The lie to that idea is given by the unmistakable figure of W. G. Grace adopting the 'secondary position' before the ball was delivered.

S. F. Barnes – 'springy, bowling consistently at the wicket.' (See p. 96.)

The incomparable Wilfred Rhodes, Yorkshire and England, who tops the bowlers' list of first-class victims with a lot to spare.

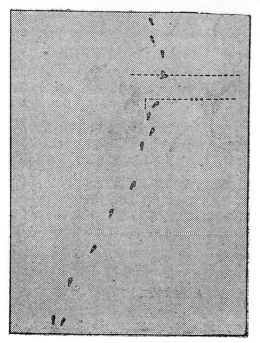

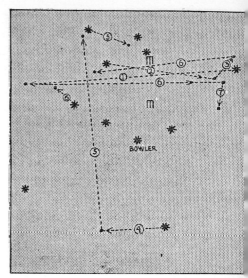

A diagram of the footsteps taken by Lancashire pace bowler Lawrence Cook in his approach to the wicket during the August bank holiday Battle of the Roses at Old Trafford in 1910. *The Field* correspondent questioned Cook's peculiar methods:

'His first step is a long stride, at the end of which he comes down on his heel; the second is not quite so long, but again he comes down on his heel. Then he breaks into three jumps, which are exactly like those made by a boy who is doing the hop, skip, and jump. Then when he has got up a great speed he suddenly changes to short steps and half his speed seems suddenly to be taken away. It is perhaps because of this that, although he has often bowled exceedingly well, he is never as fast as he ought to be.'

Cook took one wicket in a Lancashire victory.

In a drawn game between Yorkshire and the touring Australians at Sheffield in July 1909, Monty Noble, the Aussie skipper, put himself on to bowl for four or five overs during the late afternoon of the first day.

'The diagram shows the positions of the men when he began to bowl and the directions and order in which he made his changes. During this time he bowled to Rhodes, Hardisty, and Rothery, and he did not alter his field specially for each batsman. Noble dispensed with square leg and moved Ransford to a sort of deep point (1). Rhodes and Hardisty, however, placed him to leg two or three times, and so he did without a point, and sent Laver to the leg side (2). This necessitated slight alterations on the off side which are not shown. In the next over Laver was moved a few yards (3) and Hopkins about ten yards (4). Noble thought he would do without deep long-off. Hopkins was therefore moved from one end of the field nearly to the other (5), Trumper at the same time going to second slip (5). Ransford was soon afterwards sent back to the leg side (6), Laver going back to point (6) and Gregory moving a few yards (6). Finally Ransford's position was slightly changed (7). The men who were not moved at all from their original positions were Carter (at the wicket), Armstrong (short slip), Bardsley (long field off), Cotter (mid-on), and Macartney (mid-off).'

All these field changes were to no avail for Noble failed to take a wicket.

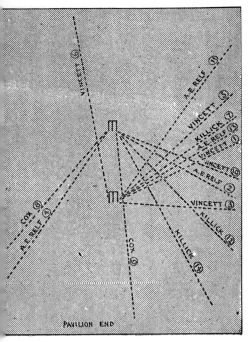

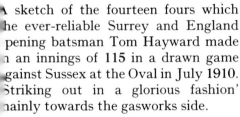

A sketch of the fourteen fours which he ever-reliable Surrey and England opening batsman Tom Hayward made in an innings of 115 in a drawn game against Sussex at the Oval in July 1910. 'Striking out in a glorious fashion' mainly towards the gasworks side.

A view of the Dudley Cricket Ground as seen in 1914. The prospect is towards Birmingham with pungent chimneys both factory and residential. It would appear the ozone layer was another prospect altogether.

Mount Scopus Cricket Ground, with the British Cemetery and Mount of Olives in the background. Only one patch of green refreshes the eye, that is the new strip of matting laid over concrete to form the pitch. (See p. 74.)

Delineations of cricketing moments that caught the artist's eye during 1939.

An impression of Paynter cutting a rising ball.

Captain J. W. A. Stephenson, the Essex all-rounder, fielding at cover-point.

ball which came along was fatal to the escaped batsman; and there are grounds for presuming that umpires and the fielding side had a shrewd idea of what was likely to happen.

In this match N. R. Udal delivered ten balls in one over, being no-balled four times consecutively. It was too hot a day for ten-ball overs, and he was taken off.

July 1917

A great individual performance was accomplished on Saturday by the Winchester bowler, J. D. E. E. Firth, medium right-hand with considerable variations of pace. Against Harrow he had secured eight wickets; against Eton he took all ten—a feat which was also accomplished in the Eton and Winchester match of 1902 for Eton by G. A. C. Sandemann.

August 1917

CONSECUTIVE TIE MATCHES

ON July 28 we referred to two consecutive tie matches, and our correspondent inquired whether such an occurrence was unusual. The instance seems remarkable enough, but cricket is an extraordinary game, and Mr A. L. Ford, whose name will be familiar to our readers, has sent the following records, adding that there are others:

Scores and Biographies, vol. xiv., p. 1093, mentions three consecutive tie matches—Motherwell Trinity v. Wesleyans, 36 each, Sept. 5, 1891; and Motherwell Trinity v. Newmans, 36 each, on Sept. 12, 1891; and Motherwell Trinity v. Ross Ramblers, 66 each, on Sept. 13, 1891.

Cricket, Sept. 3, 1903, mentions Alexandra Park Second Eleven v. Tillingham, 30 each; and Alexandra Park Second Eleven v. Friern Barnet Second Eleven, 59 each; and Alexandra Park Second Eleven v. Christ Church Second Eleven, 30 runs each, in three consecutive matches.

Cricket, Sept. 11, 1902, mentions Marchain v. Radley having played two consecutive tie matches.

Scores and Biographies, vol. xiv., p. 1051, mentions in Australia Union v. Press, 32 each, and a second match between the same teams 32 each.

A correspondent writes: 'The following incident, which I saw when playing at Hurstborne Park, may be worth recording, as it is not likely to happen again. The batsmen ran for a bye, short slip gathered the ball and threw at the wicket, hitting the top of the centre stump. That batsman was given in, but the ball rose high from the top of the centre stump, went over the other running batsman, and pitched on the other wicket, and he was run out. The fieldsman who threw the ball was some distance from the wicket nearest him.'

A correspondent writing from Sind, sends us a cutting from an Indian newspaper, the *New Times*, referring to a cricket match played recently between the Union Club of Rohri and the Europeans of Railway Shed. It is stated that the latter, with four players absent, scored $38\frac{1}{2}$ runs, while the other side scored $39\frac{1}{2}$ runs with five wickets in hand. Our correspondent says he does not know how the half runs were scored. Perhaps a reader may be able to throw some light on the matter.

Colonel B. R. Ward writes: 'While on a visit to Yelverton last week I saw what I should imagine must be unique in the annals of cricket— a double hat trick, the last three balls of one innings and the first three balls of the next one all producing wickets. Certainly it was holiday— not first-class—cricket. The ages of the players varied by as much as 54 years, the gallant admiral who captained one side being 64 years of age, his son Valentine—one of the hat-trick bowlers—being twelve, and Ivan Campbell only ten. Several ladies were pressed into the service. It would not be fair to say that this was done to make up the numbers, for one of them—Mrs Chamberlen, the vicar's wife—was the bowler who brought off the first of the two hat tricks.

'This occurred,' says Colonel Ward, 'just after the tea interval, when Admiral Le Marchant's eleven were continuing their first innings, having lost seven wickets for 33. Valentine Le Marchant, who had made 13 runs, was facing Mrs Chamberlen's bowling, and was given out l.b.w. to the first ball of her over. Michael Ward, a schoolboy of twelve, and Admiral Le Marchant, the veteran of 64, were clean bowled by the next two balls – all out for 33. Major Bundock commenced his second innings by sending Miss B. Bellamy and J. Campbell to face the bowling of Valentine Le Marchant and Challoner. The first three balls of the innings dismissed Miss Bellamy, Mrs Chamberlen, and N. Marwood Tucker, a schoolboy of twelve, all clean bowled by good length balls. I have watched a good many cricket matches, first, second, third, and tenth class, but have never seen a double hat trick before, and doubtless shall never see one again. What makes this particular pair of hat tricks even more remarkable than it would otherwise be is the fact that the hat-trick bowlers were themselves the victims of one another's bowling in two consecutive overs. Is there any record, I wonder, in the history of cricket of such a thing ever having occurred before?'

May 1923

A curious incident happened in the second innings of Hampshire. The last ball of an over by Bettington, the Oxford captain, hit Newman on the pads, but there was no appeal, and the fieldsmen began to move to their places for the next over. Newman, obviously under the impression that 'over' had been called, for in the gale of wind no one would have expected to hear the umpire at that distance, stepped out of his ground to pat the pitch. It was equally obvious that Patten, the wicket-keeper, did not think that 'over' had been called, and accordingly he removed the bails, with the result that Newman was given out. Newman thought that he had played the ball, and that he was therefore run out, but the umpire was of opinion that the ball had not been played, and so the score sheet reads Newman st H. Batten, b. Bettington.

August 1923

There was an extraordinary finish to a match at Devonport recently between the Royal Naval Barracks and Somerset Stragglers. The Barracks declared, leaving the Stragglers 302 runs to make to win in two hours and forty minutes. Two runs were wanted to win with three wickets to fall when the last over was begun. The clock struck after the first ball was bowled. One run was scored off the second ball, making the scores level. P. O. Cornish then took three wickets with his fourth, fifth, and sixth balls, for no runs, thus accomplishing the hat trick and making the game a tie.

October 1924

We are indebted to Mr Cyril Gore for a cutting from the *Sydney Referee*. It refers to a schoolboy of sixteen, Charles Sherriff, who has made a thousand runs this season without being dismissed, though he once retired. In his last innings he required 292 runs to complete his thousand, and the *Referee* says: 'Dent accompanied Sherriff to the wickets, and the latter, taking strike, chopped the first ball through slips for four, the next ball for the same, and he hit the next for six. He scored 27 from the first over. The next over he scored 4 4 6 6 4. At 64, Dent was bowled, 1–10–64, Sherriff being 54. Fraser, the next man, was caught for eight, 2–8–88. Sherriff was then 65, and showing great batting powers, had the spectators all delighted. Aitken lasted about a quarter of an hour, when he was bowled. Sherriff added 36 in the 15 minutes, which brought his score to 101. The effort was greeted with continued applause.

'After another half-hour, the score stood at six for 199. Sherriff 168 not out. He soon brought his score to 205. Three more wickets fell in quick succession, and at nine for 316, Sherriff was 252. Ogle, the last man, came in. There was a silence when Ogle took his stand at the wickets, but he played the over out. Then as Sherriff took strike the silence changed to deafening applause. From the over Sherriff scored 38—4 4 6 6 4 4 4. This brought his total to 290, and he wanted two runs for his thousand. The first four balls of the over he played back to the bowler. On the last ball of the over he flicked his wrist with a graceful movement, and with the greatest of ease sent the ball flying out of the ground for six. The applause was tremendous, and when Ogle was bowled for 1, the onlookers rushed the ground and carried Sherriff shoulder high. His 296 not out included 15 sixes and 45 fours. His series of innings this season is as follows: 56 not out, 84 (retired), 91 not out, 116 not out, 156 not out, 205 not out, 296 not out.'

This of course, reads rather like a fairy tale, but in all the ages schoolboys have done remarkable things—witness E. F. S. Tylecote's 404 not out as long ago as 1868, and A. E. J. Collins's 628 not out in 1899. If our memory serves, Victor Trumper and Clement Hill, as well as many other famous Australians, did astonishing performances as schoolboys. Probably, as Mr Gore suggests, the boundaries in many cases are small, but many of the biggest innings in first-class matches have been played on small grounds.

   While 74 is the greatest number of extras in an innings the 58 of U-Foam XI against A N Ghosh's XI at Hyderabad in 1972 has a certain claim as cricket's most trivial statistic. Is ghosh the Indian for other? And was there a non-U Foam XI? The 803 which Non-Smokers scored at East Melbourne in 1886–7 against Smokers suggests not only a moral about health but an equally serious one about sponsorship today. Perhaps tobacco companies, in danger of being legislated out of sporting sponsorship, should seek to revive the fixture. Drinkers v. Teetotallers might present a problem, rather as the Gentlemen eventually became pressed to raise a quorum, but Beards v. Clean-Shaven might persuade Gillette back into the game.

5
PLAYER
PROFILES

It is a truism to say that any game can only be as good as the component abilities of those taking part. Sometimes, however, the outstanding ability of one player can lift a match onto another plane. The following selection portrays some giants of cricket who had and have that capacity.

THE COLOSSUS OF RHODES AT NINETY NOT OUT

BY LEONARD CRAWLEY

The Yorkshire cricketer who played for England when nearly 50

'I DO appreciate your coming to see me, for what you probably do not realize is that most of my friends died about 30 years ago, and people of my age are apt to feel lonely from time to time.' The speaker was my uncle, Field-Marshal Sir Claud Jacob, more than 90 years old at the time. It might have been Wilfred Rhodes, the great Yorkshire and England cricketer.

I do not know whether Rhodes has ever experienced that loneliness in his old age, but I want him to know what a joy it was for me to see him again a few years ago at a Test match at Lord's. He was sitting between two of his great contemporaries, Sir Jack Hobbs and Sydney Barnes. Though blind, he was evidently enjoying the play as Hobbs and Barnes gave him their own graphic descriptions of it. In the long history of cricket it would be hard to imagine a greater trio, members of Lord's *honoris causa*, of infinite modesty, yet passing unrecognized by many ordinary members.

Rhodes has a great cricketing brain. He is, like most Yorkshiremen, a little reserved about his praise of others not fortunate enough to be born in Yorkshire, but when he does approve of them no-one could be louder in their praise. This I learned from once spending a train journey with him to Scotland.

I found that his pet subject was Hobbs and a right good one, too. 'Why?' he said. 'Yer can't fault 'im. 'E got as many as 'e wanted on good'uns; 'e got 'em on t' mat; 'e got 'em on sticky dogs, 'e got 'em on crumblers; and 'e got 'em all over t' world. 'E was t' best player of googly that ever lived and only reason folk ever got 'im out was because 'e could see ball spinning in t' air and 'e would get a bit cheeky.'

Next he rated Ranji for much the same reasons, namely that he proved himself a master under most difficult conditions. He has the same respect for Duleep, Ranji's nephew, from whom he also suffered. I remember Duleep getting 250 against Yorkshire at Fenner's after being dropped off Rhodes before he had scored. For once he was made to look ordinary. ''Is uncle,' said Rhodes, 'dun same thing 30 years ago.'

He had every reason to respect Sir Donald Bradman. He marvelled at his insatiable ambition to break every record in the history of cricket, but he ultimately felt that the great Australian had never proved himself on bad wickets. It is only men of Rhodes's stature that can make such statements. Again, of Frank Woolley he said, 'One of t' greatest county players of my time on any wicket, but never a great Test match batsman'; and he produced evidence of this contention that was irrefutable.

As an all-round cricketer before the days of Sobers, Rhodes had no superior. He began as a bowler, and he taught himself to bat, or rather to stay in, so well that his happiest days were spent on the cricket field opening the innings in Test matches with Hobbs. He was not a great batsman as such, for he had few memorable strokes.

When he coached at Harrow, he used to tell the boys to jab it. He did not last long there where attack has always been taught as the best means of defence. But, with Hobbs as a partner, he was a tremendous force. Hobbs taught him to run between the wickets and, as a thief of short singles, Rhodes became a comparatively fast scorer.

In the twenties he was going in to bat for Yorkshire as No 7. He used to make runs when they were wanted, but he did not do much bowling. Just when everyone was thinking that Rhodes's active career was about to end he became a Test selector, and no wiser one ever lived. There was one match to go and all to play for against Australia at the Oval in 1926. The selectors met, and one had the brilliant idea that Rhodes should be recalled at the age of 48 for active service.

Arthur Gilligan, the chairman (now president of MCC), broached the subject, Hobbs supported it, and the conversation went, I gather, something like this. Gilligan: 'Now, Wilfred, we are all agreed that we must have the best left-arm bowler in the country at the Oval. My colleagues and I feel that in spite of your age you are still oustandingly the best. Will you play?' The reply was typical of the man who knew the game from A to Z, and it was non-committal. 'Well, gentlemen, I can still keep 'em there.' He did, and no-one played a greater part in Australia's final defeat.

April 1953

THE GREATEST BOWLER

BY SIR PELHAM WARNER

S. F. Barnes, whom Australians lauded and whom 'it was a rare treat to play at the height of his skill'

THE place of S. F. Barnes among the great bowlers has long been assured. Such good judges as C. Hill and M. A. Noble, the Australians, considered him the greatest of all. On the other hand, C. B. Fry, who knows everything about cricket there is to be known, gives the palm to Lohmann, of Surrey, and C. E. de Trafford, a former Leicestershire captain, is of the same opinion. For myself, I find it hard to believe that he was a greater bowler than Barnes, but that may well be because I played more often with and against Barnes than Lohmann.

Barnes was born at Smethwick, in Staffordshire, on April 19th, 1873, and accepting an engagement in the Lancashire League in 1895 he played for Lancashire in 1899, and continued to do so until 1903, when difficulties over financial arrangements led to his leaving. 'There is no need to go into the merits of the quarrel,' as Wisden of 1910 puts it, but it may well be that 50 years ago county committees were, generally speaking, not so seized of the vital importance of ensuring the future of professionals when their playing days were over.

Barnes was not widely known until at the very end of August, 1901, playing for Lancashire v. Leicestershire, at Old Trafford, he obtained six wickets for 70 runs and was there and then chosen by A. C. Maclaren to form one of his team for Australia. His selection caused some surprise, but Maclaren, a fine judge of a cricketer, knew what he was doing, for Barnes bowled splendidly until he broke down with knee trouble during the third Test match at Adelaide and played no more on the tour.

Up to his breakdown he had taken 19 wickets for 17·00 each in the Test matches, and 41 wickets for 16·48 in the eleven-a-side matches. His breakdown split Maclaren's bowling in pieces. Subsequently Barnes paid two more visits to Australia, in 1907–08 with the M.C.C. team, captained by A. O. Jones, and in 1911–12, again with the M.C.C., with me, though owing to a serious illness I played in only the first match, J. W. H. T. Douglas taking my place as captain on the field.

The first time I played against Barnes was at Lord's in August, 1903, and I can still hear the devastating leg break with which he clean bowled me hitting the top of the off stump. It is a sound and sensible maxim that no cricketer should boast while he has his armour on, but when he has cast it aside he may, perhaps, be allowed some latitude; and in a long career two innings I played against Barnes, at Lord's, in Gentlemen v. Players in 1909 and 1919, are amongst my proudest memories. Both were small scores, 58 and 24 on very difficult wickets, the sun pouring down on a wet turf, and as Wisden wrote 'his sharp break from the leg side in combination with a perfect length being deadly.' It was just the same in 1913, and the quick-rising leg break off which I was caught off my glove by E. J. Smith at the wicket, on the level of his eyes, has gone down to history as one of the greatest catches ever made by a wicket-keeper.

What manner of man is Barnes, and what type of bowler? First—the man. He was 6ft. 1in. in height, with broad shoulders on a wiry frame.

His fingers were long, sinewy and strong. His countenance in repose was somewhat hard-bitten, but when he smiled his face lit up, 'a good face to face man' as John Nyren would have described him.

I knew him only casually before I went to Australia with him in 1911 and I was told that he was somewhat *difficile*, so I made up my mind to try to get to know him. We used to talk cricket, of course, but he also told me of his work as a checker at a coal mine in Staffordshire, and I found him easy to get on with. I noticed that he used to play with, and laugh with, the many children who were on board the liner, and I thought that a man who evidently liked children could not have much wrong with him.

I was away from the team for six weeks or more, but I saw most of the second Test match, at Melbourne. I was carried into the pavilion by T. Pawley, our faithful and splendid manager, and W. W. Armstrong, who was playing for Australia, just after Barnes had bowled 11 overs for six runs and five wickets, the first four for one run. I asked Armstrong whether there was anything wrong with the wicket, and I recall his gracious and generous reply. 'No—nothing at all. Just magnificent bowling.'

England, after losing the first Test, at Sydney, won the next four and so brought back the Ashes, and Barnes bowled superbly throughout. He never gave in for a moment and maintained a dynamic and persistent attack. He was always superbly fit. J. W. H. T. Douglas captained the side and led it with judgment, courage and determination, and if he were alive to-day, he would be the first to pay tribute to Barnes. But alas! in December, 1930, he lost his life in trying to save his father when the ship in which they were sailing from Norway was sunk in collision with another vessel. Father and son were devoted to each other and if John had to die I imagine he would have sought no other end. I owe him an everlasting debt of gratitude.

On the Australian tour the main attack was in the hands of Barnes, F. R. Foster—medium to fast-medium left-hand with an occasional very fast ball which came off the pitch like lightning—and Douglas himself. In the Test matches Barnes took 34 wickets, Foster 32, and Douglas 15, and between them they sent down no fewer than 712·4 overs, of six balls each, and the other bowlers between them only 186·1 overs. So far as our out-cricket was concerned we won the rubber with three bowlers.

All of them had the merit of extreme accuracy of length—and Barnes and Foster were described by the critics as 'the finest pair of bowlers England had ever sent to Australia.' Foster was a magnificent cricketer—and few English cricketers have achieved so much fame at so early an age. And this superb bowling was backed up by the splendid batting of the great Hobbs and the famous Rhodes, his first-wicket partner; Woolley, 'the pride of Kent'; George Gunn, an artist; J.W. Hearne, then only 21, who was called 'the young Arthur Shrewsbury'; and splendid fielding, with Hobbs at coverpoint and Woolley in the slips pre-eminent, and the wicket-keeping of E. J. Smith.

In his *History of Cricket* H. S. Altham wrote: 'But even our fine work in the field might not have availed without the comradeship that made the eleven into a team, the devotion to the game that made all minor distractions of no account, and the determination that sent them on to the field determined on victory and confident of their ability to achieve it.'

On our return to England we played the Rest of England, at Lord's, on May 23rd, 24th and 25th, and they declared that they would knock our heads off, just to show that there were two elevens in England which could beat the Australians. And it was no idle boast, for they were represented by C. B. Fry (captain), R. H. Spooner, G. L. Jessop, A. P. Day, W. Brearley, D. W. Carr, Humphreys, Thompson, Mead, Strudwick, and Dean. The match was played in fine weather on a beautiful wicket, and we beat them by an innings and ten runs. The doctor had declared that I could play some cricket, but that I must go slow. The match is fully described in *Wisden*, for 1913, but even after all these years I still recall the delight it gave me to be on the field again with the team. The late Lord Harris declared that he thought we were 'just about the best team he had ever seen.'

Barnes's approach to the crease was springy, he bowled off his toes with a lively run, and his arm was in the sky. His leg break, which he cut rather than spun, came very fast off the ground, and he made full use of the width of the crease. He bowled consistently at the wicket, which compelled the batsmen to play at almost every ball. He also bowled the off break, and had a straight fast ball. He was a very difficult bowler to drive because of the height of his delivery and his meticulous accuracy of length. He, if anyone, could dispense with an outfield.

After his trouble with Lancashire he played for Staffordshire from 1904 to 1914 and took 926 wickets for seven runs each, and during those years he appeared frequently for England in Test matches against Australia and South Africa, for the Players v. the Gentlemen, and for the Rest of England v. the champion county. There is little doubt that he profited by playing comparatively little cricket, which enabled him to keep fresh and come to each match full of energy.

His figures in the great matches are worth quoting. In 19 games against Australia he obtained 106 wickets for 21·58 each, and in seven against South Africa 83 for 9·85 each, and for the Players against the Gentlemen 45 for 15·26. He is one of the 25 professionals who were elected members of the M.C.C. for outstanding services to cricket and to the club, and when I last saw him in the pavilion at Lord's his back was as straight as a ramrod and he looked splendidly fit. It was a rare treat to play him at the height of his skill, for he tested one's defence to the uttermost.

October 1974

CRICKET'S ALL-ROUNDER

BY LEONARD CRAWLEY

Sobers retires with a record that speaks for itself

... SOBERS is to retire at 38, an age at which many of the world's greatest players have still had a great contribution to make in the annals of the game.

Perhaps it is best to retire at the zenith of one's powers like Sir Stanley Jackson, but he lived in a golden age of cricket and had other more serious matters to think about. So perhaps has this remarkable man from Barbados. Retire is perhaps too strong a word. He remains available for the West Indies if selected, and will continue to play in various matches.

On every ground of merit he is entitled to consideration as the greatest cricketer that ever lived. He can bat, bowl and field as well as the best. His record over the years speaks for itself.

He was first chosen to play for Barbados against the Indians at the precocious age of 16 as a slow bowler when he sent down 89 overs. He played his first Test match against England the next year, since when his record in Test cricket has surpassed anything ever achieved before.

The innings

He has scored 8,032 runs in Test matches in which he has made 26 hundreds, taken 235 wickets and made 110 catches. He played an innings of 254 at Melbourne which no less an authority than Sir Donald Bradman described as the best ever seen in Australia and one of the most perfect ever played.

He is far and away the most accomplished batsman it has been my privilege to watch since the war. He has all the shots, all the dash, all the cheek of the great batsmen who could fill a ground on a weekday because of their very presence 40 years ago.

Apart from his glorious batting which has brightened the grey skies on the county scene, Sobers is the most versatile bowler ever to deliver a ball in Test cricket. Alas, I do not know him well enough to say which of his many rôles as a bowler he prefers.

The versatility
A superb athlete and a perfect specimen of physical fitness, he is capable of opening the bowling with the new ball in a Test match to sting the groins of the early batsmen with vicious inswingers that hop either way from the seam. He is as happy, perhaps even happier, to use a sticky wicket and shoot out the opposition as did Rhodes and Verity in bygone days with flight and spin away from the batsman.

He can perform as a left-arm googly bowler on a broken dry wicket. In this capacity he must have derived much pleasure since the batsman at the other end has always to work out which way the red sphere is going to turn from an unaccustomed direction. It still makes me think to write about it.

Sobers is a great fielder and, like Constantine who, bless his heart, finished his days in the House of Lords, is ubiquitous and as happy in the slips, round the corner at fine leg, or at cover point with a deadly throw to the wicket for those impertinent enough to risk a short run. Even if he never plays again, the name of Sobers will live wherever cricket is played.

June 1975

COWDREY AT FACE VALUE

BY JEREMY ALEXANDER

But still a fantastic story behind his retirement

IT goes virtually without saying that there is more than meets the eye in many sporting statements. They fall out with bland plausibility but all sorts of circumstances may have influenced them. Colin Cowdrey's announcement ten days ago that he is to retire from first-class cricket at the end of the season is almost an exception.

Another man saying that with so many good players deserving a place in the side he did not wish to stand in their way might have been accused of sour grapes or being patronizing; 'just because he cannot command a regular place in the Kent team', the cynics might chorus, as well they could if dealing with a spoiled, overpaid soccer star. But, because they know their man, perhaps unique among great cricketers or great sportsmen of the day, for sincerity without side and modesty to within a snick of a fault, the commentators accept his explanation at face value.

Even so, wherefore is the need to make a statement? Is is not pretentious in itself? And will he not, regardless of retirement, be recalled next season at the age of 43 to help Kent in time of Test calls? After all, only half a year ago he was flown, in preference to all other batsmen in England, to the rescue of MCC in Australia. Can those great gifts of solid mastery and gentle power have faded so quickly? Of course not. He is simply removing from the county, with whom he has dealt straight for 25 years, any sense of obligation they may have felt towards him. That is thoughtful, not pretentious.

An invitation

But again, why now, a week ago last Monday and two days after my first innings for five years? All sportsmen have flights of fancy. Lesser sportsmen have longer flights of farther fancy. They have to. Could it be that ... no, surely not ... and yet, one must admit it is rather a coincidence. Could it really be that mine is the way he would not, nay cannot, obstruct?

It was a fortnight previously that the telephone rang and a voice which I swiftly identified as belonging to the captain of the old boys invited me to play against the school in their prestigious speech-day match. My heart missed about an over before I rounded up a response. 'You can't be serious,' I think it was. 'I am,' he said, 'I must see you bat again' and, wriggle as I did, it was no good. A man knows when he is obliged as he knows when he is terrified. I was both. Batting screws up the inside as nothing else.

Arms and armour were traced in the garage—spiders, supplementing the webbing of the wicket-keeping gloves, beetles abiding in the box, batting gloves with their protective strips of cactus and, trusty as an old bicycle, the willow. Oil for dust and the last forgave me my neglect. We were friends again as I went through my repertoire of strokes.

It was a short rehearsal. There are only two, the scoring one and the stopping one, known affectionately as the swish and the judder. One is off the front foot, the other off the back and both are founded on an initial stance not unlike a golfer's addressing a crucial putt. It cannot be beautiful. I have heard it called comic.

A microcosm

The Saturday was that first glorious one of June, almost too lovely to do justice to, the sort to make returning cricketers wonder why they lapsed, the sort that may have inspired Sir Neville Cardus, who was assistant cricket professional at Shrewsbury in 1912 and headmaster's secretary when he left in 1916, to write: 'To have lived at Shrewsbury in those days and known cricket there is to have lived in a heaven down here below.' It was all green and blue and dazzling sunlight, chapel and tea parties, deck chairs and dark glasses, smart boys and proud parents, little sisters in long dresses and big sisters trying to go brown ...

Where was I? Oh yes, the innings. Of its kind it was a gem. I was batting number 10, which was a compliment. We were 122 for eight, which was a catastrophe. I dare not have a net, lest a fragile confidence were shivered or a good shot wasted. I gained the crease, located middle and leg with the customary 'a little away from you, back a bit' exchange and sized up the field with a brisk ritual scrutiny whose apparent disdain was a mask for apprehension. What manner of bowler was this, fried by the sun and with an old ball, menacing me with a fan of four slips?

The first two balls whizzed past the off-stump a quarter of an inch wide, far enough to let go but near enough for preliminary inquiries to be made by the bat before tucking itself out of harm's way between the legs, satisfied that no action was called for. That is a variation of the judder; the slips evidently found it exciting.

The third was tickled to the fine leg boundary with an easy persuasion that Cowdrey would have coveted; the fourth received the standard judder treatment; 'over' was called and at the other end an opening batsman of little faith, followed by the last man, of little hope, committed hara-kiri in five balls. Having dominated the ninth-wicket stand, I was stranded, but even those four balls were enough to show the man of 114 Tests the writing on the wall.

A salute
Earlier in the day the real Salopian cricketers had been singing Cowdrey's praises. The previous Sunday they had lost to Tonbridge in the first round of The Cricketer Cup. The old master was playing, as unassuming in that sphere as he was courageous against Australia's opening bowlers in the winter, equally happy in both because both were cricket. They were astonished by the time he found to swat a saucy bouncer to the mid-wicket boundary with a power that came from no visible effort. They were moved by his modest approachability. They were honoured to be in the same game.

Through 25 years in the public eye Cowdrey has dealt cricket no underhand blow nor presumed favour by his eminence. A pretender, with four not out, salutes.

May 1985

QUESTIONS OVER THE CAPTAIN

BY JOHN PARKER

AS snow fell on the opening day of the first-class cricket season, I was minded to look out my version of the cricket-watcher's basic requirements—my long johns. They were acquired in dire necessity several years ago when, committed by my job to cover a five-day Test Match in Manchester I fled into the city at the first break of rain (you do not have to wait long at Old Trafford) to purchase the thickest pair of long thermal underpants I could find. They have stood me in good stead ever since on cricket grounds as far apart as Headingley and Hove.

But the long, cold spring will pass; the other cloud casting its black shadow over cricket will not, I am afraid, blow away with the changing months. I do not want to dwell on the political issues involved in the second major attempt by South Africa to seduce the world's cricketers; merely to point out the irony of the position that, as we in England welcome back the 'rebels' who have served their three-year suspension (with no remission) and for the first time since 1981 will be able to call on the strongest England team possible, so our Australian visitors have arrived weakened and riven by defectors who have succumbed to the lure of the krugerrand.

Just as in 1977 Mike Brearley's unspectacular England team was able to win back the Ashes 3–0 (two Tests drawn) from Greg Chappell's side devastated by Kerry Packer, the South African connection should ensure that David Gower and his men (whoever they may be) will go into the series long favourites to regain the Ashes lost in Australia by Bob Willis.

With Gooch, Emburey, possibly Underwood and even Larkins again in the side, to say nothing of Botham, who would take odds against England in favour of an Australia whose main strike bowler is to be the ageing Thomson (once Thommo, the terror of the seventies)?

In spite of the courageous and encouraging tour of India during the winter, when England came from behind to win the Test series and trounced the home team in the one-day internationals, Gower still has a great many things to prove as an England captain, certainly one who with reasonable success can be expected to enjoy a run at least as long as Brearley's four years.

The first is in his own form as a batsman, which had little to do with England's wins. From an armchair in front of the all too brief television summaries permitted us by the BBC, the batting of Gatting and Fowler and the bowling of Foster and Cowans appeared to be the main inspirations, with the steady bowling of Edmonds the backbone of the side.

Many people believe that a captain is worth his place in the side only if he can justify it by his ability on the field. That is Australia's way. They choose their team and then find a captain from among the players—on the first among equals principle. England waver from one theory to the other. No one can doubt that Hutton, May, Cowdrey and Dexter were worth their places as players. No one would argue that Freddie Brown, Illingworth, Denness and Brearley were chosen for their prowess as players before their potential as leaders. As for Greig, one can argue both ways for hours.

If the cares of captaincy have really robbed Gower of that magical certainty which, at his best, has made him the natural successor to Woolley, then it is highly doubtful whether he will survive as England's skipper. For there are two other question marks over his head. How will he cope with genuine cricket crises on the field; and can he control and meld his team into an homogeneous fighting cricket unit? The signs are mixed.

On the credit side are Gower's remarkable coolness, his undoubted intelligence and his increasing confidence in dealing with the importunate press. The English touring party to India was reported to have been one of the most happy, contented and dedicated teams to have toured abroad for many years.

But when things were not going so well against the West Indies last year, the Gower coolness manifestly gave way to the glazed look of a punch-drunk boxer waiting for the knock-out; and at least one leading cricket writer has wondered publicly whether England's successful tour of India was due not so much to the presence of David Gower as captain as to the absence of Ian Botham from the dressing-room. He suggested that had Botham been a member of the England party, then England might have lost the series, notwithstanding his great performances in the past.

Which brings me to the second great question of the 1985 season. Certainly England needs a Botham. But does she need the one she has got? It is impossible now for Peter May and his fellow selectors to leave Botham out of the team, after his spectacular batting at the start of the season—particularly against the Australians. He is certainly needed at number 6. His bowling form, however, is another question.

We want no more repeats of the spectacle, seen seven times last season, of Botham bowling away to his heart's content while the opposition hit him for more than 100 with Gower standing zombie-like at mid-off. If the Indian tour has given Gower the strength and confidence to put the dressing-room bully-boy in his place, then, to misquote Kipling, he will be the captain England have been looking for.

August 1986

A SEVEN-YEAR WAIT FOR HICK?

BY JOHN PARKER

NO cricketer in these days of mediocrity plays such an extravagant stroke as the draw, which was a sort of ugly reverse cut in which the ball was drawn away to leg between pads and wicket-keeper. I suppose the nearest modern equivalent is the reverse sweep, much favoured by Messrs Gatting and Botham until Peter May put a stop to it – in the name of security rather than aesthetics.

One esoteric stroke which keeps coming back to mind is Denis Compton's late cut, played off the front foot in defiance of all the rules of batting, probably from a yard up the wicket and wickedly placed to bisect the slip field. It was an individual gem, the hallmark of a genuine Compton innings that no one in my experience has ever had the wit or the ability to imitate.

Some years ago I had the pleasure and privilege of watching the great Barry Richards towards the end of his career when, on his own admission, he was bored with the game and would invent strokes with which to torment the bowlers.

This particular effort was another late cut, similar in outrageousness to Compton's, but this time played off the back foot. Nothing new in that, you may say, but this cut went to the third man boundary between the stumps and the wicketkeeper. Even the other Richards, Vivian, has not tried that one yet.

This is not a lament for the golden oldies, though I will admit to more than one overdose of melancholia recently when watching the truly dismal performances of England's cricketers against both India and New Zealand this summer. But the memories came flooding back, and with them all my conviction that there is no game in the world to touch cricket, as I watched a young man batting at Hove this summer.

Graeme Hick is a fourth-generation Zimbabwean, born in 1966, the year Ian Smith declared UDI. His father farmed at Banket, a small town about 100 miles outside what was then Salisbury, and was himself an all-round sportsman who introduced his son to cricket at the age of six. He had injured his back badly playing rugby, so he pointed young Graeme to hockey instead, which is probably just as well for opponents – now, at 20, Hick stands 6 feet 3 inches and weighs around 15 stone.

His schoolmaster quickly noticed that Hick had been born with a natural eye for ball games, and had the intelligence not to force a style on his batting but to help him develop his own talent at his own pace. The results are now being seen on English county cricket grounds.

Hick has never seen Barry Richards play, but he is being regarded as the great man's natural successor in the game. Comparisons are unnecessary and usually unhelpful, but the memory of Richards is still fresh enough to make it, in this case, valid. Hick has a similar stance, easy and unconcerned, at the wicket. He has all the strokes and, like Richards, he finds the gaps in the field without seeming to try.

Evidence, as often in cricket, lies in the figures. In mid-August Hick had scored more runs than any other cricketer this summer – and this in his first full season with Worcestershire. He was third in the averages, with 1,578 runs from 29 innings, including two double centuries and a top score of 227 not out. (His highest score in any cricket, last winter in a club match in Harare, is 309, made in an afternoon.) [*Subsequently overtaken by his 405 not out v Somerset at Taunton in 1988.*]

Hick first visited England at 17 with a junior Zimbabwe hockey side and liked what he saw. When it became clear that he had an exceptional talent as a cricketer, he decided to try his luck in England. If it did not work out, there was always the farm in Zimbabwe. 'Half-way through the season I decided that cricket would be my life,' he says with some diffidence but complete certainty.

He came back to England in 1984 with a scholarship and the idea of working on the ground staff at Lord's, but decided instead to look for some second-team cricket with a county. Worcestershire had a place open and after taking a good look invited him back the next season. Last year they began talking about the new Barry Richards.

It is a plot for a playwright. South Africa, by refusing to accept a Cape Coloured, Basil d'Oliveira, as a member of the touring England side, found itself ousted from the international cricket community. Zimbabwe, after independence, does not as yet have Test status. And here is a Zimbabwean cricketer, unable to qualify for England for the next seven years, being coached at Worcestershire by none other than Basil d'Oliveira and playing alongside d'Oliveira's son Damian.

'I've learned a lot from Basil,' says Hick, 'particularly about building a long innings. In the second team I'd make a hundred and get out, and Basil would shout at me that that was no b..... good if I wanted to play for England.'

And that is his ambition, even if he has to wait seven years. 'I'm hoping that they'll understand that in my country they can't play Test cricket at all, so perhaps the rule can be relaxed in my case.' He does not mention Zola Budd but, looking at the desperate state of English Test cricket, Messrs May and Co might consider that Hick has arrived at precisely the right moment.

July 1987

IMRAN'S LAST SUMMER?

Pakistan's cricket captain against England has said he will retire in the Autumn. He talks to Andrew Fraser about conservation as well as cricket

'TIGERS — they fought like tigers.' Lying back on a sofa in his London flat Imran Khan's voice vibrates with passion as he describes the team that has rewritten cricket's record books. India were defeated at home by Pakistan in a Test series for the first time ever, and defeated in five out of six one-day matches. 'You see, we are such a young team; myself and Javed Miandad are the only senior players. Our batting was inexperienced and completely at sea on slow wickets. Our bowling relied on pace throughout and it was neutralised by the spinning wickets. In the Indian team the first seven batsmen had 90 Test centuries between them compared to only 16 in our top order. Our success was in team spirit. It was a total team fight. For me the most satisfying aspect was the team spirit.'

Imran was being typically modest. His captaincy of this young team, now in England for a five-Test series this summer, was outstanding. Given no choice by the Pakistan Board of Cricket Control in the team selection, he experimented fearlessly with the batting order right to the last game. He called up three replacements, each of whom proved to be a match winner. In each Test match Pakistan fought back from a seemingly hopeless position. They drew the first five, then won the last. Imran, with a batting average of 64, was voted Man of the Series. In Pakistan he earned the title Fateh Hind, Conqueror of India, and 150,000 turned up at the airport to welcome his team home.

Imran was born in Lahore in 1952. His family is old in land on both sides although his father is a successful civil engineer. Imran is a Pathan and his ancestors came as mercenaries to help Sher Shah Suri conquer northern India more than 600 years ago. They were rewarded with land in the fertile Punjab and have resisted all attempts to move them ever since. Two of Imran's first cousins, Majid Khan and Javed Burki, have also captained Pakistan at cricket. Majid's father, Jahangir Khan, was a Cambridge Blue in the thirties while his brother, Asad, played for Oxford. Imran's own game was learned at Aitchison College, the Eton of Pakistan, and with his cousins playing in Zeman Park, the residential suburb of Lahore.

He was 18 when he played his first Test, against England. In 1972 he went up to Keble College, Oxford, to read politics, philosophy and economics and in 1974 he was elected captain of the University team, the first overseas captain since the Nawab of Pataudi in 1963. Imran loved his Oxford days and hit some big scores for his team including 170 against Northamptonshire and 160 against the Indian tourists. 'I am not sure if I was a popular captain,' he says. 'In cricket my attitude as captain used to be very straightforward: I would go out and try my best and I would expect everyone else to do the same. I would get very cross if I found someone wasn't. A lot of times I would lose my temper.'

In 1975 Imran went back to Pakistan for the first time in four years. 'I found it quite strange going back. A man grows up in the years from 18 to 22. I suddenly found that I had no friends in Pakistan; they were all out of town or working or married. It was a big change. I just got involved in cricket from then onwards.'

Since 1973 Imran had played county cricket for Worcestershire. In 1976 he was batting number 4, averaging 50 in the John Player League and topping the bowling tables. Worcestershire took it badly when he left them in 1977 to play for Sussex but he was bored and wanted more stimulating surroundings. He had to wait. Worcestershire had him banned from playing with Sussex for virtually the entire season. Imran still feels that Worcestershire broke their promises to him and took advantage of his naivety. 'The irony is that what I then stood for is freely allowed now; Botham was allowed to go from Somerset to Worcestershire, Dilley from Kent to Worcestershire, and Mendis left Sussex for Lancashire. I am still insulted and abused when I play in Worcester. I find it quite bizarre.'

In the same year Imran was banned from the Pakistan Test side for joining Kerry Packer's World Series Cricket. In their 1978 tour of England, Pakistan, without their Packer rebels, were thrashed and General Zia, President of Pakistan, ordered the Board of Cricket Control to relent. 'I don't regret playing for Packer. It made the cricketing public and establishment more aware of commercialism and the players' need to be treated as professionals. I am just sad about the bad blood it caused.'

Imran was back in the Pakistan team when India visited in the winter of 1978. Recriminations were forgotten in Pakistan's triumph and the team became national heroes. In 1982 Imran was made captain and, though his team lost 2–1 to England, they followed this with decisive victories against Australia and India. He had been Man of the Series against England. Against Australia, in another three-match series, Pakistan won 3–0, a margin repeated in a six-match series against India when Imran took 40 wickets and scored 250 runs.

He probably pushed himself too hard. Playing three series in less than seven months took its toll and Imran developed a stress fracture in his left shin. Bad advice from doctors, and his refusal to stop playing aggravated the injury and put him out of cricket for nearly two years at the peak of his career. Yet when Imran came back in 1985 Javed Miandad stood down as captain; in 1986 Pakistan became one of few teams recently to beat West Indies in a Test.

Imran believes he is playing as well now as he ever has. His bowling may not be as consistently fast as it was 'but sometimes it clicks.' The batting, he feels, is his best ever, certainly against India it was superb. His ambitions now are to defeat England, win the World Cup in the autumn and become the third player to have scored 3,000 runs and taken 300 wickets in Tests, following Ian Botham and Kapil Dev. 'I need only ten more wickets but I shall have to bat very well as I need another 400 runs.' Apparently prematurely he is retiring at the end of this season, though he is being pressed to change his mind. 'I shall be 35 in November, so it is best to leave while I am still good. Pakistan is a place where they do not tolerate fallen idols.'

Off the cricket field Imran is also a considerable sportsman. I spent three weeks in Pakistan last year when he arranged a feast of sport, from pig-sticking to partridge shooting. His prowess with a rifle had rather startled the ghillie when he came out on the hill with me in Scotland: we had just come out of a small corrie and could see the beasts 250 yards or more away. The ghillie settled himself comfortably for a spy and to work out the best route to get us in closer. 'Is the one on the left the best?' Imran asked. 'Aye, we'll be shooting that one,' said the ghillie, who was pretty surprised a second later to see the stag he was peering at through his glass drop dead, shot through the heart by an impatient Imran.

Like all true sportsmen Imran is keen on conservation. Pakistan has a wealth of wildlife but sadly not much respect for preserving the rarer species. One of Imran's dreams is to start a sanctuary for wildlife at the base of the Salt Range where the Chenaab River flows through the fertile plains of the Punjab. 'There is a lot of game in the Salt Range. There is urial, a lot of partridges, chuckor, another variety of partridge called sissy, there are quail there, bears, plenty of wild boar, monkeys, baboons, panthers might come ...'

Imran's more immediate concern, however, is to defeat England in the present series. I asked him about the great players he has known. 'Viv Richards is the greatest batsman I have ever seen. The most outstanding bowler is Dennis Lillee; his comebacks from injury, his guts, his skill. John Snow was a superb fast bowler. Boycott, despite not being flamboyant, is a very intelligent and gutsy cricketer. You need someone like him in a Test team.

'The present England team is very professional and Botham stands out as a match winner. His performance has been incredible for England.

The only thing is that he has not done himself justice against the West Indies. To me the one test of a cricketer is to perform against a team such as the West Indies have had in the past decade. John Emburey is a superb bowler who always utilises conditions. Phil Edmonds is probably bowling at the best in his career. Dilley has come back and is bowling superbly. Chris Broad has done a lot to strengthen England's batting.

'England will be a hard team to beat; I have no illusions that we will start as underdogs. But I really do feel that the way our team fights we might start off badly, as we did in India, but then as the tour progresses, we will master local playing conditions and, if we excel, can win.'

Apart from Javed Miandad, Imran is the only member of the Pakistan side with English county cricket experience. Nevertheless his young team won its spurs in India and Mike Gatting had better look out for Imran's tigers.

6

FROM THE PRESS-BOX

Cricket has a very different perspective thro'
binoculars in the correspondent's conclave
from that on the field of play. A number of
distinguished reporters convey their views on
cricketing moments and matters that exercised their minds.

CRICKET AND THE SPECTATOR

BY NEVILLE CARDUS

I HAVE often wondered why somebody does not write a short book for the average spectator at a cricket match showing him how to watch the play, what to look for, and why. Even in the pavilion at Lord's I have heard strange questions concerning some obvious procedure in the field.

'Why doesn't he take the new ball?'—a criticism directed at a captain who preferred to use the old ball because at the moment his best spin-bowler was doing well.

Such a question would not, of course, have been unintelligent once upon a time, when slow spin-bowlers cheerfully opened the attack with a fast bowler at the beginning of a match; recollect the famous 'opening' combinations of Mold and Briggs, Hirst and Rhodes, Wass and Hallam, to name a few. Not many seasons ago I saw one bowler polishing the new ball on his trousers, and at the other end of the pitch the slow bowler rubbing the same ball on the ground, a procedure which probably puzzled even the most expert observer in the crowd. It should always be remembered that cricketers, like most human beings, are subject to fashions and to spell-binding phrases. And what is the custom in one period becomes obsolete in the next, not necessarily because of a development in the technique of cricket, but simply as a result of a shibboleth or craze.

No doubt all of cricket's procedure and ritual has had some practical origin, but in many cases the outward form of it has survived the first useful purpose. I have actually seen an English batsman patting a cast-iron Australian wicket between overs—a clear case of the habit of a lifetime. When I was a boy I never saw a wicket-keeper returning the ball to the bowler via point or short square-leg.

Nowadays the ball is seldom sent directly back to the bowler, especially if he is a quick bowler; indeed, I am expecting any fine morning to see, say, Wood 'take' a ball from Bowes and then to see it tossed from backward point to third-man, and so on, all round the field. I suppose the modern idea is to return the ball from the wicket-keeper in a way that will safely get it back to the bowler without risk of the seam suffering damage by contact with the ground; the bowler might miss holding a direct return! Besides, we must protect our bowlers' fingers at all costs.

The 'average' spectator varies in knowledge considerably in different parts of the country. My primer on watching would have a special edition for Yorkshire, where they know most of the tricks of the trade. Yet it was in Yorkshire that a dear old writer on the game achieved a precious gem of innocence. Shortly after the War, Yorkshire on a soft pitch would begin attack with Robinson and Waddington. Then, as the new ball waned, Macaulay would come on, over the wicket, just to get the 'feel' of the turf. But as soon as his off-spin started to 'bite', he went round the wicket. And then our beloved scribe sent off his message: 'Macaulay, obviously experiencing some difficulty in obtaining a foothold, was compelled to go round the wicket.'

The 'average' spectator at Gloucester still wonders why Goddard bowls 'round' rather than 'over'—at least, I recently heard puzzled remarks at Gloucester on this subject. And under the 'new' l.b.w. rule, is it as advantageous for an off-spin bowler to exploit his spin from *round* the wicket as it was under the old rule? Have we not here another case of necessary procedure changing into mere custom?

A few years ago it was a familiar thing to see a slow left-handed bowler on a hard pitch choosing over the wicket as his point of attack, against all 'classical' precedence. Did Rhodes or Blythe, not to mention Peel, ever bowl over the wicket in all their lives? I recollect that Sir Pelham Warner once deplored in print that so naturally gifted a slow left-handed bowler as Roy Kilner frequently bowled over the wicket. No doubt it was a 'trade secret'.

In Lancashire, during the great Makepeace regime, the left-hand over the wicket tactics were employed whenever on a hot day the spear-head of McDonald had been blunted. A widespread on-side field supported good length bowling aimed at the leg-stump, and thus the batting side's merry-making (and that of the crowd if the batting side was playing at home) was spoiled. A favourite complaint against Lancashire in those days was: 'You won't score quickly yourself and then you bowl tight and make it impossible for batsmen who *have* got strokes to make them!'

Oh, the lovely summer afternoons I have seen ruined for patriots at Hove by those 'dour' Lancashire clods of the bad old times! I have heard retired colonels fuming; I have seen them helpless with mortification as Lancashire put into effect the two match-saving specifics—the 'dead' bat one day, and 'Hopwood over t' wicket' the next. But I am not sure that Rhodes was not as much the prophet of the 'dead bat' (on bowler's pitches) as Makepeace himself, though no batsman has played 'dead bat' more skilfully than Makepeace. The 'dead bat' meant a passive stroke to the abrupt spinner, so passive that the ball fell harmlessly off the bat to the ground almost at the batsman's feet. Thus was the expectant close-up 'leg-trap' thwarted. The 'dead bat' prevented the ball from spinning, or ricochetting, from any part of the bat to the fieldsmen.

The close-up leg-trap is a post-war 'gadget'. (I do not refer to the packed leg-side field for the so-called 'body-line' stuff; I mean the legitimate supports for off-spinners on a 'sticky' wicket, or for Root's inswingers, which never threatened anything except a batsman's innings.) Who was the first off-break bowler to employ a short-leg field?

Hugh Trumble once told me he used such a field at Manchester in the 1902 Test match which Australia won by three runs. My memory cannot confirm this point. Did Spofforth ever bowl off-breaks from round the wicket? By going round the wicket, post-war bowlers of Parkin's or Macaulay's order hoped to thwart the batsman's defensive pads; by going round the wicket, the angle of the spin was, as the saying had it, got at the bowler's end. As I have already asked in this article, is it any longer necessary to bowl off-breaks from round the wicket? I should have thought that the new rule would favour the angle of spin occurring at its abruptest at the batsman's end.

The spectator's guide should certainly be written. And one of the first things it must explain is the general absence of a fieldsman in the straight deep nowadays when a slow bowler is on. A few years ago, old Bill Howell, the Australian, visited a cricket match at Sydney, the first he had seen for many years.

He watched in silence, then after half an hour he spoke: 'When did this new rule come in?' 'What new rule, Bill?' 'Why, the one which stops the batsman from hitting a four in front of the wicket!'

August 1935

FROM THE PAVILION AT LORD'S

BY LIEUT.-COL. CYRIL FOLEY

Smith Punishes Kent Bowling

ON July 24th the pavilion habitués could talk of nothing but the results of the county matches completed the day before. These were generally voted to have been the best both in quality and quantity which had appeared this season in their respective morning papers. First we had Lancashire's glorious performance against Surrey at the Oval, in getting 240 runs for the loss of two wickets in ten minutes under three hours, at the rate of 85 r.p.h., and so winning by eight wickets with 25 minutes to spare. Then we had Sussex scoring 62 in 27 minutes to beat Warwick by eight wickets with seven minutes to spare; and to crown all a really desperate encounter towards the termination of which Sims of Middlesex hit Freeman for what looked like a perfectly safe four, which would have made the match a tie had not Valentine, appearing out of the blue, caught the ball knee high at square-leg in front of the pavilion, and so won the match for Kent by five runs. And if anyone cannot, as I could not, visualise the picture, let me add that the wickets at Maidstone are now pitched parallel to the pavilion, and not at right angles to it as they used to be.

Jim Smith who, in the same match, scored 50 in 14 minutes, 49 of them off Freeman, was sad that he had not hit 'just one more six', which would have won the match, and explained to Mr. Findlay in the most serious manner possible how, when he found himself opposite Marriott, he 'saw a great open space on the off side', and 'tried to place the ball there,' and then added rather naïvely: 'But you know I can't *place* the ball.' No, Jim Smith, we *do* know you cannot place the ball, and we hope you will never try to do so. You are quite good enough value as it is.

Other good matches were a win by Worcester over Northants by 30 runs, and a great effort by Glamorgan (242 for nine) which enabled them to draw with Hants. Eight first-class matches out of ten were finished.

On the subject of remarkable matches, Mr Percy Perrin recalled one, so remarkable indeed that I looked it up, as I could only vaguely remember it. It certainly does take some beating. It was between Essex and Derbyshire, and was played at Chesterfield on July 18th, 19th, 20th, 1904, just 31 years ago. Essex batted first and made 597 and lost the match by nine wickets, for Derby scored 548 and at lunch time on the third day actually had six Essex batsmen out for 27, and four afterwards for a total of 97, leaving themselves 147 to win. These runs were knocked off for the loss of one wicket. For Essex, Percy Perrin created a world's record for a first-class match, for his 343 not out contained no fewer than 68 fours, or 272 by boundaries! He would have made 12 or 14 more runs under present-day conditions, as he thinks he hit six or seven 'sixers' which were at the time only reckoned as fours. His innings occupied five and three-quarter hours, so he scored at the rate of 60 r.p.h. For Derbyshire, C. A. Ollivierre, whose brother recently played for the West Indies, made 229 and 92 not out. I think that must be one of the most remarkable matches ever played.

The Middlesex v. Hampshire match of July 24th, 25th, 26th interested me perhaps more than any other match played at Lord's this season. As the average rate of scoring all through the match was about 48 r.p.h. this may seem curious, but so much depended upon results and there were so many surprises during the game that one forgot the slow progression. Had we lost we should have dropped to eighth place instead of being, as we are now, third in the County Championship. Something happened in the match which no doubt has been noted by Mr John Wisden's statistical department. In three consecutive innings in one match over 50 runs were added for the last wicket. That is surely a record? Middlesex had made 184 and Hants had lost nine wickets for 177 when the last wicket, Boyes (28) and Hill (29 not out) added 56, bringing their total to 233. Middlesex at the close of play had made 143 for five wickets, and so led by 94 with five wickets in hand, and the match was an even one.

On the Friday Hendren, who had scored 81 not out overnight, succeeded in completing a really splendid century, but nine Middlesex wickets were down for 189, which meant that they led by only 140 runs, a situation definitely in Hampshire's favour. However, Hulme (37) and Young (19 not out) added 59, leaving Hants exactly 200 to win. And then to cap all, when Hants had lost nine wickets for 93, Boyes (22 not out) and Hill (27) almost emulated their first innings performance by adding 53 for the last wicket, Middlesex winning by 53 runs at three minutes to six o'clock. Needless to say the last wicket stand in Hampshire's second innings was easily the best of the innings, and the other one only failed to be the best by two runs; while the Middlesex effort of 59 was only nine runs short of that made by Hendren and Newman for the fifth wicket. Uncommon as the whole thing was, had all three stands been the longest, as they so nearly were, in their respective innings, it would have ranked as one of the most extraordinary things that ever occurred in first-class cricket.

When Young joined Hulme in the Middlesex second innings and we were only 140 runs on, I said to my neighbour: 'I'm afraid we can't expect more than ten runs from this last wicket.' If they had actually added that number Middlesex would have won in the end by four runs, but I tremble to think what our feelings would have been as the Hants score, with 151 to win, steadily rose from 93 for nine, to 146. Personally, I should have probably become unconscious at 5.53 p.m., some four minutes before the end. Scores: Middlesex, 184 and 248; Hants, 233 and 146.

July 1939

ROUND THE WICKETS

BY HUMPHREY DANIEL

IT was so cold at Lord's for the first day of the Test match that it might have been snow on the seats instead of white paint. The wind blew bitterly, in icy stabs. The sky was a wash of grey, cloudless, dreary, as smooth and as cold as a slab of stone. The elders in the Pavilion enclosure crouched huddled together in groups, vague reminders of partridges in coveys. The only warm spot on the whole ground was The Tavern. It glowed in that windy waste like a fire in a Victorian drawing room. People crowded round it, they drank in its warmth. Their faces beamed red with it. From the shelter of its comfort they looked out on a game played by men burly and bulging with sweaters, watched by people immersed in the top-coats of winter. It was a terrible day for cricket. There was nothing of the sunny south about this, and nothing of the bright happy-go-lucky cricket which the sun of the south brings. It was dour, grim, vigorous cricket. The wind cut like a knife. It frayed tempers. Batsmen hit hard, bowlers bowled fast. It was the cricket of the north. And it was two north-countrymen who held its stage.

They opened the attack, both bowling extremely fast indeed. But there was something more than sheer speed in the bowling of Bowes and Copson. It seemed to have something vicious, something awe-inspiring about it. It was something entirely different from the genial thunderings of Jim Smith or the boyish energy of Gover; maybe it was just that they both had red-coloured hair and suggested sting. But their bowling was hostile—it had spirit behind it.

To look at, Bowes is anything but terrifying. Caricaturists have put him behind a desk with a mortar-board on his head with great effect. But his cane has always seemed out of place. His glasses, his complexion, his almost chubby face all give it the lie. But a friend of mine once batted against Bowes. He was a good bat, brilliant for a schoolboy. Apparently Bowes hit him many more times than he hit Bowes; the ball seemed to be made of rubber, it kicked all over the place; but his hands proved that it was cork and leather all right—they were bruised blue.

But Bowes does not depend entirely on his height and making the ball 'bump'. He does not depend on anything, except his own ability; to him, the wicket is only an accomplice. He can swerve the ball so much and so accurately that he can beat a batsman before it has even touched the turf. That is why he is the best bowler on all wickets in the country, and, possibly, in the world.

Copson, at the other end, was a complete contrast. Small and thin, almost frail-looking, he is in the line of Larwood. Also, like Larwood, he is incredibly wiry. The ball leaves his hand rather like a stone from a catapult. His whole body whips behind it. He, too, can make the ball fly at times; but his counterpart to Bowes's bumping is a terrific break back. It must rival any of Kortright's.

The wicket which Bowes and Copson had to bowl on was about as stubborn as Russia's policy towards the Peace Front. It was sodden with rain—almost drunk with it. It was insensible, lifeless; but it could not frustrate them. For over after over they pounded at it; occasionally a spark of life would make the ball lift; more than often they managed to make it turn quickly, and while the shine was on it they swung it for all their worth. Between them they captured eight wickets. It would be interesting to watch the combination of Bowes and Copson on something else than a feather-bed wicket—on a fast Oval wicket, for instance. It is ripe time that England found another pair of fast bowlers. Since the days of Larwood and Voce, fast bowling has not been too popular. We have seen very little of it. It is suspected of being unsporting, dangerous. It is supposed to be unfair. It has gone out of fashion. But it must come in again. We cannot do without it. No game can be a great game without that element of risk, that test of courage. We want fast bowlers. Bowes and Copson may be the men we are looking for.

Away from the dust and din of the main conquest, news kept coming through of the minor skirmish going on at Sheffield. Yorkshire were falling—they were 22 for 3, they were 32 for 5, they were 62 for 6. Yorkshire were down. They were all out for 83. The Pope brothers of Derbyshire had bowled out Yorkshire for 83. Well, well, we thought, it had to come sooner or later. We were still thinking, when the next news came through. Derbyshire were all out for 20. Not one of them had reached double figures. Five of them had made nothing at all. Not one out of that great array of run-scorers had been able to raise a bat to stop the onslaught. The relentless machine, with four of its driving wheels missing, had swept them back into the pavilion in 40 minutes, in 67 deliveries. Then we looked for the name of the man of the moment, the hero who had so nobly filled the breach. Smurthwaite, we read. Smurthwaite? A misprint for Smailes, someone suggested. A railway porter, perhaps, picked up on the journey and put in to make up the team.

And then a picture from the past sprang into view in my mind. A picture of a stocky little man with a red face and small blue eyes close-set. He looked like a general who had lost his monocle and forgotten to grow a white moustache. And that is just about what George Hirst is to Yorkshire—General-in-Chief of all their forces. Year in, year out, he picks them out. He trains them. He puts them into the field cricketers, as perfect as Yorkshire can boast. Everywhere he has nets, looks out for the cricketers of the future. And George Hirst standing in front of a group of boys with a net in the background has become as familiar to the the pages of Yorkshire papers as any pictures of royalty.

It was at one of these nets of his that I remembered him. So vast was his organisation, so thorough and painstaking, that even my moderate ability was to be considered. I put on my pads. I went in to the net, faced the bowling. Presently Hirst himself took the ball; two steps and the great man had bowled it. Down it came slightly outside the off-stump. Just as I was congratulating myself on having hit a ball from George Hirst, it disappeared. It reappeared behind me somewhere to lay back the leg stump. It must have swerved not only very much but very late. Two more steps and the ball, apparently the very same one, was on its way again. I waited for the swerve, played for it. It did swerve—uncannily; but it also spun, just enough to curl round the bat and send the off-stump shooting out of the back of the net. I was desperate, and in my exasperation rather angry. So that when Hirst's next ball came down I went to meet it, struck at it, caught it (*mirabile dictu*), sent it skimming out of the mouth of the net. 'That's better, lad,' said Hirst 'now you've got your back up. That's much more like a Yorkshireman.'

At the end of the practice he talked to us. He showed us how to hold the ball, how to make it swerve and spin. He took a bat and demonstrated strokes. The usual pictures were taken for the Press. (Most of us spent many a penny before finding the paper it adorned.) He then called out the names of the lads he wanted to see again. We listened for those names, because we knew that one day they might be talked of wherever cricket is played. I believe Smurthwaite was one of them.

ROUND THE WICKETS

BY HUMPHREY DANIEL

WICKETS fell all day long at Maidstone the other day when Kent were playing Gloucester. The small boys in front of us got a lot of fun out of filling in their score cards. So, apparently, did the man in the bowler hat sitting next to me. He put down everything so neatly and correctly on his card that he might have been filling a ledger. And at the end of the day he asked his friend—a red-faced man in a cap—whether it was a record for the lowest aggregate in a day. The man in the cap could not tell him. No wonder. He had sat all day, his arms folded, his score card in his pocket. The score did not mean a thing to him. Just as the game did not really mean a thing to his friend.

A game is pretty obviously whatever its followers make it. If, for instance, England played Australia, not at the Oval, not at Sydney, but away out in the country somewhere before a handful of villagers, it would, I think, be a very different affair indeed. There would be no doped wickets, no body-line bowling nonsense, no trouble about fast bowling or slow batting, no record mania. In all probability it would be a very peaceful affair. So that any unpleasantness can, to a great extent, be suspected from the spectators. And I do not think there is much doubt which of the two types of spectator is the most suspect— the man who loves the game and what it stands for, or the man who loves its figures, its scores, its records, its sensationalism—the man in the cap or the man in the bowler hat. When the first two Tests had been drawn the bowler-hatted one thought he was not getting his money's worth. In no uncertain terms he demanded results at all costs. Timeless Tests became his watchword, his banner with a strange device. And so eventually we went to Kennington Oval to witness his invention. Those who survived went abroad to recuperate—and ran head-first into the biggest farce which the game of cricket ever conceived—the ten-day Test at Durban.

But then the man in the cap intervened. He had been ready to put up with people who had evidently never heard of Hirst, who stormed that something called 'body-line' would assuredly wreck the game. He had been ready, too, to look on both sides of the 'barracking' controversy. But he was not going to stand by and watch the game made into something like a Six-day Cycle Test. He demanded that cricket should be governed by time, because if it were not its pace would come to a standstill; that cricket should be played on English turf and not some product of science; and that it should be played with a spirit worthy of the game, its players and its followers. And people listened to him. So long as they continue to do so, cricket will always be a game worth watching.

We were watching Townsend bat. Rain had made the wicket a mat of black rubber and the ball was leaping about all over the place on it. Every now and then one would rear up and smack him on the hand. And every time the little man sitting next to me on the seat would stir uneasily. He had come a long way apparently to see Derbyshire play and Townsend bat. So that when a particularly vicious ball suddenly flared up at Townsend, rapped him on the gloves and then settled down again, nestling quietly in the hands of first slip, he was moved to a degree. But not beyond words. As the wiry form of his idol, banished to the obscurity of the pavilion, grew smaller and smaller he grew more and more heated. It was, it seemed, all about gloves.

Townsend had been wearing the wrong sort of gloves. They were, I had noticed, somewhat out of the ordinary. Instead of horsehair padding wrapped in leather or spikes of rubber for protection, they had what looked like strips of solid rubber. The little man was claiming that Townsend would never have been out, would still be on view if he had been wearing the right sort of gloves. It was ridiculous to wear such things—the ball bounded off them higher than it did the bat. Horse-hair gloves were no better. What was wanted was something which would check the ball, put the break on it, put it on the ground. Rubber spikes were the things. The ball had not half the chance of going up and being caught if it hit rubber spikes.

I thought a lot about the little man's theory during the next few days. I kept an eye on all the cricket pictures in the papers. I noticed what kind of glove the batsmen were wearing. Almost to a man they wore gloves with rubber spikes on them. I was just thinking that there might have been some scare in the fury of the little man's exaggeration when I came across three pictures—one of Hammond, another of Bradman and another of Hobbs. They were all wearing gloves backed with horse-hair padding, great things which looked like bolsters. But then, I realised, the three greatest batsmen which we have seen since the War were so rarely hit on the hands that they might never have worn gloves at all except for their peace of mind and confidence. Besides, if a bowler hits Bradman on the hand he must almost be tempted to appeal for l.b.w.

Wilkinson was toiling in the blazing sun of a July afternoon. The Old Trafford wicket was as hard as iron, the batsmen in their element. He had been bowling for over two hours. And he had taken but a single wicket for well over 100 runs. Not a very imposing feat—from the figures. But in point of fact Wilkinson was bowling very well indeed, well enough to be kept on in spite of all the runs he was costing his side. The fast bowlers were finished. He was holding the fort until the new ball came along. It was a thankless task. The dice was heavily loaded against him. Almost his only hope was his googly, in trying to trick the batsman to think the ball was going one way when it was really going the other. The wicket hardly helped. It was as shiny, as unresponsive, to the bite of a ball as a sheet of glass; and just about as icy in its relentlessness.

Wilkinson had beaten his man more than once, had deserved more than one wicket. Four times he had lured him out, spun the ball round his bat, watched it go on—and hit the pads. And four times he had plotted in vain. The ball had not pitched on the wicket. And because it had pitched on the leg the batsman had not been given out. That is the law. Don Bradman has suggested that the words 'that part which is between wicket and wicket' should be cut out of the new l.b.w. rule. I will be extremely rash. I will go further than he. When that is a rule, as I think it will be soon, and when it has proved insufficient, as I think it may quite possibly prove to be, then, I suggest, make anything which is going to hit the wicket count as if it had hit it. Make a ball good enough to beat a batsman, but simply not good enough to pass clean through his pads to hit his wicket good enough to count him out. Do let us give the bowler a fair chance.

August 1939

ROUND THE WICKETS

BY HUMPHREY DANIEL

ONE of the gunners had found a cricket ball in his kitbag. Prospective players, in ammunition boots, overalls and khaki shirts, had taken the field on the narrow stretch of mud which lies behind the group of huts officially known as Hyde Park Camp—and unofficially as anything under the sun. We recognised it at once. It was the Oval. There could be no doubt about it. There was the Pavilion, four of them in fact. There, undoubtedly, was the Vauxhall end with the camp's four boilers smoking themselves black in the face in their efforts to look like gasometers. There was the enormous crowd—a bunch of gaping faces peering round the fence and looking as if they had taken the wrong turning for Regent's Park. And there, too, was the sight-screen—a lone tea-cloth of doubtful hue which some trusting soul had hung out to dry outside the cook-house.

Only one thing suggested that it was a game of cricket, and that was that it was played with a cricket ball. The wicket at one end was an edifice of two billycans, one perched perilously on top of the other; at the other end, nothing—with the batsman at the mercy of the bowler's generosity—and direction. For bats there were a variety of inventions. The first man in tried an ordinary piece of wood. When at last he did make contact he had to leave the field wringing his hands like a maiden in despair, but hardly with the language of one. The next man tried a broom—one of those things which always remind one of 'black and midnight hags'. He was equally unsuccessful. As he had perforce to use a scythe-like motion, because every attempt at playing straight resulted in a blow on the chin, it was not very long before the crash of the billycans behind him were ringing his fall. The next man had the best weapon of all. It was a large and heavy Army spade. The batsman dealt out blows right and left like some mighty Vulcan at his forge. The game became even more complex, even more devoid of rhyme or reason. The stoppages became even more frequent because where before the ball had merely to be poked out of the dixie of potatoes behind the wicket it now had to be retrieved from under the huts—a game in itself. It was on one of these quests into the nebulous unknown that a speculative pole struck a bottle—and we, in turn, struck beer. And it was here that Alby appeared on the scene.

Alby, known to his few enemies as Albert, held the position of assistant to the cook. In other words, Alby was not only a very wise man but also a very resourceful man. And it was not beer this time which had drawn him from the cookhouse. In his arms he bore what at first sight appeared to be a small tree and at second proved to be the roughest of roughcasts of a cricket bat. It was so large that it covered the entire wicket, and as Alby was so small that he could put his legs behind it and defy the world in general, we had some difficulty in getting him out. Just as we were getting rather tired of Alby, and Alby's position was looking rather unhealthy, the bowler happened to notice a large saucer-like hole, made possibly by some unfortunate gunner in the face of the sergeant's wrath to encourage the earth to swallow him up, about 2 yds. from where the leg-stump is normally rooted. It was so large that his first attempt went straight home. Alby, seeing the ball sailing innocently down somewhere outside his rear, turned his attention to more pressing issues (I suspect it was what had happened to the bottle of beer). We were quite unable to convince him that the crash of his wicket had been made by the ball and not the boot of an exasperated wicket-keeper. And so we finished, in true army tradition, in hot argument—and the canteen.

There was a time, well within memory, when Worcester was amongst the down-and-outs of cricket. They were always at the bottom of the table; they never had any batsmen, never made many runs, and they never had any bowlers and never got many sides out. When they won a match, it was almost headline news. The only time they touched the threshold of fame was when the Australians came and used them as a sort of bicycle to try out their paces at the beginning of the season; when Bradman used to come to score an inevitable double century which broke the hearts of their bowlers for many a day. Poor little Worcester it always used to be. Today poor little Worcester are sixth in the county championship. They are above strong Surrey, above great Lancashire. They have swamped sides like Sussex. They have beaten Yorkshire. Poor little Worcester are getting up. They are not only on their feet again, but taking on the might of the game. Why is this? What has turned the weakling into a side to be respected and even feared? There is, true, the fast bowling of Perks, and the thrilling batting of the boy C. H. Palmer. But that is about all. And it cannot account for everything. Worcester's rise is one of the great surprises on which the game of cricket is nourished.

Not even the most sensational of co-starred comets from Hollywood can challenge the popularity of Compton and Edrich nowadays. They are doing a great service to the game. They are bringing back youth into it. Compton can hardly move off a cricket ground now without an admiring train to uphold his greatness. (The other day I saw a gentleman come out of the gates of a county ground simply howled out of existence when he put forward quite a creditable pretence to a crowd of small boys after autographs that he was indeed the one and only Denis Compton.) Edrich has not been so fortunate, or rather he has been too cherished by fortune, almost bewitched by her smile. One day I have no doubt the less intelligent representatives of the press will say of him: 'Failed, because he had too many chances.' People are still speculating about Edrich. What is the matter with him? Is he really a great batsman? Is he going to prove us all wrong in the end and the selectors right?

The answer, I think, lies at the other end—when Compton is batting. Watch Compton drive a half-volley. The strike is decided without hesitation, is perfectly balanced, instinctively timed; the ball fairly skids over the ground to the boundary, *all along the ground and between the fielders*. Now watch Edrich play the same shot. There is not the same quick decision, the same balance, the same timing. And more often than not the ball goes straight at a fielder. And how many times in an innings does Edrich stir the hopes of opponent spectators by being caught off 'bump' balls? He is always doing it. He obviously gets too far over the ball, nullifies the power of his shot by driving the ball into the turf. The difference between Compton and Edrich is the difference between a great batsman, an immortal player and a great county batsman, someone to be remembered when all the deeds of a Compton have been told. The ingredients of a great batsman are an uncanny pair of eyes, a brain behind them which can read instantly the message they telegraph, a comprehensive array of strokes perfectly geared and timed, an ability which is almost an instinct to put the ball anywhere, and the fortune to be born a great batsman. Compton has them all. Three years ago, when I first saw him bat, I did not think so, but he has turned out to be the greatest discovery since Hammond. He has proved me wrong. I hope Edrich will.

July 1947

THREE 'CLASSICS' OF THE YEAR

BY E. W. SWANTON

Comment on the University Match, Eton v. Harrow and Gentlemen v.
Players

THE past week has seen the height of the season at Lord's, with the three classic matches (beside which Tests and the County Championship are new arrivals) fought out on the field, and, of course, in the pavilion. The University Match was still suspended when the last *Field* went to press, so a note must first be made on that. Several reasons could be adduced for Oxford's failure to bowl out Cambridge on the third day, and so bring to full fruition their previous large advantage. For instance, they might be said to have paid the price for not including a bowler with any serious pretentions to beating his opponents in the air: a really slow spinner, either from off or leg, is one of the nearly-essential attributes of a University side.

Again, it could be urged that, even as things were, the match would have been won had one of the two catches offered by G. Willatt in the second innings been taken. A. W. H. Mallet, it should be recorded, was the bowler in the picture, in each case. Then there was the sickness of M. P. Donnelly, who might have been expected, if thoroughly well, to deal much more savagely than he did with the Cambridge bowling on the Saturday evening. These are items of reasonable conjecture, but the fact was that Cambridge did achieve their draw, and showed much resolution in doing so.

Having had the pleasure of playing against both sides this summer I did not approach the Eton and Harrow match in the expectation of seeing anything particularly scintillating, and so I was not unduly disappointed. If there is an A. W. Allen, a Macindoe, a Hayward, or a Pawle in either of the present elevens, to hark back no further than the thirties, he is lying darkly hidden. Good and grave reasons why the war should stand the blame for the level of school cricket have been given in these Notes before. We must not expect too much too soon, and that is all there is about it.

The first Harrow innings had its good points. T. J. M. Skinner and D. C. Prior showed some pleasing strokes, and R. H. Thompson defended with phlegm and patience, while R. la T. Colthurst exuded a gay spirit. One thing could hardly be overlooked, the performance of the slow left arm bowler who, on a soft pitch, aimed consistently a foot and a half wide of the off stump to a wicket-keeper already stationed there. The wicket seemed to bear no part in the whole operation. The Gentlemen's bowling a few days later only emphasised once more that there are few better balls to bowl on sluggish turf than spinning half-volleys *straight*.

No match in all the year comes under a more powerful microscope than the Eton and Harrow, and it was hardly to be expected that Harrow's declaration almost directly after tea on the first afternoon would escape the critics. But surely these gentry had a case to argue that even the most contentious might be chary of. The pitch was not thoroughly easy, or rather it was difficult to force accurate bowling for runs on it. To give Eton a hundred minutes' batting after the best part of a day in the field seemed to me the only sane thing to do. At the close Eton were 78 for four, or nearly two hundred behind, and but for an exceedingly narrow shave they would have been 74 for five, the ball brushing the bails before it went to the boundary for byes immediately before T. Hare and S. D. D. Sainsbury came in for the night. Next day both made hundreds: by such short inches is the course of history determined.

Hare, by repute, was the best Eton batsman, and very nicely did both he and C. W. R. Byass play. But the hero of the 'human story' was Sainsbury, who was chosen as a bowler after only two matches for the XI, and was promoted from number ten merely, or rather at worst, to feed the lions. To hit a century in such circumstances was to play the hero in the school story with a vengeance. Sainsbury's moments in the nineties were the best of the match, and his partner abetting with such enthusiasm that there seemed at least once every likelihood of the melodrama ending in the sorry anti-climax of a run-out.

The Gentlemen's performance against the Players, apart from M. P. Donnelly's glorious innings, was generally disappointing, but at least there was an indication that amateur cricket is not so sterile as some may suggest. It is important that young amateurs of promise be encouraged to play for other counties, and I do hope, if I may say so, that those who are anxious to play will be given a fair run, for there are tricks of the trade to be learned, and they do not always come quickly. Before the War it was often difficult for the counties to give an amateur a generous chance, for the ranks of their staffs were pretty full. There should be no such difficulty now, when everyone is crying out for young players, and each county has several old gentlemen just carrying on until reinforcements arrive.

Incidentally, the occasion seems equally ripe for the introduction of a school cricketer or two, if any good enough are to be found. One name at least suggests itself, that of P. B. H. May, who has been doing phenomenal deeds at Charterhouse, and has impressed everyone. By the School qualification clause his county is Surrey, for whom, so I am informed at the Oval, he is anxious to play.

August 1953

DUST AND THE ASHES AT THE OVAL

BY F. I. WATSON

How Australia fell to spin on a crumbling wicket, and how England hit off the runs to win the final Test

NOT yet has a Test match at the Oval between England and Australia failed to produce a chapter of its own in cricket history, and there has certainly been no more tense or fluctuating struggle than that by which the mythical Ashes have now been restored to England for more than a week. This was a match worthy in spirit, if not in technique, of the succession of great contests of the past, dating from that calamitous day in 1882 when England were for the first time beaten at home by Australia (by seven runs) and were consigned by the *Sporting Times* to the indignity of cremation, 'deeply lamented by a large circle of sorrowing friends and acquaintances.'

Twenty-seven years ago I was at the Oval when England last beat Australia on her own soil after the first four matches had been drawn. No one who was there could forget the gripping intensity of the last day, when Larwood and Wilfred Rhodes, recalled to the England team at the age of nearly 49, broke the back of the Australian batting in a hushed aura of strained unbelief among the spectators. Not until six wickets had fallen for less than 100 runs did the crowd really let themselves go in the scent of victory. This year's match reached its climax earlier, when Lock and Laker spun Australia out on a wearing wicket and it was realised that the Australians themselves had no comparable bowlers to exploit the conditions when England went in to get 132 to win.

Let us for once praise that small band of men who cheerfully suffer so much criticism—the English selectors. With the sides poised so evenly after four drawn matches and a possible six days' play at the Oval, they showed both courage and vision in choosing Trueman, short of match play as he was, and including the two Surrey spin bowlers for the later part of the match. This policy largely nullifed the luck of the toss, which Hassett won for the fifth time. However it went, England were equipped with Bedser, Trueman and Bailey for a first Australian innings that would presumably be played while the wicket was reasonably good, and whether Australia played the third or fourth innings, it could be expected that the wicket would give some help to Lock and Laker.

The way in which Trueman broke through Australia's middle batting was one of the most promising auguries for the future. Without much doubt he is the best fast bowling prospect England has had since Larwood. But the man whose influence was greatest in this Test series is certainly T. E. Bailey. He is apparently one of those players who thrive on adversity. On the English tour in Australia in 1950 he bowled with lion-hearted determination and resource in the first two Test matches before he broke a thumb, and in the present series the same fighting quality turned him into a match-saving batsman at Lord's and Leeds and the architect of England's hard-earned lead on the first innings at the Oval. It is, indeed, a salutary reflection that but for Bailey's stubborn resistance at Lord's or Leeds, the Oval match might not have been all to play for. This has, without question, been Bailey's series.

Bailey has an ideal temperament for the big occcasion, and the hardened experience of Bedser, Evans and Edrich has apparently been proof against the modern blare of publicity which now seems to accompany overseas tours in general and Test matches in particular. Much of the England batting was of an ineptitude that can be explained only by nerves. Hutton succeeded more by virtue of an inner instinct for self-preservation, though it was an odd spectacle to see him run out in the England second innings in an eagerness for a second run that was never there. The most heartening factor in the England batting was undoubtedly the success of P. B. H. May, who seems to be in full possession of the confidence which he seemed to lose for a time. Seldom has an Australian team been more unstable in batting in Test matches, but more will certainly be heard of Hole, De Courcy and the mercurial Harvey.

But the Oval match was really won and lost on bowling. That the Australians should rely almost entirely on pace bowling was a strange departure from the pattern of past Australian teams, which have almost invariably included at least one class spin bowler. How Hassett must have sighed for a Grimmett or a Mailey or an O'Reilly in the second English innings.

The wonder is that Lindwall and Miller were able to carry so heavy a burden so successfully and continuously while the versatile Johnston was out of the game through injury. In the Oval match Johnston used both his styles as a fast medium and slow bowler with great skill; but he is not a true spinner and could make little use of a wicket on which Lock and Laker had proved their worth. Out of their long experience

Lindwall and Miller kept going for long spells by their accuracy and variations of pace and direction, which they use more than most English bowlers.

It was no more than Bedser's due that he should bring his total of wickets in this season's Tests to 39, exceeding by one M. Tate's record of 38 in the English tour in Australia 28 years ago. Whether Bedser is a better bowler than Tate can never be proved. He has probably had a larger share of bowling to do, since Tate was contemporary with Larwood and other outstanding bowlers, such as Woolley and Kilner. Tate at his best had tremendous fire off the pitch and accuracy, but fewer variations than Bedser, whose subtlety increases with experience.

In the first four Tests the English fielding was something to remember—with regret. In the last match it was a good deal better for the introduction of Lock and Trueman and was infused with more activity and purpose, but it suffered lapses in catching when the later Australian batsmen in the first innings began to play free with the bowling, to turn what looked like being a moderate score into the reasonable one of 275. Australia made their mistakes, but they were less important and in many respects their fielding touched brilliance.

Certainly there is to-day no cover point to equal Harvey, whose excellence in that position recalls the mastery established by Hobbs. Not only is he sure in technique and anticipation, but covers ground so quickly that very little escapes him and he is a constant menace to the short run. Hole was an outstanding fieldsman at slip, and the whole team gave the impression of being more on their toes, physically and temperamentally, than England. They had the advantage of all touring sides in binding together more as a team than the changing English side and, like most Australian sides, their bowlers bowled more consistently to the field set for them than did the English bowlers, with the exception of Bedser.

It is as true now as ever it was that catches win matches, and no more so than in Tests. Fortunately for England some very good catches were held in the Oval match, and it is perhaps better to forget those that were missed in the earlier matches in the hope that some useful precepts have been driven home by them and will be put into practice in the future.

Before the next Test series against Australia is played in England, in 1956, changes will have been made in the composition of both sides. We have probably seen the last appearance in these matches of Compton and Edrich, perhaps of Evans, who is being understudied by the promising Warwickshire wicket-keeper and batsman, R. T. Spooner, on the tour to the West Indies this winter. There will be room in the next English team for young players along with such as May and Trueman.

Of the Australians, we may not see here again such masters as Lindwall or Miller or Johnston, and Hassett, at the age of 39, must be thinking of honourable retirement. But we shall almost certainly see more of the young players Archer, Davidson, Hole, Benaud and Craig, who, in spite of his failures on this tour, has impressed good judges with his possibilities as a true stroke player. Among these players Australia already has the makings of good all-rounders—a type that England needs very badly.

The best we can hope is that the present victory after so many years may herald the dawn of a new spirit in English cricket—a spirit that will give attack free play along with the necessities of defence. And that needs not only the skill of the player but the inspiration of leadership. Hutton has done all that could be expected of the phlegmatic Yorkshireman of long experience on the field. He is by nature of the dour, calculating type and it is late in the day to expect touches of genius from his captaincy.

The laws of progression apply to captains as well as to players and the Selection Committee must always be on the look out for a new captain as well as for new players. Meanwhile, our players, old and young, may take inspiration from possession of the Ashes once more and the need to prepare to defend them in Australia in 1954–55. They may perhaps now and then look in at Lord's and see the famous urn. It is the only symbol we have of a glorious victory.

August 1957

THE TEST THAT NEVER WAS

BY A. E. R. GILLIGAN

The West Indies, despite their brilliant individual performers, were no match for the best England team since the war

THE Fourth Test match at Headingley, Leeds, last week, was scarcely a test of the England team. Their superiority in all departments of the game was even more marked than the scores suggest. The time taken to win the game, two and a half days, was a fairer indication of the extent to which the West Indians were outplayed.

They were also out-captained. P. B. H. May is to be congratulated, not only on winning the rubber, but on a great exhibition of captaincy. The experience he gained last year against Australia, and in South Africa during the winter months, has stood him in fine stead. He will, I believe, rank as one of England's best captains. He handled his bowlers extraordinarily well, and I noticed that he had made a particular study of each of the West Indies batsman's favourite strokes, and placed his field accordingly.

I consider that the pitch was the ideal one for a Test match. It was helpful to the bowlers, and to the batsmen who were prepared to make strokes. I noticed that the ball, at times, though coming slowly off the pitch, was inclined to lift, and the batsmen had to watch closely, and make up their minds what stroke to play. When one looks back at the huge scores at Edgbaston and Trent Bridge it is interesting to note that the highest scores last week were 69 by P. B. H. May for England and 47 for the West Indies by R. Kanhai.

The low scoring was probably due to the heavy atmosphere and strong cross-wind blowing from the west, which favoured good swing bowling. Both Trueman and Loader exploited it to the full.

I regard Loader as the finest swing bowler since the late J. W. H. T. Douglas in his prime. He bowled magnificently in the West Indies first innings. He bowls with his head, and I like his slow ball, which he disguises very cleverly and which, incidentally, completely deceived Weekes, who went out without scoring—clean bowled.

Loader's hat-trick was the first one I have seen in international cricket. It was a splendid outswinger which knocked back Goddard's off stump; then there followed a mashie shot by Ramadhin, who was easily caught at mid-wicket close in. There was tremendous excitement as Gilchrist walked in. Loader made no mistake. He bowled a swinging full toss straight at the stumps which deceived Gilchrist completely.

It is some 25 years since England had such a wealth of fast bowlers, and our selectors are fortunate in having such a quartet as Trueman. Loader, Statham, and Tyson to draw on. I would say without hesitation that England now has the best attack in my memory. May himself told me what an easy job it was to captain a side with two such great fast bowlers—aided by Bailey (who missed the Leeds Test owing to a split hand), and then to have two spin bowlers of the calibre of Lock and Laker.

Lock, strange to say, took only one wicket in the match, but his fielding helped to lay the foundation of our victory. I never hope to see a finer catch than he made at short leg, diving to his right, to send Sobers back to the pavilion. Again, in the West Indies second innings, when Sobers had opened brilliantly against Loader and Trueman, it was Lock, fielding in the covers, who made a great stop, and Sobers, thinking he had hit a certain four, found himself half-way down the pitch. Lock's return to Evans, right over the stumps, saw Sobers run out, and the whole game turned England's way from that moment.

Here again was a splendid piece of captaincy by May. He had replaced

Loader with D. Smith, with his left-hand deliveries over the wicket, and at the end of Smith's second over, with Sobers dismissed, he brought back Loader at once. With his first ball Loader had Kanhai plumb l.b.w.

A word about the English fielding. It was really one of the best performances any England team has put up for years, and I could fault not one of our side. Cowdrey made three good slip catches, the best being when he caught Worrell out in the second innings, taking the ball one-handed to his right. Evans kept wicket in his usual brilliant fashion. He is still the world's oustanding 'keeper.

Loader, in addition to his great bowling performances, made many saves on the boundary, and he returned the ball like a bullet, straight over the stumps to Evans. P. E. Richardson was brilliant in the covers, and saved many runs, and the Rev. D. S. Sheppard made a very fine catch at the second attempt to send back Walcott.

There used to be a feeling that Leeds was England's bogey ground, but May has now surely dispelled it with two consecutive victories there—against Australia and now the West Indies.

As for the West Indians, I give the fullest praise to that great all-rounder, F. M. Worrell, who, after making 29 and going in first, proceeded to bowl 38.2 overs and take 7 English wickets for 69. No man tried harder than he, and he was well supported by Gilchrist, who has vastly improved since the beginning of the tour.

Gilchrist, for a small man, is the fastest bowler in the country today, and he found two beauties which sent Graveney's and Lock's stumps somersaulting—both these deliveries turned back very sharply and could be considered virtually unplayable. Alexander was this time preferred by Goddard to Kanhai and the old Cambridge Blue kept wicket exceedingly well.

In a previous article I mentioned that the big stand by Cowdrey and May at Edgbaston in the first Test match had paid handsome dividends to England by showing that it was possible to tame Ramadhin. His innocuousness was again evident at Leeds when he failed to take a wicket.

Finally full praise to our Selection Committee for bringing back Sheppard who, after a sketchy start, again showed real class batsmanship; and for bringing in Loader for the injured Statham, when many thought that they would choose Tyson. It will be interesting to see who will be Trueman's partner in the Fifth Test at the Oval on August 22nd. I have an idea that Loader will get the vote.

August 1957

CLOSE-OF-PLAY CRICKETERS

BY ROBIN MARLAR, *Cambridge University and Sussex*

TUESDAYS and Fridays are the most eventful days in a county cricketer's week, for the last day of a match usually sees the most action. But at the drawing of stumps there is no time for a breather. Both teams barely have time for the niceties of congratulations before bodies, and minds, are switched to the business of moving on to the next engagement.

After a few years, the panic which normally precedes a journey begun in a tearing hurry ceases to afflict the county player. Hair's-breadth catching of trains, and the swift packing and disposal of innumerable cricket bags, are bi-weekly occurrences. Hence one often sees cricketers creaselessly clothed! A parent trying to hustle his family through the barriers at holiday time would marvel at the phlegmatic behaviour of the scorer baggage-master of a county cricket side.

Nevertheless, the actual travelling is a bore, and eventually many of the older players even become *blasé* about the opportunities which cricket presents for touring in this country. They prefer to stay at home, no matter how attractive the prospect of playing, say, Lancashire at Blackpool during Wakes Week.

Opinions differ amongst the counties as to the best, and the most economical, means of moving the cricketing circus. Over the last seven years there has certainly been a swing away from the railways, though there can be little doubt that the longest hauls are quicker by train than by road. Several of the Midland counties, whose average distance per trip is less than those at the extremities of the country, have adopted coach travel, but car trips are rapidly becoming more popular, despite a pre-war reputation for mishaps. To some extent this reflects the desire for a little freedom and relaxation. Bradshaw's discipline is hardly conducive to ease and comfort after a day's play which has used up a certain amount of nervous energy. A quiet pint at a roadside pub works wonders in these circumstances.

One of the best of recent cricketing stories is told by Laker. In his autobiography he describes a stop he made at Lichfield after the 1956 Manchester Test. The public bar re-echoed to the name of Laker, and yet the only question the landlord asked England's hero was 'How far are you travelling, sir?' Moments such as these tend to make cricketers philosophical.

Long-distance driving has its own habitués and its own manners. Outsiders, i.e. ordinary motorists, find it hard to become initiated. At night the lorry-drivers—the Americans know them as teamsters and for once their linguistic tradition is pleasantly old fashioned—have a Morse code of their own. A car-driver who ventures into a transport café is as far from his *milieu* as a lascar seaman in an airline pilot's hostel. Snatches of their overheard conversation are as incomprehensible as the flashing patterns of their headlights. On one black night *en route* for Manchester, having used up all the daylight and all the opening time as well, I stopped for a break at a roadside café in North Staffordshire, far from any built-up area. A fish out of water quickly searches for familiar objects, but there were few; a juke box was the main article of furniture, and the only literature was a copy of the *Daily Worker*.

Three days' rain at Manchester recently, and the team was on the road again and due for fresh shocks to the system. The week-end following was due to be spent at Ashby-de-la-Zouch. Anyone who believes that a cricketer has only to play the game in order to lead his pleasant life does not take account of the adjustments such changes of scenery demand. To be pitchforked from a busy centre of business and industry into a decayed nineteenth-century spa town requires adaptability even on the part of those who are convinced that the only health-giving liquid comes out of a barrel marked XXX. To move from the most up-to-date pavilion in the country, where one cannot turn round in one's quarters without being aware of glass doors marked 'Ablutions, Home and Visitors', to a worm-ridden shed where ablutions are almost non-existent, is to realise that cricket is a game which makes light of material things.

But the hospitality and kindness are always the same, and so are the characters. At Manchester, during one of the intervals between the showers, the captains decided to inspect the wicket with a view to making some contribution to public relations. No groundsman—no covers removed. Presently, a breathless man of Kent emerges. 'Sorry, skipper—I didn't think it was due to stop, so I sent the lads off for a bite of lunch.'

'Aha! Trusting southerner,' says the northern weather man, 'I caught you napping that time; if you stay here for 20 years, I'll bet you never understand my ways.'

Seventy miles away at Ashby Fred Garratt is applying the finishing touches to his wicket. For him there will be no more important visitors this year than Sussex. His next task is to prepare an agricultural show ring. It is not raining, but the clouds are piling up over Ashby's ancient monument of a Greek-porticoed British Railways station and, as he hammers long spikes through his canvas sheets, Fred recalls the Surrey match a few years back. The Surrey players arrived on the Monday morning to find 'one of the covers up a tree', as Stuart Surridge graphically described it, and conditions just right for Jack Walsh, who spun the visitors to defeat after Leicestershire had been put in to bat on the Saturday.

'What happened, Fred?' I asked him.

'Well, it was like this. You see, they had no proper covers—not that we have now,' he added, pointing a derisive finger at two porous tarpaulins, 'and they sent some people over from Leicester, seeing as how it were my first year at it: and when seven o'clock come they fixed them down in a helluva hurry, 'cos they wanted to catch the bus back, and on the Sunday they blew off no trouble. Coo, it were funny really, for there was a huge wet patch just right for Jack.'

Bad luck, Fred. This year the rain flooded your entire square, rushing through, under and round the covers. Had it not, I believe, as you do, that your pitch would have proved itself a 'beauty'. It had certainly had loving care lavished upon it, by one of the friendliest men in all Leicestershire.

January 1964

ELEVEN MEN TO BEAT MARS AT CRICKET

BY LEONARD CRAWLEY

THE recent efforts of the Fédération Internationale de Football Association to get together a World team must have re-awakened in countless minds the intriguing question of whom to select for a World team at cricket. There are two varieties of such teams. One can play tricks with time and bring great players back from the past. Or, as I prefer, one can imagine that a team of current cricketers has been challenged by Mars, for example.

In choosing any cricket team a certain balance must be preserved between batting and the various types of bowling, and an accredited wicket-keeper must be included. Accepting this proviso, let us set about our task.

We begin with the opening pair. Australia, West Indies and Pakistan all have their opening batsmen. So had South Africa until McGlew retired. England alone has not. We have tried various combinations, and finally forced the unwelcome distinction on Cowdrey. He, having occupied this position unwillingly for his country, must now be made to do so for the World.

Cowdrey is something of a paradox. Almost anyone would concede that on his day he is among the world's greatest batsmen. But sometimes he is unaccountably ineffective. He is not so much tied down by any one bowler, as by his own diffidence. But he remains a great batsman, great enough to bat in the wrong position and still survive. Whatever place in the order he occupies for Kent, he is the greatest No. 1 in the world.

If Simpson of Australia is chosen as his partner, many eminent players must be left out. But Simpson has other strings to his bow. In the absence of Sharpe of Yorkshire, he is the greatest slip-field in the world. Perhaps he is that anyway. And as a leg-break and googly bowler alone he could be played in any representative side. We will hear more of this side of him over here, as Benaud fades from the scene. Finally he is a run-stealer of a high order. And, as Cowdrey is also of an anticipatory nature, they should form a pair well calculated to keep their opponents on their toes.

Neil Harvey having retired, Kanhai has earned the title of the World's No. 3. His brilliance at The Oval alone entitles him to it, and he 'came off' consistently in last summer's tour. But Kanhai, in the class of cricket in which he plays, is something of an inspired amateur. Making the game look easy, as any great performer should he sometimes dazzles even his own eyes. It is the price one has to pay for including a West Indian. They play in a different spirit from our men. But that spirit has done more than anything to keep the game alive.

What has May done to earn his dismissal? He had long been our own No. 3, and often a premature one, in view of some early disaster. About two years ago he announced his resignation from county and country captaincies, as he no longer felt able to travel. His appearances since have been spasmodic and not very successful. A few matches in succession would probably restore those glories of old. But on balance, Kanhai's preparedness to go wherever he is required must make him preferred.

Norman O'Neill is a natural athlete. If he had not chosen cricket to excel at, it might have been any one of half a dozen other sports. His century in the Fifth Test at the Oval in 1961 gave such pleasure to all those who associate enterprise with a vanished age, though Burge went on to overtop it, that it alone would earn O'Neill the position of No. 4 in this team.

Dexter may or may not be the world's greatest batsman. Certain critics have suggested vulnerability against spin bowling, and often when he appears set he gets himself out. But he is indisputably the most exciting, particularly against fast bowlers. The faster they bowl, the harder he seems to hit them. Add to this a few quick overs when a long-desired wicket is liable to fall, and the majesty of his fielding in the covers, and you have a claim for inclusion at No. 5 that none can gainsay.

At No. 6 we look to Sobers, not only a great left-handed batsman, but the greatest all-rounder in the world, still more undisputed in this claim since Davidson retired. The only man who could possibly challenge him is my choice for No. 7, Reid of New Zealand. If he existed in a team of giants with only himself to support, one could more easily assess his stature in all departments of the game. As it is, he bears the responsibilities of his side on his shoulders, just as May once bore the early indiscretions of England.

South Africa's John Waite is at No. 8. Murray of West Indies shares his record toll of victims. But he is young, with many seasons still before him. Waite is mature already, and he combines with wicket-keeping such a class of batsmanship as we have not seen since the days of Ames.

Benaud is shortly to retire. But first we must claim him to direct operations from mid-off. The Martians will surely succumb to his stratagems and deliveries on the field, and equally be charmed by his affability off it.

There are just two places left, and those must be filled by fast bowlers. Who is to stand down? All I have said of Murray as a wicket-keeper, I say of Griffith as a bowler. He, too, had a wonderfully successful first season in this country, but has many years before him. Instead, I prefer Trueman, who no longer relies on sheer pace. In any case, the crowd must have someone to talk to on the boundary! Lastly there is Hall, still probably the fastest bowler of his age.

So my team for the first interplanetary Test Match is: M. C. Cowdrey (England), R. Simpson (Australia), R. Kanhai (West Indies), N. O'Neill (Australia), E. R. Dexter (England), G. Sobers (West Indies), J. R. Reid (New Zealand), J. H. B. Waite (South Africa), R. Benaud, captain (Australia), F. S. Trueman (England) and W. Hall (West Indies).

July 1972

CRICKET DUTY AT DUSK

BY JEREMY ALEXANDER

Some who watch their blocks by night and play their strokes by day

IT is about a quarter to seven at Kidderminster. Worcestershire are all out, Middlesex have just lost their first wicket, and Parfitt is next man in on the score card. But wait. This is not Parfitt coming out to bat. It is an altogether shorter man, slighter of build and darker. This surely is Latchman, Harry Chand Latchman in full, the county's resident nightwatchman come to play out time. He does it—as he has done on each of a score of occasions when so called upon—but the other opener does not, so Parfitt comes to the wicket after all.

It might be anticipated that this is to be used as illustration of the futility of the nightwatchman tradition, but that is not my purpose. The tale is yet half-told. Next day Middlesex were put out for 192. Latchman made half of them, 96. He watched by day as well as by night. Parfitt stayed a while, but Radley, Brearley, Murray and Jones, the batting heart of the county, went quickly. When Latchman was eighth out—he is usually ninth in—the score was 177 and he had hit 13 fours. He had gone beyond his term of duty and done overtime of three and a half hours.

A batsman within

So what? you may ask. In the fourth Test at Leeds in 1948, Alec Bedser was sent in No 4 as nightwatchman and the next day took 79 off the unbeaten Australians, keeping pace with Bill Edrich and putting on 155 with him. There must be many such cases. The point is that deep in most batting orders are so-called rabbits, men who bowl or perhaps keep wicket, and deep in most of these rabbits is a batsman trying to get out. The nightwatchmen are the fortunate few, albeit possibly volunteers at first, who once in a while can let the batsman among his own kind higher up the order.

Latchman applied for the job six years ago and has not failed in it yet, which is four or five times a season. You can't sack a man like that. Previously his highest score in this rôle was around 30, though last year he made 65 not out against Cambridge University from his normal lower position. He calls himself a collector of runs, but he does not hide his relish of the chance to build an innings. No wonder, with such incentive bonuses, he puts no foot wrong as nightwatchman.

This, of course, remains his first concern. The nightwatchman's hour, when in autumn the owls are beginning to stir and bats are on the wing, comes about half an hour before stumps are drawn. His is shift work, only 20 minutes at most, but he must be ready if called. He fastens the locks, takes up his torch as it were and waits for an alarm which may never come.

Latchman explains the next requirements. 'The nightwatchman must be unflappable; he must have a sound defence; and he must be beyond temptation.' With 20 minutes to go, Latchman will have a go at a bad ball; with five minutes left he will leave it alone. And he takes as much of the bowling as possible, even if the other 'real' batsman is played in and seeing the ball well. In short, he has most of the qualities of his namesake in factory or office block.

Unafraid of the dark

He is the security man, a guard, a blocker, a protector of the team's jewels. He must be watchful, stubborn, single-minded, as unafraid of the dark as the shadows round the corner, for the odds are that the fieldsmen will be crowding round him and shadows, if there is sun to make them at all, will be long and eerie.

Latchman, incidentally, sharpened his eyes last winter coaching rackets at Harrow, a post he assumed in October as assistant to the professional there, Roger Crosby. In previous years he had coached cricket and been an assistant car salesman. Now he is learning real tennis with Henry Johns, the Lord's professional. I wonder if any other West Indians—Latchman was born in Jamaica 29 years ago yesterday—play these court games. The wristy stroke-play of some of the cricketers would surely lend itself to rackets.

But to return to nightwatchmen, for diversion is forbidden to them, other members of the union include Gifford (Worcestershire), who does the job for England, Pocock (Surrey), Hobbs (Essex), and Wilson or Bairstow (Yorkshire). Pocock, Wilson and Hobbs are naturally big hitters of the ball, using a long handle. Gifford and Bairstow are more subdued. The latter is an example of the wicket-keeper watchman. If a side must bat for just ten minutes or so, the wicket-keeper is used to the light and pace of the pitch; often he keeps his pads on.

Into the breach

I cannot resist ending with a personal tale, for I used to keep wicket myself, albeit on a loose rein and at low level—all of which is here irrelevent, since on this occasion tea fell between the opposing village's laborious 135 in two and a half hours and our reply. There was great debate over the sandwiches and shop cakes as to who should open our innings. We had one of our best line-ups—men of pomp and plump averages, men of circumstance and straight bats—but one, just one, was prepared to open. Real batsmen are terribly fussy about the number on their back. No 7 will happily face the last ball of the first over, but nothing will induce him to go to the crease after an hour if he is batting No 6.

Anyway, on this occasion I was clearly destined for no innings in my normal No 10 (which is where I belonged) or, if all those stars above me had been put out, for an appearance of such brevity that it would be less embarrassing to come over queer or something. It was a strong cup of tea that day. 'All right. I'll open.' 'Good on you,' cried the stroke-makers with one accord. 'Don't worry,' comforted No 3. 'If you can just last an over or two.' So off I went as a kind of first-ball watchman,

watchman, feeling like John the Baptist preparing the way for one, nay eight, greater than me.

Knowing the knock

Well, our Lord never got a look in. He was still stomping about with his pads on and all his disciples with him as we returned an hour later at 136 for o. The regular had made 70, I 66. It was ridiculous, of course. My stay had not been charmed; it was the stuff of dreams. If I hit the ball at all, I hit it in the air (it goes that way by nature) unless I went for the handsome off-drive and squirted it through my legs which is another of my specials. In the air the ball mostly flew among the people with the sense of a bird among branches. When it went to hand, it found the fingers more buttered than the sandwiches.

They don't make fielders like that now, except in the England side. But the moral of the story needs no pointing. Our Lord now opens the batting. Nightwatchmen everywhere know the knock of opportunity.

November 1972

CRICKET, AN ART THAT IS OUT OF FASHION

BY LORD COBHAM

How present conditions stifle the game when before, even the masters broke the rules

EVERY games player soon realizes that there are certain principles which are common to all. The golfer knows that when he begins to address the ball, until he starts his back swing, neither his body nor his hands nor his club should be entirely stationary. His muscles are in a state of 'controlled tension'. His weight shifts slightly as he 'waggles' until he finds the best position to be able to turn his hips and shoulders away from the ball.

Similarly, the tennis player, preparing to receive a service, dances on the balls of his feet. Both are 'standing up'; no ball can be hit from a hunched or slouched position. The boxer is also on the move, weight on the balls of his feet, stance half-open, weight shifting so he can hit quickly with either hand at any moment.

Secret of power

In golf, it is also axiomatic that the ball should be hit under the eyes; in tennis when the ball is passing the body and opposite the eyes. The same is true of racquets and squash. 'Sideways' is the rule; the ball should be hit as late as possible, without ever being too late. This is the true secret of power. In golf it is a combination of width of arc and the late uncocking of the wrist. In the moving ball games it is to hit the ball in the position where the instrument can develop the maximum velocity.

The Nawab of Pataudi once said to me: 'An Indian is taught from birth the virtue of relaxation. The more urgent the occasion, the more relaxed he must become. With most Englishmen it is different. Faced with fast bowling he tends to become tense and motionless, presenting a solid, chunky stance. Generally, an Englishman has a high back-lift (correct), but starts to lift the bat too late. The bat must be moved before the delivery stride of the bowler, and the weight must not be thrown forward on to the toes during the back-lift. Otherwise, one can play anything on or outside the off-stump but everything else hits you!'

Both W. G. Grace and Charles Fry adopted a 'secondary position'. As the bowler reached the end of his run, they both stood up and lifted their bat. All they had to do was to bring it down. There was no chance of 'stripping the gears' (bringing the bat down before they had finished picking it up).

Sir Donald Bradman was perhaps the great exception. I never saw anyone who stood so still while the bowler ran up, but his footwork was so quick and certain that the movement of the bat seemed almost perfunctory. The ball seemed attracted to it as if by a magnet. I remember once thinking at Worcester that had there been no fieldsmen on the ground, every ball would have reached the boundary fence.

Parrot fashion

Coaching can so easily degenerate into a series of parrot-cries, rendered wearisome by reiteration and false by experience. 'Lift your bat over the stumps . . .'; few of the great players of my generation lifted the bat straight. It is better to lift the bat crooked and bring it down straight than to lift it straight and bring it down crooked.

Few ball games demand that the arc of the back swing be in the same groove as that of the down swing. As the hips and shoulders take up their new position the instrument adjusts itself to a new arc. Sir Donald Bradman, Walter Hammond and Peter May, three of the greatest, all lifted their bats towards third slip. S. J. McCabe lifted his bat immaculately over the middle stump.

'Hit with the tide' is only half true and perhaps one of the least-understood principles of batting. Nobody would dispute that it is sheer suicide to play into the 'new line' of a leg-break, but the reason is that one is attempting to hit a moving ball with the bat moving in a curve, as the right shoulder swings round to meet the ball.

Thus the cardinal sin is created of 'crossing the line'. Should I ever have the misfortune to see a motor-car slanting towards me out of control, I hope that I would have the nerve to steer towards it. Had the master of the *Andrea Doria* altered course towards the *Stockholm* instead of away from her, the ship might still be afloat.

On anything but a turning wicket the off-spinner should be played or driven on the off-side. Even on a sticky or broken wicket the best players of off-spinners are those who have taken guard outside the leg-stump and played the ball into the empty off-side field.

R. E. S. Wyatt played the best spin-off with relaxed ease from a stance a foot wide of the leg-stump while his less skilful partners were providing a battery of short-legs with hope and exercise.

On a hard wicket, batsmen like Hammond and Ames gave off-spinners the full face, driving them mercilessly wide of mid-off's left hand. When they went for the big hit, the ball usually soared over the bowling green or on the off-side of it.

When bowling, 'Let your right arm brush your right ear' is nonsense. Some great bowlers had 'high' actions, but some of the greatest (Ray Lindwall) were distinctly not over the top. Wilson, a fine fast bowler in his day and one much feared by C. B. Fry, was frankly, a round-arm bowler.

The top-class batsman is one who can score off good bowling. It is good practice, and certainly enjoyable, to drive a series of half-volleys into a net. I maintain, in all humility, that more attention should be paid by coaches to scoring strokes off the back foot.

Few boys, and fewer first-class players today, make use of the crease. I have seen Hammond force a medium-paced bowler to the off-side boundary with his right foot level with his leg stump, his body still slanted forward and his left shoulder pointed at impact at mid-off.

C. F. Walters, another beautiful driver off the back foot, used to move his right foot a few inches towards his leg-stump to almost every ball. If the ball was well up, his weight flowed smoothly into the forward stroke.

The modern English batsman's first movement is often a short shuffle forward of the front foot. If the ball is short of a length, he is left between wind and water, able only to leave his bat close to his pad and hope that the ball hits one or the other. Some move across their wicket before the ball is bowled, but this leaves them out of position if the ball is straight.

Wretched law

The combination of bad wickets and this wretched 1935 l.b.w. law has combined to kill English back-play for a generation. On good hard wickets, the 'new law' is not so restricting, since batsmen have learnt

145

to make full use of their front pad. It does tend to produce dull cricket; if the pad is put outside the line of the wickets, the batsman is forced to play round it with half of the face of the bat to mid-on or forward short leg.

Batting is being stifled by artificial measures designed to defeat the l.b.w. law. On the dead, dusty wickets, alas so prevalent today, the 'phantom seamer' and the 'cutter' rule supreme. The fast wicket bowlers, the leg-spinners, and the flighty left-handers and off-spinners have been virtually driven out of the game. Bowling, even spin-bowling, is fast, flat and accurate.

The Worcestershire slow left-hand bowler, Dick Howorth, used to get half his 100 wickets a year at Worcester using subtle variations of flight and direction. Today, on the modern Worcester wicket, he would be bowling at medium pace and turning the ball farther with the rolled ball than he could in the old days using full finger-spin.

The modern ball loses both its shape and hardness before 200 runs have been scored. It has become mandatory for captains to 'take the new ball' when it is due.

For not even spinners can make use of a soft and shapeless one. Few opening bowlers today like using 'the new ball' but, by rubbing one side on their trousers, they find that they have greater control over the swing.

December 1986

TURNING POINTS

BY WILLIAM DEEDES

THE first battle for the Ashes to capture my imagination was the 1924–25 M.C.C. tour of Australia. Their captain was A. E. R. Gilligan and the batting order opened: Hobbs, Sutcliffe, Woolley, Hendren, Chapman, Gilligan and Tate.

It was not the happiest series in which to get engrossed; we lost four of the five Tests. But it seemed to me then an historic event, on which much depended. Hobbs and Sutcliffe secured a permanent place in my heart.

I find it hard to imagine what my reactions would have been had, say, Hendren or Tate announced at the start of the tour not only that he is quitting Test cricket, but that he had made a contract which in future years would offer six months in Australia, playing for Queensland.

'Dad, why is Hendren going to play for an Australian side?' 'Because, my son, he will be well paid for doing so—and his family will be able to winter out of England.' 'But he's playing there now against Australia to win the Ashes for England?' 'Yes.' 'Then, dad, which side is Hendren really on?' 'His own, my boy.'

My innocent state of mind would have been akin to that of the old squire who was in his country house library when news reached him in September 1939 of the war with Germany. 'Bring me the atlas,' he directed his son. Then placing a stubby forefinger on the Austro-Hungarian empire, he declared, 'Mark my words, that will be the key to it all.' 'But father, it isn't there any more; it went after the Kaiser's war.' The old man was dumbfounded. 'That,' he said bitterly, 'reduces the whole thing to a ruddy farce.'

I suppose all this sounds unfair to Ian Botham. To be less unfair almost exactly the same sort of transaction was made by an Australian before the 1924–25 series, about which I was so starry-eyed. Australia's fast bowler, McDonald who, with Gregory, had wrought havoc over here on Armstrong's tour of 1921, had settled in England and was no longer available to Australia in 1924–25. He had contracted to play Lancashire league cricket.

So there is nothing new in leading cricketers making the best arrangements they can for themselves. Cross-fertilisation is now universal. West Indians play for most of our counties – and for Kerry Packer in Australia. Allan Border, who declared himself to be weary of the game after leading a fairly disastrous Australian tour to New Zealand earlier this year, spent his summer making runs for Essex.

Each of six countries now plays two or three Test series a year. To some, England's tour of Australia still occupies a niche of its own; personally I find it hard to get worked up about the outcome. It is often observed that we play too much international cricket, and so we do. But it cannot be pared down without enormous loss to the game. I went into the figures not long ago. These international games heavily subsidise first-class cricket in this country and elsewhere.

We have to accept that times have changed and we must contrive to enjoy it the way it is, or must we? I have one strong reservation about that approach. As the game loses natural excitement, so it becomes essential (if the gates are to be kept up) to inject artificial excitement. That is a deadly trend.

The embodiment of artificial excitement is Packer, the television tycoon who invested floodlit cricket in fancy dress for his frightful channel. Packer now has his imitators. The marketing men in Sydney reckon they can improve on some of Packer's earlier ideas. There is to be even more Disneyland and even less Lord's.

England may well escape the worst of these delights, which are at present designed for Australia's inter-state cricket. But they will certainly not get through this tour without involvement in artificial excitement because that, unfortunately, is the money-spinner.

Natural excitement is being lost to cricket, not simply because players have become mercenaries, because international boundaries have been blurred, or because there is too much cricket. It is being lost primarily because tactics on the field have changed.

Broadly spinners are out, fast bowlers in – preferably a battery of them. The West Indians set a pattern which all desire to emulate. It leads to victory – and far duller cricket, not least because the over rate (designed to keep the pacemen fresh) has become a disgrace. Worse still it has led to indiscriminate and intimidating fast bowling at tail-enders. That tells one where cricket is sliding.

I can think of no better way of restoring at least some natural excitement to the game than by getting spinners back into it. No one was bored when Mailey, Grimmett, Freeman or Verity was bowling. To lure the spinners back we shall have for a start to stop covering wickets. It would be better for the game than Packer.

May 1989

TIME TO CALL IN THE SENIOR CRICKETERS

BY COLIN COWDREY

ALLAN BORDER'S Australian Cricket Team is on the way and another battle for the Ashes will be joined in June. We are in for a good summer of cricket. After a lean spell, we are desperate to see England win again. Yet, as Ted Dexter, the new Chairman of the England Committee, was bold enough to declare at the outset, the winning is not everything.

The truth is that while the game flourishes around the world, more and more people playing and falling under its magic spell, Test cricket does not appear to be much fun.

There is no shortage of talent, and a number of great players. Sadly there is a meaner approach abroad and less warmth and humour. All too often the umpires are at the heart of the acrimony. Test cricket, the golden goose and still the aspiration of the young, simply has to look to its image. The leading players of the day have to address themselves to this impending crisis and make a contribution.

Committee Rooms can hum away, old players pontificate, cricket managers huff and puff and Boards of Control can finally decree. But the change that we all long for can only come effectively through the co-operation and good will of the captains and best players of the day in each Test-playing country.

I lie awake at night and imagine being able to wave a magic wand, summoning a meeting in the M.C.C. Committee Room at Lord's of two or three of the best players from each country. I would add to their number one from each country who was a senior player; their experience would be valuable if my think-tank was to be a success.

Several vital questions press for discussion. First, where are the spinners and will they ever come back? I would call on Viv Richards—no mean spin bowler himself, but owing the success of his West Indian team to a battery of fast bowlers—for a paper on how we can reintroduce the spinner into a full place in top-class cricket and so restore a proper balance to the team in the field. There are precious few class spinners in the game, and to my mind cricket—both to watch and to play—is poorer for it.

I would ask Allan Border and Mike Gatting to talk to the subject of fast short-pitched bowling. Both of them have for some years now faced the nastiest of onslaughts. Allan Border commented recently that if he withstood the bombardment for three or four hours to play a fine innings for his side, he would have a mass of bruises to show for his expertise, and be discomforted for several days. Is this the type of game we want to watch, or want our sons to play?

Speaking for myself, I never want to see another helmet on the field again, and I believe 'helmeted fielders' smells of sharp practice.

I would ask Richard Hadlee and Kapil Dev to talk about the aggravation caused by the front-foot no-ball law. This may have led to a reduction of genuine outswing bowlers, a breed we want to preserve. This is technical stuff, about which only the bowlers, and perhaps the umpires too, are able to advise the game.

Dickie Bird would have something to contribute on this subject. He believes that the change from the back-foot to the front-foot no-ball law has, in forcing umpires to watch the bowlers' feet for vital split-seconds longer, reduced their span of vision in other areas, to the detriment of their decision-making.

Imran, of course, will say a lot about fast bowling; he has a good cricket mind and should be encouraged to make his responsible contribution. He feels strongly about the deterioration, as he and some others term it, in the standard of umpires in top-class cricket. He feels that the formation of a world panel of umpires and the selection of independent umpires for each Test series is a priority.

I would like to hear him talk about the players' attitude and behaviour with regard to umpires, and what powers he would give them in the face of bad language and open defiance and dissent. I would ask him to produce a comprehensive plan with regard to the selection of those umpires and of that body which would have the unenviable task of selecting them, monitoring them and occasionally standing them down.

These discussions could be invaluable, although there would not be total agreement on everything. But the Test match scene cries out for the Test-playing countries to come closer together, and for a breaking down of deadlocks.

Ted Dexter has made a clarion call for heroic deeds and a more chivalrous approach to cricket from his England players. We are lucky to have Allan Border leading Australia for he has a real feel for the game and a warm regard for English cricket, having had a season or two in County cricket. I am confident that Border will respond and work hard for a good series played in a healthy competitive spirit. So, too, will England's present captain David Gower. The combination of Gower and Border is good news. As for heroic deeds, there is no reason why our best players should not produce more of these than the enemy. When it comes to heroes, however, few could match some of the memories I have of Peter May. I am personally sorry that he has chosen to stand down just at a time when a new Test match charter has to be drawn and England's fortunes are going to change.

It is now to Ted Dexter that we look for inspiration—a close partnership between him and Gower. This liaison is one in which I have enormous confidence, both for the success of the England team and in the broader interests of cricket. As a player, Dexter was a man for the big challenge; he had the capacity to pull himself to his full height, take a deep breath and play out of his skin. I can see his smile now when the England team does just that against Australia.

7

FROM THE
NOTEBOOK

The Field always had the happy knack of
finding room for intriguing snippets of information that escaped the daily press with
their more frequent deadlines and greater
demands on space.

A CAUTION

WE have been requested to caution all who may be applied to by a man falsely representing himself to be John Painter, of the Gloucestershire county eleven. Already several persons have been victimised.

July 1909

On the whole it may be said that time has dealt kindly with the historic Bramall-lane cricket ground at Sheffield. The wonderful background, as seen from the pavilion in days gone by, of factories, tall chimneys, and churches is now partly hidden by the practical but by no means ornamental grand stand of the Sheffield United F.C., built on the site of the old drinking booths. The only other apparent changes consist of better accommodation for spectators and a new and commodious press box designed on common-sense lines. But the chimneys still continue to belch forth dense smoke, the light is still of the kind peculiar to Sheffield, and the soil which peeps here and there through the turf looks blacker than ever. It is more than likely that the bad reputation which the ground has gained of recent years for its wickets is due to some extent to the vast football stand, which must tend to prevent the turf from drying in a natural way.

The rural charm of the St Lawrence ground at Canterbury, which makes it unique among the arenas devoted to county cricket, asserted itself strongly on Thursday, when it was possible from a raised seat to see hay being carted in one field and wheat in another. It is not many years since a hop garden came down to the boundary. The size and character of the attendance, and especially the number of ladies, gave the scene the character of a second edition of the Thursday in Canterbury week.

July 1914

The Dudley cricket ground is finely situated and commands some remarkable and even wonderful views. Most impressive is the fine old castle, peeping through a break in the trees above a dense wood. The appearance of the town itself is quaint and pleasing, although it is somewhat spoiled by the pavilion, which is of a different style of architecture from the houses of the town. Many visitors, however, will prefer the distant prospect towards Birmingham, with its thousands of houses and factories and tall chimneys. This in certain lights has a beautiful and mysterious charm. A nearer view, represented in the sketch [*which appears in this book in the section of illustrations*], has its attractions, for although the lines may be severe, the colours are such as would make an artist yearn to put them on canvas.

August 1922

During the Eastbourne Week the Sussex captain, Mr Arthur Gilligan, gave a cricket lecture to the members of the Y.M.C.A., and said that he would like to describe the Saffrons as the prettiest ground in England, but could not very well do so because in a lecture at Horsham he had said that the ground there was the prettiest. In any case there is no doubt that the Saffrons is one of the prettiest grounds in the country, with its beautiful trees and its decorative pavilion, which was looking very gay with scarlet geraniums placed on suitable points. It may be that the trees are not an ideal background for batsmen, but the light is nearly always good, and the wicket is nearly always as good as skill and care can possibly make it.

July 1909

The height to which a cricket ball has been, or is commonly, thrown is a question propounded by a correspondent. It is a matter of some speculative, if of little practical, interest, and there may possibly be cricketers who can furnish authentic data from which some estimate may be formed. In Hertfordshire and Bedfordshire villages the church tower was formerly a standard of measurement, but the feat usually attempted of throwing over it was limited by the requirement that the thrower should place one of his feet against the masonry. Another test was the throwing of a hundred yards from a bushel basket. A mathematician accustomed to ballistic problems, starting from the basis that a maximum range of 100 yards entails an initial velocity of projection of 98 ft. per second in a non-resisting medium, estimates that a velocity of 150 ft. per second would be required to give the same range with air resistance taken into account. This velocity he computes would give a height of about 85 yards. But, inasmuch as a thrower could hardly apply his force to the same advantage in a vertical as in trying for maximum horizontal range, it would be safer to assume an initial velocity of 100 ft. per second, and this gives a vertical range of a little over 53 yards, which accordingly may be taken as a rough theoretical estimate of the height to be attained by a thrower capable of 100 yards in an ordinary competition.

July 1910

An amusing little comedy was played at Leyton on Wednesday during the ten minutes preceding the luncheon hour. It was obvious that in common decency McGahey must declare the Essex innings closed at lunch time, and it was equally obvious that A. L. Gibson, who had made about 35 runs, was very anxious to get his second 50 in the match. Everybody on the ground recognised the situation except Buckenham, whose chief objects in life seemed to be to keep the bowling to himself and to curb the impetuosity of his youthful partner. In vain did Gibson try to get the bowling and the spectators shout 'Go on' when there was an easy run; Buckenham would have none of it. Two or three times by good luck Gibson got the ball, and with two overs to go he had made 44. Buckenham hit the last ball of the first over past the bowler and the long field, who evidently knew what was in the air, did his best to give a two, but although Gibson was halfway up the pitch for the second run before the fieldsman had begun to make his throw, his partner waved him back. Gibson did not get a chance again until the last ball of the last over. He made a desperate effort to hit a six, but the ball was hardly up far enough, and was skied over the heads of the slips for three.

August 1910

Everyone knows that many famous batsmen have had the strongest objection to bands on cricket grounds, arguing that the noise put them off their play. Mr C. I. Thornton, the most remarkable hitter ever seen on a cricket field, tells a story against himself that, once when he was taking part in an important country house match, the band began to play when he was at the wickets, whereupon he approached the owner of the ground and pointed out that music interfered with his batting. The band was promptly silenced; Mr Thornton walked triumphantly on to the wicket, doubtless bent on a few sixes, and was bowled next ball. It is said that the soul of Killick, the Sussex batsman, is so filled with music that when he hears a good tune he can think of nothing else but the music. It is also said that at a recent county match the band began a waltz just as he was comfortably settled at the wicket, and that when he unconsciously began to move his feet in strict time, he discovered with disastrous results that the bowling was in another pitch.

September 1917

CRICKET AT THE FRONT

CRICKET at the front affords a welcome relaxation from the cares of modern warfare, and is indulged in whenever circumstances allow. Some capital performances have been put up this summer, but probably the scoring of a century under actual shell fire is unique in the annals of the game. The match in question took place somewhere in Flanders on Sept. 6 between teams of 'Gunner' officers (eight aside) captained respectively by Colonel C. B. Browne, D.S.O., commanding the —th Division D.A.C., and Major C. Fowler, commanding 'D' (Howitzer) Battery of the —th Brigade, R.F.A.

Losing the toss, the D.A.C., who were playing at home, took the field, Capt. T. W. Thwaites and Capt. J. Warham bowling to Lieut. G. P. Brooke-Taylor and Second-Lieut. M. Selby-Lowndes. Both batsmen quickly started business and runs came freely, until the former got in front of a straight one from Capt. Thwaites with his score at nine. Major Fowler added a couple before being bowled by Capt. Warham, and Lieut. M. E. Todd was dismissed for 21, after making a spirited stand with Lieut. Selby-Lowndes. This latter partnership added some 60 runs. Capt. Pride-Jones, A.V.C., hit two sixes in his unfinished innings of 30; Second-Lieut. Worsdale added ten, and the closure was applied with the score standing at 206 for four. Towards this total Lieut. Selby-Lowndes (who is a son of the well-known Master of the East Kent Foxhounds) contributed an exact century, which included no fewer than five sixes. He was finally bowled by Colonel Browne.

Four D.A.C. wickets had fallen for 47 runs when Boche shells, which had been intermittently falling in the neighbourhood throughout the game, came uncomfortably close and caused a cessation of play. Failing light prevented a resumption, and the match was left drawn. The following were the D.A.C. scores: Col. Browne, not out, 3; Capt. Warham, not out, 4; Capt. Thwaites, 0; Lieut. A. E. Bishop, 11; Second-Lieut. Culverwell, 8; Second-Lieut. R. Symington, 1; extras, 15. For 'D' Battery Major Fowler and Capt. Pride-Jones bowled well.

The rain on Saturday afternoon played some amusing tricks with the players and spectators at the Middlesex v. Hampshire match. To start with there was a steady drizzle which lasted upwards of an hour, but, nothing daunted, a considerable crowd, including many small boys, gathered in front of the pavilion near the professionals' room. When at last the rain ceased, the welcome sound of the bell to clear the ground sent them scampering in all directions to resume their places to the accompaniment of enthusiastic cheers, but the groundsmen had scarcely removed the first wicket cover when the rain started again. Another crowd gradually grew in front of the pavilion, and when the bell announced another effort to resume the game on the cessation of the shower off they went again with renewed cheers and enthusiasm. This time about seven minutes' play was possible before rain forced the players to retire, but they had hardly got into the pavilion when the rain stopped as if by magic again. After much clapping of hands and other indications from the crowd that a resumption would be welcomed, the umpires reappeared, and the players were preparing to do so when the rain once more came on. But the players had apparently had enough of these antics by then, and after hesitating a minute or two the game was resumed in the rain and carried on under impossible conditions for a few minutes before being finally abandoned for the day.

HOW L. P. HEDGES WAS OUT

AS often happens in cricket the stroke which brought about the dismissal of L. P. Hedges in the first innings of Oxford against Cambridge last week was so unexpected, and the movements of the fieldsman (Hubert Ashton) so quick that onlookers have described the catch in all sorts of ways. We give a few extracts from the daily papers:

Sportsman: Hedges was out to a fine catch off Allen by Hubert Ashton at forward short-leg, the Cambridge captain diving sideways at the ball and catching it close to the ground as he fell.

Morning Post: Hedges was splendidly caught at short-leg by H. Ashton. Allen, who was bowling at the pavilion end, made a ball short of a length cock up, and H. Ashton, throwing himself forward on his right shoulder, brought off a great one-handed catch.

Sporting Chronicle: In the morning Hedges fell to a wonderful catch by Hubert Ashton at forward short-leg.

Evening News: Hedges got Allen away to square-leg for four. Two balls later he tried a similar stroke and was magnificently caught by Hubert Ashton, who was fielding at forward short-leg. Hedges hit the ball hard enough to reach the boundary, but Ashton made a jump and threw himself sideways at the ball. He reached out with his right hand and caught the ball two inches above the ground as he fell on his shoulder. It was a grand catch, and Hedges was a very unlucky batsman to lose his wicket from the shot he made.

Times: Mr Allen's slow ball hung a trifle, and Mr Hedges put it up nearly square with the wicket on the leg side. Mr Hubert Ashton anticipated the direction of the stroke, and moved to his right. Although the ball rose no more than two or three feet off the splice of the bat and dropped quite close to the wicket, he got his fingers under it by flinging himself at full length on the ground. A child, or even a cricket reporter, could have caught the ball, if placed on the line of it. But to get there was great fielding.

Our own impression is that the ball was short and that Hedges would have banged it to the boundary if he had not been afraid of the presence of Hubert Ashton at silly mid-on. He hesitated and tried to place the ball square, but put no force at all into the stroke. Ashton threw himself forward and, when on his right elbow, made the catch apparently with both hands.

May 1923

The following extracts will show the difficulty of making cricket history:—

Cook stonewalled with considerable success (at Cambridge). Occasionally he got the ball away, but nothing would tempt him to hit. After he had been at the wickets for an hour and three-quarters, he was still showing just as much caution as he was when playing his first over.—*Times.*

Indeed, the only batsman who showed any inclination to take risks was Cook.—*Daily Telegraph.*

The curious point about these two statements is that although they may appear to be contradictory, they are both right. It is true that Cook played as if he were an Alec Bannerman, but he frequently showed that he would like to hit if he dared.

November 1923

Nothing in the recent general election was quite as astonishing as the fact that C. B. Fry, a Liberal candidate, entirely unknown to the electors except as a popular cricketer, polled more than 22,000 votes in an Unionist constituency. It may be taken for granted that so remarkable a circumstance will not be forgotten by the organisers of the various parties when the next election comes, unless, indeed, they show an entire inability to recognise the signs of the times.

The Hon. F. S. Jackson and Mr M. Falcon have been again returned to Parliament, and another old cricketer who has gained a seat is Sir G. R. Blades, a Surrey man.

December 1923

The Rev. F. H. Gillingham, the Essex cricketer, who has been Rector of Bermondsey since 1914, and served as Army chaplain during the war, has been presented with the living of St Margaret's, at Lee, near Blackheath, by the Lord Chancellor.

May 1923

We have frequently watched football matches with far less discomfort from the weather than was experienced on the first day of the Surrey v. Hampshire match at the Oval. A bitterly cold wind and threatening clouds made the players, like footballers, glad to dance about on their toes during intervals of waiting, and a double sweater covering was adopted by at least one bowler. In the middle of the afternoon, when a particularly thunderous-looking cloud had shut out all possible warmth from the sunshine, spectators were surprised to see two attendants issuing on to the field from the pavilion equipped with what appeared to be coffee pots and cups, but before they had gone far they retreated. The next minute a heavy shower of hail and snow commenced, and in a short time the ground was white. Very old habitués of the Oval could not remember another occasion on which snow had laid on the ground during a county match.

When G. T. S. Stevens bowled the first ball of the last over before lunch on the first day of the Middlesex match there was not a daisy to be seen on the ground in the Parks. Before he had time to deliver the second ball the players had fled, and the ground looked as if it had the most luxurious crop of daisies ever seen on a cricket field. This was due to a violent hailstorm, which, accompanied by a hurricane of wind, lasted for about a quarter of an hour, and then turned to rain. On almost any other wicket in the country further play would have been impossible until the morrow. In the Parks, however, play was resumed only a quarter of an hour after the usual interval for luncheon, although the bowlers for some time had a wet ball. Another storm, almost as severe, only delayed play for about half an hour.

September 1924

A week or two ago we referred to an incident at Worcester in which a hit was made which would have produced three, but the players had to run for shelter, and afterwards the umpires allowed two runs. It seems that the exact facts were as follows: H. A. Gilbert hit a ball to the lower corner of the ground in front of the Press box, but it did not quite reach the boundary. At the very moment the stroke was being made a cloud-burst caused the whole of the fielding-side and the umpires to make a bolt to the pavilion. The batsmen ran one and were turning for a second when they saw that they were alone on the field, and they, too, incontinently fled. The ball was eventually picked up by a small boy and given to one of the staff. We see no reason to alter our opinion that only the run which had actually been made should have appeared in the score.

May 1923

Some old cricketers were talking last week at Oxford about the big hits made by Stevens, Taylor and Hewetson in the Middlesex match. The conversation turned to past hitters at the University, and naturally the name of R. O. Lagden soon cropped up. George Quelch, the old University umpire, said, 'Once when I was umpire at the bowler's end Mr Lagden drove back a ball so hard that I thought it best to jump. The ball hit the top of one of the stumps and turned out of its course sufficiently to hit me on the ankle, and hurt it pretty badly. The next ball came back even harder, but I just managed to turn in time and it caught me in the middle of the back, leaving a mark for weeks.

Mr. Lagden came up to me at the end of the over and said, "I really haven't any evil designs against you, George!" On the next morning I was riding a push-bicycle and had to pass a cart. At the moment when I was about to pass, it turned to the right, leaving me only just room to pass between the cart and some iron railings. Then I saw that Mr Lagden, also on a push-bicycle, and riding as hard as he could, was close upon me, and a bad collision seemed inevitable, for of course I was helpless. But Mr Lagden simply let the bicycle go and clutched hold of the rails. The bicycle just missed mine, and Mr Lagden, strange to say, was not hurt in the least.'

July 1924

It is said on all sides that more schoolgirls than ever are playing cricket and that they like the game infinitely better than any other. Certain it is that when small schoolgirls and schoolboys are seen playing together the girls frequently hold their own. Last week on the sands at Weston-super-Mare, in a party consisting of five or six boys and one girl, with the average age of about 12, the girl was much the best player, although she was not the oldest. Most of the boys had modelled themselves on certain county players who very seldom pick up the ball at the first attempt; the girl might have studied Hendren. She was the only bowler who could keep a length. Very obviously she was very grateful when occasionally she was allowed to bowl, but for all that her interests as a cricketer compelled her to get the other people out, to their intense disgust.

To anybody who had never experienced the fascination of a game of cricket, the play would have seemed absolutely devoid of interest. The boys bowled all sorts of lengths, in all sorts of directions, and the batsman, for ten minutes at a time, would smite the air valiantly with his bat without touching the ball. But what of that? There was always the chance that he *might* smite it, and every now and then, by a fortuitous combination of circumstances, a ball would not only be within his easy reach, but he would even time his stroke so well that he could hit it. Still more thrilling was the possibility that he might even get out, and, strange as it seemed, this is exactly what sometimes happened, and so the noble game went on, to the joy of the players, and the occasional spectators, until the calls of hunger reminded the players that this is a prosaic world.

In the interests of young cricketers of both sexes, to say nothing of their fathers and uncles who join them in the game, the Weston-super-Mare authorities ought undoubtedly to make a bye-law prohibiting motorists and motor cyclists from using the sands for pleasure riding. It is bad enough to have a game of cricket interrupted by perambulators; it is something like a public scandal that young fieldswomen and fieldsmen should have to fly for their lives from motorists. It is true that at present motorists who use the sands are not numerous, and that although the marks made by their wheels spoil many prospective pitches, no attempt is made to invade pitches which are actually in use. But next year sand-motoring may be the fashion, and the lives of young cricketers would then become unendurable.

August 1934

I am indebted to Mr H. Carter, the famous Australian wicket keeper, for the following amusing story. Sid Gregory, who was well known for his speed between the wickets, was once batting with a colleague who refused to run the longest run. Gregory eventually played a ball slowly to deep extra mid-off and called. His *vis-à-vis* declined to budge, so Gregory ran down the pitch, whispered in the timid one's ear. 'We'll run the next one' and then ran back again.

January 1949

HIT FOR SIX

IN a legal action of wide interest at Manchester, judgment was given in favour of a cricket club which was sued for damages by a woman who was struck by a ball hit out of the club ground. The judge said that considering the prevalence of games in Britain, there was a dearth of legal authority on the matter.

November 1950

AUSTRALIAN CRICKET INCIDENT

REPORTS from Australia of an umpiring incident in the second match of the M.C.C. tour should not be taken too seriously. It appears that a young West Australian batsman complained about the way in which R. Berry, the Lancashire slow left-hand bowler, runs up to the wicket from behind the umpire, claiming that because of it he did not have a fair view of the bowler. The umpire is said to have asked Berry to alter his run up, but after discussion waived the point and subsequently reported the matter to the Western Australian Association.

The M.C.C. note on the duties of umpires can hardly be mistaken. It reads: 'The umpire shall stand where he can best see any act upon which his decision may be required. Subject to this overriding consideration, the umpire at the bowler's end should stand where he does not interfere with either the bowler's run up or the striker's view.' Any possible question of the bowler's run up is thus subservient to 'the over-riding consideration' of the best position for the umpire, and Berry follows a long line of bowlers who have run up from behind the umpire—in fact, most bowlers bowling round the wicket do so.

June 1955

MAIDEN OVER?

ARTHUR MILTON, the Gloucestershire cricketer and Arsenal foot-baller, saw Pettiford secure two wickets with successive balls and then Miss A. Hattrick by inches before he himself fell a victim to the offspinner. But Milton had hit 85 in three and a quarter hours.— *'Egyptian Gazette,' May 22nd, 1955.*

U BIQUE

May 1967

BOWLERS' KNEES

SHORT trousers for cricketers, suggested in a letter to *The Times* which challenged 'the ridiculous spectacle of fast bowlers tearing up to the wicket with long flannel trousers flapping round their legs,' met a mixed reception.

Mr M. J. P. Grace, of Lillywhites, feels that 'as one gets on, one's legs become less physically attractive.' He said that cricket flannels have become narrower in the last five years. They now measure 19 in. instead of 21 in. at the turn-up.

Mr Alec Bedser, the former Surrey and England fast bowler and now a Test selector, regrets this. He prefers roominess to style. Mr S. C. Griffith, secretary of M.C.C., revealed the dark secret that in some English summers players wear pyjamas under flannels.

August 1970

IRISH CRICKET

CRICKET could not, by any stretch of the imagination, be considered an Irish game. It seems strange, therefore, that Messrs Guinness should have presented a trophy to the winners of the recent series between England and the Rest of the World.

But Mr Dermot Guinness, a member of the firm, assures me that the company sponsors the game in Ireland to great effect. Their national side skittled out the West Indies for the alarming total of 25 runs last year. During the final Test match last week the trophy was on view at a party at the Oval. It consists of a silver harp, the company's emblem, on a plinth of green Connemara marble. It is to live at Lord's.

March 1971

A CATCH IN CRICKET'S LAW

How long must the ball be held? The villages at Lord's

A READER, apparently having watched those potted television Test matches—wickets and boundaries only—has not unreasonably asked how long the ball must be held for a catch to be deemed caught. So often, particularly by the close fielders behind the wicket, the ball is tossed into the skies in the same movement in which the hands receive it. Just suppose no-one catches it when it comes down.

The Law is clear but unhelpful. Experimental Law 35 says: 'The striker is out "caught"—if the ball, from a stroke of the bat or off a hand holding the bat, but not the wrist, be held by a fieldsman before it touch the ground, although it be hugged to the body by the catcher, or be accidentally lodged in his dress ...'

Note 2 adds: 'The act of making the catch starts from the time when the fieldsman first handles the ball.' No mention of when the act of making the catch finishes, which is surely the relevant point, though a new clarifying rider includes: 'The fieldsman having caught the ball must retain control of the ball within the field of play.' But that is catering for cases on the boundary.

And so via Lord's (it's up to the umpire) to 'Dusty' Rhodes, a Test umpire last season and former Derbyshire player. He confirms that no time is set and that, 'in the opinion of the umpire', the ball must be held—which seems to mean 'held under control by a part of a fieldsman who is himself under control'. This allows for the catch cleanly held but jerked out on an arm's impact with the ground. That is not out.

Rhodes has 'never in his playing or umpiring days seen a catch disallowed through the ball being thrown in the air'. So, while bearing in mind that cricket is creating precedents at every turn, those who intercept a stinger in May, when the hands are not yet ready to receive, may like to make a passing gesture at the ball and trust to their own umpire's understanding that it was really caught and that it was missed only in its fall from a celebratory toss.

February 1971

EARNED INCOME?

A FINANCIAL postscript for statisticians—has anyone ever taken more for less? The salary, including bonus, for a man on his first major tour, is about £1,450, with £25 extra for each previous major tour. In four months in Australia, nearly an English season, Wilson bowled 95·7 overs (one-tenth his English quota). Disregarding his two innings, he received about £15 an over, and bowled less than an over a day. No discredit to him, but no wonder he was described as a 'cheerful' tourist.

April 1971

MUCH ADO

BETTER still is Basil Easterbrook on the 'dreaded cypher', less for Easterbrook's own humour, pleasant but unexceptional, than for his quotes from essays on the subject by R. C. Robertson-Glasgow. Was there ever one who expressed himself more felicitously? I commend:

'The essence, the aristocracy of o is that it should be surrounded by large scores, that it should resemble the little silent breadwinner in a bus full of fat, noisy women. Indeed, when the years have fixed it in its place, so far from being merely the foil for jewels, it should itself grow, in the fond eye of memory, to the shape and stature of a gem.'

August 1971

SNOW FALL AT LORD'S

Another regrettable incident and more clumsy handling

THEY were out in the playground, the big one at Lord's, and they were playing cowboys and Indians. But it was not like children playing, all shouting and tearing about and shooting each other and dying. It was like the grown-ups in the films, drawl and dust and slouching and nothing happening.

Then suddenly there was a rustle, a flare-up. Big John knocked an Indian from his horse, then picked up his gun and tossed it to him with a kind of disdain. And the dust settled again and they drawled and they slouched and the music mounted in a rallentando of volume and the titles came up and it was just like any other western and one remembered the fight and forgot the rest.

And that, it seemed, was that, all very convincing and pointless, until the headmaster popped out and reminded us all that he was headmaster and it was only a game and the children must not get too worked up about it as though it were real, but they must none the less stick to the rules because even games teach lessons. 'Now, Johnny, you're to tell them you're sorry and you didn't mean it.'

And Big John rather spoiled it because, though he is a bit of a bully like most of the best fast bowlers, and though he is a bit mixed up at the moment, writing poems and things, he didn't throw a tantrum and say he wouldn't apologize, nor did he go all meek and shamefaced and recite the headmaster's apologies without thinking.

Instead, with courage and grace, he admitted his offence, made no attempt to justify it and apologized for it with an obvious sincerity. The Indians accepted it as man to man and put it behind them. But headmasters will be headmasters, frightened of their image if not their authority and therefore labouring worthy points about the right and wrong thing to do. So Big John has been punished too. He was not let out to play. And soon he may find that he likes writing lines more than playing with the other boys.

May 1973

The Editor, in his notes, is traditionally predictable in his condemnation of gamesmanship, in particular the badgering of batsmen by bowlers and the fashion for frivolous appeals . . .

'Nowadays,' writes the Editor, 'sometimes the whole eleven in the field leap in the air. This is unfair to the umpires who have to put up with such antics for six hours on each of the five or six days of a tense Test Match. Unless commonsense prevails, silence may have to be enforced and the whole matter left wholly to the umpires, without appeal by the contestants.' And so I suppose we head again for the silent, spiritless ceremony of the sixties.

I deplore the appeal which is a demand with menaces, as I do on any sporting field. An impassioned inquiry, however, is reasonable. But can anything be unfair to an umpire? As long as he is in doubt, be it for six days or a season, he can go on saying 'not out', and he is more likely to be doubtful if most of the appeals are far-fetched. The subtler approach, weighing up the situation before asking politely, gains judicial respect and often better verdicts.

July 1973

That Greig and others can be posted with impunity six feet or less from the crease on a fast true pitch is but a sign of the impotence and thinking of the modern batsman. 'What would Hammond have done to this fellow?' demanded the President of M.C.C. 'He would have killed him and so would you,' I replied. 'No,' he said, 'I would not without warning the umpire that I would hold him responsible if there was a serious accident.'

December 1973

CRICKET'S EXAMPLE

SIR JACK HOBBS, the cricketer, was a modest, gentle creature who from the humblest of beginnings rose to leave a record of batsmanship behind him unsurpassed in the annals of the game. I once asked him why his greatest innings were all played in Test matches or on bad wickets. He replied: 'Well, sir, on such occasions I expect I feel a bit nervous.'

February 1974

CRICKET CRISIS

IN the incident in the first Test in Trinidad last week whereby Kal-licharran, having made 142, was run out off the last ball of the day and reinstated two hours later, only Greig, the fielder who performed the dismissal, can know whether he intended something outside the spirit of the game or whether an instinctive action led to events running away with themselves. The decision to reinstate was, sadly, probably made in fear. By then, in any case, the damage was done.

It is interesting to speculate on whether an English batsman would have been so favoured and, for that matter, whether he would have been so dismissed. In general, crowds will best learn to take rough with smooth and to respect the law in spirit if it is not bent in letter. Cricket's authorities have set a precedent which may be immediately expedient but later embarrassing.

March 1974

BY JEREMY ALEXANDER

... An incident in the second Test last month in Port of Spain shows the absurdity of appeals. In England's second innings, the West Indies appealed, as it later transpired, for l.b.w. against Denness. He was given out caught in the slips. The umpire could clearly have made the decision without an appeal at all. If he knows enough to give a man out, he does not need to be asked. Furthermore *the* incident in the first Test could have been averted if Greig's appeal had not forced the umpire to invoke the letter of the law. Greig, not least, would have been glad.

Every ball

Officially (Law 47), 'the umpire shall not order a batsman out unless appealed to by the other side'. And (Note 1), 'an appeal covers all ways of being out unless a specific way of getting out is stated by the person asking'. So, to take no chances, the fielding side should appeal on every ball just in case an umpire has spotted something they have missed. And, if they are going to do that and to accept his verdict, they may as well never appeal and accept it just the same.

Cricket sets great store by its code of conduct and the honesty of its participants. The practice of appealing casts doubt not only on that honesty but on the competence of umpires. Their decisions will be no less final without appeals. As they say in cases of batsman's indignation, justified or not, look in the score book.

8

OUT IN THE STICKS

Any real cricket lover will tell you that the true game is only to be found far away from the metropolitan and provincial centres. The locations for *essential* cricket are where the rooks are always cawing in the rectory elms and the hedgerows constantly flowering, where the painted tin plates on the rickety scoreboard relay the total in tens and where the pub and the church provide more than a mere backdrop for the Porsches parked around the boundary edge.

After all, the vicar is likely to be the opening bat and the inn comes into its own when everybody is out . . .

THE REAL TEST

CRICKET is the language of our village. At the centre of refreshment, where the affairs of the local team are decided, there is no one who cannot tell a Test match captain what he should have done and what he should do. There is also no need for a Wisden. At least four of the regular attendants can quote with accuracy the details of play and scores of county matches for years back.

But now the discussions do not centre so much upon Test matches as on the very important forthcoming match against a visiting team. 'You see,' explained the landlord, 'we get a team together to meet ours and nobody knows much about it until near the day. You'd be surprised at the visitors we can muster. Why one year we had a Test player who could show our lads something. And they could show him something, too. One county batsman was out for two. I reckon we could match those Tichborne people.'

One of the listeners was injudicious enough to say that the local team was so rich in talent that they could afford to leave out the best batsman. 'Why,' he added, 'he has never made a duck yet.' The landlord withered him. 'W. G. Grace,' he replied, 'of whom you may not have heard, was once told that. What did he say? You don't know, but I do. He said a batsman who had never made a duck was no use to him.'

Waiting for that remark to sink in the landlord continued, 'And you, instead of wasting a week at Lord's, might do better to come and see some real cricket on the green. When were you there last?'

'This morning, and long before you were up,' was the answer. 'Ah,' replied the landlord, without a pause, 'then there's one thing you had better realise before you get into trouble. All the mushrooms round the cricket ground are private property.' No one seemed to think July early for mushrooms.

CRICKET CURTAIN

IT was a great day for the village. The local cricket club were to entertain, in a close-of-the-season game, a team captained by a county player. The village were anxious to do him well, for he had this season been given a benefit by the county club and his team was to be composed of county players, past, present and possible.

For a week before the game sheep were banned from the cricket ground and the roller was over-worked, moaning in its travail. The team was chosen with care and a proper regard for its sartorial appearance on the field. But apart from that, the village side had no inhibitions, knowing from cheerful experience that anything can happen in a country match. Was not the great Wilfred Rhodes once persuaded to play incognito in an up-country game in Australia, only to have his bowling slammed all over the field until his agonised friends at last shouted: 'For heaven's sake, Wilfred, tell them who you are.'

At least the members of the county team were known by repute to the village, but—'we'll play 'em at our game and see what 'appens,' said the village captain. What happened was that the county side, batting first, were rescued from ignominy by a youngster, still at school, with the eye of a hawk and a determination to go out to the pitch of bowling that kept low or rose high according to the contours of the pitch. The villagers loved it, for this was cricket they understood. Of the side's total of 103, the youngster scored 58.

The village began to lose wickets at once. There was a hurricane recovery for the fourth wicket, a collapse for the fifth, sixth and seventh. With three wickets to fall they wanted 32 to win. With two wickets to fall they needed 20. With the last man in they needed 8. 'Two fours 'll do it,' someone shouted. Gallantly the last man waded in to the county slow bowler—with a dire result that echoed the poignant exclamation of an old Essex player, as he heard the clatter of bails behind him: 'I'd have given it Johnny-up-the-orchard if I'd known which way it was going to break.' And that was the end. But it was a great day for the village.

April 1954

HOW'S THAT!

HARD is the lot of the arbitrator, for he can seldom please both sides. He can only suffer criticism with dignity, repudiation with philosophy. In both respects the cricket umpire generally sets an impeccable example. 'I wasn't out, Reevo,' said a batsman once, as he passed the old Essex umpire, R. Reeves, on his way to the pavilion. 'Oh, wasn't you,' replied Reeves; 'you look in the evening papers and see if you wasn't.'

No one is likely to complain that umpires in first-class cricket do not deserve the increase in pay which they are now to receive. They earn every penny of it. Not for them the glory of achievement. No one has yet heard an umpire applauded on the field. And yet his duties demand a prolonged concentration of purpose, which must be proof against, for instance, the soporific effects of a match in the doldrums, after lunch, under a broiling sun, when suddenly he is confronted with a raucous 'Z'at!' and must give an instant decision.

He may on occasion temper justice with discretion. In the more spacious days of county cricket, Robert Thoms, famed for his umpiring *mots,* saw Jessop run out by a couple of yards and, on appeal, answered 'Not out—not out,' adding, 'Sixpenny crowd—Saturday gate—can't disappoint 'em—near thing—near thing—not near enough for the occasion.'

But it is when we come to village umpires that we find the real autocrats of the white coat. Once when George Lohmann, the famous old Surrey bowler, was playing in Hampshire for Under Wallop against Upper Wallop, an incoming batsman, taking his guard, said to the umpire: 'Be my toes in front of the wicket?' The umpire replied 'Thee keep 'em out. *I* shan't tell'ee whether they be or not.'

August 1955

FOXHUNTERS' CRICKET

FOX and harehunters have, I hear, been taking to organised cricket in a large way.

The ladies of the Vine Hunt, under Mrs Frank Mitchell, who is Joint-Master with her husband, challenged the gentlemen of the Hunt to a cricket match—the gentlemen to bat and bowl left-handed. The gentlemen, with Lieut.-Colonel Frank Mitchell as their captain, accepted the challenge, and a most enjoyable afternoon's sport followed. Each innings was limited to one hour, and almost everyone batted. The gentlemen won.

With Kimpton Hoo, in Hertfordshire, as a setting, a South Herts Beagles team played against a Hertfordshire farmers' XI. After scoring 178 runs for seven wickets, the farmers declared. The beaglers pinned their hopes on the Master, Mr Peter Woodbridge, their amateur huntsman, Mr Bill Vaughan Williams, and the kennel-huntsman of the Aldenham Harriers, Ben Wilkinson. However, Ben could not repeat the performance which he put up at a previous match of scoring a century.

In fact, the farmers had the whole side out for 57, and I could only conclude that, as a training for cricket, haymaking is better than harehunting.

I was told that this match has been an annual event for the past four or five years and that, in 1954, it was held in spite of heavy rain. This time, the sun shone brightly.

June 1966

CRICKETERS OUT OF THE SADDLE

BY SIDNEY ROGERSON

A National Hunt team loses to the home side in a game marred by the weather

BY all the portents this should have been one of the more unusual and entertaining matches of the season, exceptional in its setting and in its clash of contestants. It was played at Ascot on Sunday, May 22. One side was the Royal Ascot Cricket Club, a local club of respectable middle-age and membership which rejoices in the privilege of having its ground in the middle of Ascot racecourse, where the playing area, spacious as it is, is dwarfed in the vast acreage of the racecourse in its mantle of bright shining green grass now being brushed and curry-combed in readiness for next month.

The club's opponents were an XI, or, better, a XII, of men, all under 30 years of age, and all bound together under David Nicholson, in the tie of the profession of being National Hunt jockeys. The nature of the opposition, the setting for the contest, the time of the year, and the implied challenge between maturity and youth, all should have combined to guarantee a match of interest and excitement. But weather, the curse of the country which invented the summer game which above all others most depends for its success and its enjoyment on fine weather, effectively intervened to destroy any hope of reasonable cricket conditions throughout the day.

Nicholson gathers up his players from all corners of the country, and even though they assembled on Sunday under lowering skies and rain-swollen clouds they were little prepared for what was to greet them.

Play was to have begun at 11.30 a.m. and at 11.35 a fine, fiercely driven rain began to fall and within no more than a few seconds the emptiness of the course almost made itself felt. A few rain-proofed golfers plodded on through the rain, but the stands must have looked down in wonder at the flannel-clad figures who on a sudden dashed for the cover of the pavilion as the first of a succession of storms lashed the players from the field.

By that time, however, Ascot had taken first strike on a hard and fast wicket. Also Nicholson had opened the bowling at a nice easy medium pace. In his second over he claimed the wicket of Murdie, Ascot's opener, by trapping him l.b.w. to a ball which came very fast off the pitch, freshened by rain.

After lunch the sun broke through to give the longest period of uninterrupted play of the day, during which there ensued the longest stand of the match, between the two Ascot stalwarts, Pank and Bishton, who kept up a steady though unexciting rate of progress. Pank made valiant attempts to score quickly, but after the storm the ball travelled slowly and the occasional ball rose sharply. Pank sent up the 90 with a single to third man, but the going was slow until after scoring a three to mid-wicket Pank was l.b.w. to Wates for 40.

Thereafter, with efforts being made to accelerate the scoring, wickets began to fall fast, chiefly to Wates, who took five for the Jockeys with a mixture of slow off-spin of assorted lengths. Bishton was at last out to an excellent catch in the gully by King off Wates, and the big, florid Sharpe, after a brief innings, fell to an equally brilliant catch by Gifford off Wates. With play again interrupted by a storm, this time accompanied by thunder, and with wickets still tumbling, Ascot at 3.40 p.m. declared at 161 for nine.

The Jockeys made a disastrous start, their first wicket, of J. Hindley, falling at 11 when Hedges had him taken at the wicket for six by Moses. Worse was to come and the tall, powerfully built Butler, who seemed to bowl off the wrong foot, bowled Dale for two. King got off the mark with a push to mid-wicket before he, too, fell to Butler, whose curious action seemed to enable him to get much pace off the pitch.

At this stage, the youthful-looking Dartnall was joined by Arthurs, and these two, batting with some confidence and ease, made one of the minor stands of the innings. Any hopes that they would take command were dashed when Dartnall after tea followed a ball from Hedges wide of his wicket and quite unnecessarily cut it into the hands of Allen in the gully—a pointless stroke which the Jockeys could ill afford, and which I regret to report was, on the day, of too frequent occurrence.

Dartnall's innings was the high-spot of the afternoon, but after he had gone there were only a few blows from his brother, V. Dartnall, and a spirited effort by Josh Gifford to relieve the gloom which was beginning to settle over the ground.

ROYAL ASCOT C.C.		NATIONAL HUNT JOCKEYS	
M. Murdie lbw b Nicholson	3	J. Hindley c Moses b Hedges	6
A. Pank lbw b Wates ..	40	G. Dartnall c Allen b Hedges	22
J. Bishton c King b Wates..	53	P. Dale b Butler	2
W. Allen c Nicholson		C. King b Butler	6
b Arthurs	0	I. Arthurs c Hallman b	
P. Mathews c Dartnall		Murdie	15
b Wates	4	A. Wates b Hedges	1
D. Sharpe c Gifford b Wates	5	V. Dartnall c Sharpe b	
P. Halman c Wates b Arthurs	0	Murdie	16
W. Delany c Walthew b		L. Walthew run out ..	7
Arthurs	2	J. Gifford b Delany ..	10
R. Hedges not out	24	Jeff King not out	4
G. Moses c Gifford b Wates	0	T. Biddlecombe c Hedges b	
B. Butler not out	3	Bishton	1
Extras	27	D. Nicholson c and b Delany	0
	—	Extras	3
			—
Total (for 9 wkts dec.)	161	Total	93
A. Hitchcock did not bat			

July 1985

MERRIFIELD'S MIRACLE

BY JOHN PARKER

IN the days before video, the film camera reigned supreme in television; and the king of the cameramen, so far as cricket was concerned, was George Richardson, of Independent Television News. George used forearms like the average man's thighs to hump his great camera and tripod up countless ladders in various cricket grounds of the world, and he never missed a trick through his dark-grained reflex viewfinder. No one else could find the wicket through it, let alone a four-and-three-quarter ounce cricket ball moving at 100 mph. His maxim was: 'The moment you think you've got cricket taped, it'll sit up and bite you.'

This is not the tale of George, but of a batsman with a delightfully rural name, Bob Merrifield. His club is Clyst St George, which plays in the Devon League and at the moment is second from bottom of the table. Clyst St George is a village of some 200 souls but lies in a large catchment area of hamlets outside Exeter. Its cricket ground is a gently sloping field surrounded by hedges and magnificent broad oaks. You cannot see the village church through the foliage but you can hear the bells ring loud and clear.

The pavilion was once a water tower, which the club bought cheap; perhaps in honour of the pavilion's origin the roof leaks. There is an artificial practice strip at the bottom of the ground, but that is as far as modernisation goes. The club's 22 members use an old petrol can as a wicket when they practise in the nets on Friday evenings.

August 25 last year was the wish-it-could-be-forgotten day on which the full England team crawled its way to 161 in six hours, batting against fledgling Sri Lanka. In Clyst St George it was the never-to-be-forgotten day on which Merrifield scored 255 runs out of 330 for three wickets declared, in a minute under three hours, and so ensured that his team would play in Devon D and not Devon E this year.

Merrifield is an easy-going six-footer who makes a living as a freelance photographer. At 39 he has been a botanist, a teacher and a market gardener, but he prefers buzzing round the Devon lanes in an ancient Morris Minor and taking pictures—and playing cricket. He is particularly easy-going about his great innings.

'I hardly remember a thing,' he says. 'I just went out and hit the ball. Everything I did came off.'

But the Clyst scorebook, and Merrifield's team-mates, recall the events with devastating accuracy. Clyst had to win or get a 'favourable draw' in order to keep in the D section of the League. They had already had one tough match with Cornwood, their opponents, and expected stiff opposition. So the first thing to do was to win the toss and bat on a wicket that had been bone hard all that sunlit summer. Eric Richardson, the captain, obliged and duly elected to bat first.

Merrifield, opening the innings, hit his second ball for four and took seven off the first over. Before he was 20 he drove the ball off the meat of his jumbo bat straight into mid-off's midriff. Mid-off dropped it, and Merrifield never looked back. Tim Read, who shared a century partnership with him, says, 'Bob wasn't slogging. He was just trying to ensure we won. But he went so fast.'

He did indeed. He progressed like this:

Runs	Minutes	Balls
50	33	32
100	84	74
150	125	102
200	149	119
250	176	142

They have lost the chart of the innings at Clyst, but it showed that most of the runs came square off the wicket, on both sides. A left-hander, Merrifield plays strongly off the front foot, and has the left-hander's natural pull. He hit nine sixes and 37 fours. He was bowled out off the penultimate ball of the 46-over innings, trying to block it.

It is kinder not to record the Cornwood bowling analyses. Suffice to say that the most economical of the six bowlers conceded only 25 runs—off three overs. Cornwood, thoroughly demoralised, made 80. Clyst stayed in the D League. And Merrifield has a mounted cricket ball on his mantelpiece to remember it all by.

But remember George Richardson's maxim. On the same day, in the north, another village club batsman scored 256, one more than Merrifield. And this year Merrifield's top score is 21.

May 1970

VILLAGE CRICKET GROUNDS, BY A COLLECTOR

Edward Hart recalls some he has played on, where deeds great and small were wrought

OTHER boys outstripped me at philately, cigarette-card collecting or accumulating brass rubbings. Later, no compilation of ancient firearms, no muster of rare orchids or tropical fish came my way. But I was always an assiduous collector of those most English of places, cricket grounds.

Lord's, Headingley and Old Trafford have, of course, been included. But even more precious are the host of village grounds where I actually played, and did not merely applaud the experts. In those days of limited travel immediately following the Second World War, village cricket was an organized method of seeing the countryside, and meeting other enthusiasts, the keener for years of deprivation from their favourite game in home surroundings.

Each ground had its idiosyncrasies. Who that played there will forget the giant stone horse-trough at Normanby, in North Riding's Ryedale? Standing eternally at square-leg or extra-cover, it had insinuated itself so far inside the boundary as to be counted two runs when smote, to the chagrin of the mighty hitter robbed of four and the delight of the craftsman aiming gently at its unyielding exterior.

Most of my cricket was played in this area, where dale meets lowland. Not only the grounds, but the players, were different. At school I was taught that the game's the thing, that if one lost it must be cheerfully done.

Joining a Yorkshire dales team, I soon learnt that it was much better not to lose at all. This was especially so if the opposition was from 'the low side'—the fertile arable country—and had once brought with them an umpire who awarded six l.b.w.s against us in a semi-final.

That this was 25 years ago was irrelevant; their present captain's father used to flick off the bails with his pad when wicket-keeping, and they are all tarred with the same brush.

Some rivalries were friendly. There was Gillamoor, with green, long-peaked caps like the Australians, and a ground where one could stand at mid-off on a summer's day and watch the purple heather of the north Yorkshire moors stretching for mile after folding mile. Here a retired farmworker told me how they would walk 12 miles to a match, after following horses all the week.

Ripe for toppling

More intense was the battle with Harome, firmly fixed at the top of the league and thus ripe for toppling. We played there after the Coronation celebrations, and feasted on a huge tea which had ensued from the village festivities.

We lost the toss and, surprisingly, were asked to bat first. Came the vast repast and we could neither bowl accurately nor run in the field, and lost by a large margin. What was this but Glencoe in a minor key? In memory, I prefer that glorious meal to the two vanished points, but dark were the inferences at the time.

Alongside our home ground was kennelled one of the oldest packs in the country—the Bilsdale. They were always a source of interest to visitors in that keen hunting district, and a cause for concern if a six threatened to land near a favourite hound's living quarters.

On a hillside

The ground itself was on a hillside; it could scarcely be otherwise in that area. Thus normal field settings went by the board, and two extra men were posted on the lower boundary. To score above the wicket called for a lofted shot, hardly the best training, yet some of Yorkshire's most notable village cricketers were nurtured here.

Nearer the sea, I played many games at Lockton, also adjoining the moors. A forestry worker who lived two miles down a rough track came in to bat. The opposing bowler was the local postman. 'Give me a long hop to leg, or I'll send myself a postcard every day for a fortnight!' was the batsman's sally.

Some grounds were well kept, others rough and positively dangerous, but there was the same delightful ride to reach any of them. May with banks of bluebells merging into hay scents of June, corn fields ripening under August sun, and heather drawing visitors and bees in September.

Dropped catches

As the season wore on, league championships were resolved, cups won and lost, and some of the keenness departed. We looked forward to the easier atmosphere, but memories of those 'friendlies' are hazy as heat shimmering on the heather, while the sharp edge of cup battles remains.

Once on holiday in the south-west I played for the local team. But I did not really enjoy it. They were too carefree, those chaps with the foreign burr. They skylarked between wickets, chaffed the captain, and laughed uproariously at dropped catches.

I recalled missing the opposing opening bat at first slip in a Yorkshire cup tie, and the countenances of my colleagues counting the cost.... As Herbert Sutcliffe (or was it Emmott Robinson?) is reputed to have said: 'We don't play this game for fun.' Yet I am very glad to add that ground overlooking the Bristol Channel to my list, with its red soil appearing through turf burnt by a Cornish sun.

Woods at Hovingham and Malton are picturesque, but no help to the batsman in late evening. Other grounds have their trees inside the boundary, range of nearby farm buildings on which to register big hits, ponds or rivers taking annual toll of an increasingly costly item.

The umpires

But added to these natural features is the character lent by generations of keen players, kindly or sharp tempered, good losers or those who 'couldn't bide being beaten'. And umpires. 'He was more out t' first time,' said one in response to my appeal; previous occasion was the very first ball of the game, when my yorker struck an unmoving boot right in line with the middle stump, but before our umpire had adjusted his faculties to the match.

But all are forgiven. They are an indispensable part of a rural cricket match. As Sir James Barrie said: 'Seen and heard through the trees, it is surely the loveliest scene in England and the most disarming sound.' Long may it continue so.

Arthur Wood anticipates the decision to an l.b.w. appeal.

Townsend, of Derbyshire, about to bring off a late cut through the slips.

Edrich, the most discussed cricketer of the moment, glides to leg.

H. M. Garland Wells dives at a hard chance in the slips and succeeds in knocking the ball up.

Harold Gimblett jumping to the pitch of the ball.

Democracy in cricket. These two spectators, seen at Lord's, might
be colonel and batman.

The Free Foresters pictured during their tour of Germany at the stadium in Berlin built by Hitler for the **1936** Olympic Games. They played occupying service elevens. (See p. **75.**)

Four runs from the moment the ball left the bat. P. Walker (Free Foresters) hooks to the square-leg boundary during a two-day game against the Gentlemen of Sussex at Bury St Edmunds in **1962**. The Gentlemen won by six wickets. (See p. **251.**)

Bob Merrifield, the saviour of Clyst St George in the crucial game against Cornwood in 1984. (See p. 178.)

The downs and ups of cricket enhanced by the caricaturist Donald E. Green.

'Who that played there will forget the giant stone horse-trough at Normanby, i
North Riding's Ryedale? Standing eternally at square-leg or extra cover...'

'Came the vast repast and we could neither bowl accurately nor run the field, and lost by a large margin.'

The dropped catch . . . and the countenances of colleagues counting the cost.

Sentry and century: Harry Latchman, primarily a leg-break bowler, was resident night-watchman for Middlesex. On one occasion against Worcestershire he stretched his brief duty of survival and sentinel by three and a half hours to make 96. (See p. 140.)

Graeme Hick, the answer to the prayers of the England selectors for the 1990s? (See p. 106.)

April 1963

CRICKETERS IN SUFFOLK

BY SIDNEY ROGERSON

When Rickling Green faced a total of 920 by the opposition, and Fuller Pilch played for Bury St Edmunds

EAST ANGLIA is today only remotely associated with cricket in the public mind. It boasts no first-class counties. It is a dry region specially suited to the growing of wheat, barley and sugar beet, but so ill-adapted for grass that good wickets and cricket grounds are few and far between. Yet studies of old records and ancient score books prompt the speculation whether East Anglia was not one of the cradles of English cricket, treading closely in the footsteps of the pioneers of Hambledon and Broadha'penny Down. Certain it is that nearly 200 years ago the Eastern Counties were much more active and important in the realm of cricket than they are today.

The first mention of organised cricket at Bury St Edmunds is in 1767, when the local club was beaten by Ely by 63 runs. By the earliest days of 1800 matches were being played in the district with some regularity. Thus in 1806 Bury twice played Thetford, winning the first and losing the other. Two years later they played a home and an away fixture against Newmarket.

A red-letter year was 1823, which saw the great Fuller Pilch's debut for Bury and his engagement as professional to the club. Pilch had been born at Norwich and had played for Norfolk at Lord's when he was 17. Before the advent of W. G. Grace, Pilch was the greatest batsman cricket had produced. He was the pioneer of forward play and he taught cricketers the art of placing the ball in front of the wicket with a stroke which became known as 'Pilch's Poke'. He remained with Bury until 1831, when he returned to Norwich, before joining Kent at £100 per year.

In 1827 Bury played a home and away fixture with Mary le Bone, Mary le Bonne or Mary la Bonne—it is variously spelt—the Londoners losing both matches. After the first day's play at the Bury St Edmunds match, there was a dinner at the Angel Hotel for upwards of 30 people. The fare included 'a turtle weighing 100 lb., two fine haunches of venison and several large salmon contributed by a player of the Bury Club.'

Bury's victory in this match seems to have been the occasion of a minor benefit to Pilch, who was presented with a silver watch and a gold chain. Whether he received any share of the '£173 taken at the gate, besides what was taken by the landlord of the Chequers, who erected a large stand in his yard' is not specified. The account does record that 'the last hour was occupied in scoring the two notches wanted to beat, and 33 balls were actually given without a run.'

In those days cricket was, of course, very much a betting game, and we are told that in the first of the two 1827 matches the betting opened at 6 to 4 on M.C.C., but after Bury's first innings had swung round to 7 to 5 in their favour. In a note on the 1828 fixture played at Lord's it is noted that when Bury went in for their second innings it was found that 'Mary la Bonne had six fielders who had not played the previous day—a circumstance that caused many bets to be disputed.' This irregularity notwithstanding, the 1829 match against M.C.C. was played at Bury, the stakes being 1,000 guineas!

A few years later we find in the Bury ranks the names of the celebrated Alfred Mynn and William Clarke, of the All-England XI. Alfred Mynn, the 'lion of Kent' stood over 6 ft. and weighed between 17 and 18 st. He was reported to be a terrific hitter, but when he assisted Bury against M.C.C. in 1847, the only note is that Mr Mynn got all his runs by singles—and he made only ten of them.

In 1849, when 18 of Bury played the All-England XI at Bury, both Fuller Pilch and Alfred Mynn were arrayed against them, and All-England won by 123 runs, despite the local side including George Caffyn, of Surrey and England, who went to Australia with Parr's XI in 1863 and coached there for seven years.

The foregoing details have been extracted from the old score books of the Bury and West Suffolk Club, now in the custody of Miss Lake, whose family, brothers, nephews and others have from the beginning been the pillars and patrons of cricket in this area and who, through their Westgate Brewery, donated to the club the handsome Victory Ground, one of the best in East Anglia.

Away to the south of Bury is the famous Rickling Green, which is something unique in cricket grounds. Here, according to the memories of the ancients and the accumulated legends from the past, cricket has been played from time immemorial. So I had heard and, after a visit to the Green, had readily believed. Alas! the Rickling Green Club does not appear to have had a Lake family or a brewery to keep its records, with the result that the first score book goes back only to 1880, though it is well known and attested that cricket was being played on the Green at least 50 years before that date.

In 1882 Rickling Green figures in a match of record high scoring made by the Orleans Club. This club first outed Rickling for 94 runs and then proceeded to make no fewer than 920. The score book makes odd reading, as it shows that Orleans's first wicket fell at 20, the second at

623. The heroes of the occasion were G. F. Vernon, who made 259, and A. H. Trevor, 338. . . .

Rickling is an area where the cricketing names are the same today as they have always been. The same families are playing today as were playing when the club was founded.

9
CORRESPONDENTS' FILE

Some people are compulsive letter-writers, even in these days that have technological alternatives. They are of the same breed as those who shout loudest when seeing a driver go in the wrong direction down a one-way street. They are the first to advise, suggest, complain, take issue, tell a story, give an opinion and answer their own questions. Their thoughts can provide vicarious amusement when read dispassionately and removed from the physical personality. They are a boon to any anthologist. Mind you, some letters and writers are not like that at all ...

LETTERS OF COMPLAINT

September 1865

SUSSEX V. KENT—THE DEGRADATION OF CRICKET

SIR,—Believing *The Field* to be the gentleman's sporting organ, I lose no time in apprising you of practices tending to the dishonour of a game noble in itself, and maintained in nobleness by the purses and personal skill of English gentlemen.

I have always understood that Kent and Sussex were two of our most distinguished counties in reference to their cricket, and that their clubs were principally supported by the membership and management of gentlemen belonging to those counties. I wish to inquire whether the practices I witnessed during this week's 'conquering match' between these counties had their knowledge and tolerance? I heartily admit that during the three half-days consumed by the sides, there was some first-rate play; but there appeared (especially on the third day) to be a combination to prevent any decision of this deciding match, and to show 'how *not* to do it;' in fact, to make a drawn game, and bring it to nothing, after a contest of three days—a long time to take for working out such 'a lame and impotent conclusion.' This was effected by cutting time to waste in the most flagrant manner. There appeared to be no presiding authority, or no effective one, but certainly an absence of the usual element of control. I suspect that the principal gentlemen of the two clubs were absent during this 'out of season' time, and that the mice went to play. I came away impressed that hirelings are not to be intrusted with the maintenance of that character which this English game has achieved in England and over the Continent. Never till at Hastings this week did I see the game interrupted at short intervals (two mates being in) by 'the pewter pot' being brought out to the players, who coolly left their places and passed it round; or left the game suddenly and ran off to drink in the booth.

Kent, at two o'clock (the dinner hour), on the third day had obtained 179 runs for second innings, with nine wickets down; Sussex had to go in after dinner and get through her second innings (after getting Kent out) by six o'clock, when the stumps were to be finally drawn. Accordingly (!) both sides disappeared from the ground, adjourning, it was reported, to a new tavern close by, with the name of G. Wells on the front. The two sides reappeared at half-past three o'clock (an hour and a half for dinner!), Sussex to get nearly 170 runs in two hours and a half—if they meant to try and win for their county. During their absence the hat was carried round among the company for Bennett, who had made a good innings—and I suppose was engaged for good pay—and a sum of £2. 8s. was collected in the hat in silver and coppers.

Now I ask the gentlemen subscribers to the Kent County Club whether we are to infer that their professional players are so poorly paid as to have any excuse for this resort to public charity? And whether these gentlemen maintain their club and provide themselves with the amusement of cricket partly by sending round the hat for their retainers? After dinner a ball was bowled on the Sussex side by the said Wells, and knocked up into the hands of mid-wicket in a most accommodating style; and then a long delay again took place before Sussex went in for second innings. The negligence of the fielding (especially in the missing of catches) was now remarkable, and can only be referred to the performances being post-prandial. As a set-off to the example set on the Kent side for Bennett, the hat was again carried round, this time for Charlwood, one of the Sussex eleven, who also had made a fine innings. But I also ask the above questions of the subscribers to the Sussex club. As to a good innings, is it true that the pay of each paid player is higher if he play on the winning side? In the prize-ring (not admitted by *The Field*) I have read of the hat going round for the beaten man. He, poor devil, has no such provision made for him in the way of regular payment in any event. Are cricketers—paid members of county clubs, and fellow members of gentlemen—on his level, or on that of the street tumbler? 'Twopence more, and up goes the donkey!' used to be the cry of Joe Muggins only!

At six o'clock yesterday (Wednesday), when Sussex had made 112 runs with six wickets down, the stumps were drawn, the match was drawn, and my conclusion was drawn that the parties engaged had shown no desire to maintain the honour of their respective counties, or the high characters they had long ago acquired. I hope that cricket will not, like too many of our sports, be made subservient to the public-house interest.

VIATOR
St. Leonard's-on-sea

June 1873

THE CONDITION AND MANAGEMENT OF LORD'S GROUND

SIR,—I trust that in the interests of cricket you will allow me a short space in your columns to enable me to draw attention to the present management of the Marylebone Club, and the condition of Lord's.

I had the misfortune to be one of the players in the match between the M.C.C. and Ground and the Civil Service at Lord's on Friday and Saturday June 13 and 14. On resuming the match on the second day we found, to our very great surprise, that no less than three other matches were about to be played in various parts of the ground, which of course rendered the game an absurdity, our long leg having to field almost between the wickets of another match. On remonstrating with the ground keeper, we were informed that these matches were being played by Mr Fitzgerald's orders.

Now I submit that this was either a deliberate violation of the courtesy due to the Civil Service Club, who were the guests on the occasion, or the result of gross carelessness.

I am informed that there are various clubs who are allowed to play their matches at Lord's on non-match days on payment of 1s. for each player. This seems to me to be a very bad arrangement, interfering as it does with the already few occasions on which members can practice, besides unnecessarily cutting up the ground.

The condition of Lord's is now most disgraceful; the practice wickets are positively dangerous, and the whole ground in a state which would hardly be tolerated by a second-rate village club.

A MEMBER OF THE M.C.C.

July 1896

UNPUNCTUALITY

SIR,—That unpunctuality and waste of time are the curses of second-class and club cricket, is, I think, well known to all who play that class of cricket. There are many hundreds of cricketers in the same position as myself. At a public school or university we have learned to love the game and play it according to its best traditions; then we go into business or profession, and are restricted to the day a week, and then how our souls are vexed and our keenness tried by waste of time, is, I think, well illustrated by my own case.

I belong to a club of high standing in my district, and play regularly on Saturday—to do this I work late on Thursday and Friday and very early on Saturday. Eleven o'clock is the nominal hour to begin, and at 11 I am there, and perhaps two or three others. At 11.30 there are six of each side; at 11.45 perhaps eight, and at 12 or 12.15 the game begins—one hour wasted. Almost an hour is taken for lunch—half an hour wasted. At 6.30 stumps are drawn, whereas in June and early July the light is nearly always excellent up to 7.30. In this way two hours and a half are wasted over every match, and the result is often an uninteresting draw, instead of a good finish. A little keenness and trouble on the part of captain and players would soon stop this. Surely cricket is worth an effort, and the difficulties in the way of coming punctually are rarely insuperable, but in most cases it is sheer slackness which is at the root of the evil.

B. A., *Oxon*

ADVICE AND SUGGESTION

June 1890

ATTACHING BAILS TO WICKET

SIR,—Will you permit me to suggest through the medium of your paper the following simple means of avoiding the many accidents that occur in cricket through the bails being driven in the wicket-keeper's face by the ball. Let the middle stump have a gimlet hole drilled through it parallel to the plane of the wickets, and about 6 in. below the bails, and through this hole draw a fine cord about 16 in. long, with a slip loop at each end to go round the bails, which, therefore, can easily be removed by the ball but can travel no distance. Many very nasty accidents might be avoided by the adoption of this simple device.

J. E.

July 1880

CRICKET UMPIRES' COATS

SIR,—When a bowler bowls over the wicket, the batsman generally suffers disadvantage through the umpire standing behind the bowler's arm. Why should not the umpire be compelled to wear a white jacket instead of the conventional dark coat of his species?

FITZBOB

Some months ago we published a letter from the Rev. E. L. Browne, the headmaster of St Andrew's School, Eastbourne, on the subject of fast bowling at preparatory schools. We made some comments on the letter, and these are printed in the June number of *The Preparatory Schools Review*, together with some remarks by Mr H. C. McDonell and Mr A. C. Maclaren, who were not fast bowlers, and Mr P. H. Morton, who was one of the very best fast bowlers of his time. In substance Mr Morton agrees entirely with what was said in *The Field*. He says: 'It is really too silly to imagine that fast bowling is more effective by taking a run of 20 yards, *à la* Hitch, than by taking one of 7–8. Nothing to do with it. A fast bowler ought to bowl with his body and not merely his arm. The captain of the Cambridge XI (who used to nickname me Dorsals) wrote in *Whitaker's Almanac* in 1880 of me: "Not only do batsmen tell us they are deceived by his pace being faster than expected, etc., etc., etc." *I* certainly never took a run of more than 7–8 yards, if that. On the other hand, I cannot quite see the M.C.C. framing a rule, as Mr Browne suggests, to prevent this absurd practice; but surely it is up to the headmasters of Preparatory Schools to see that neither in practice, nor in a game, nor in a match, should their boys be *allowed* to take more than, say, an eight-yard run. A school refusing to conform could be dropped from the fixture list.'

Mr Morton also gives the following practical advice to young fast bowlers:

1. Aim so as to hit the wickets. If you can make the ball turn from the off so much the better. Pitch the ball accordingly. And, if you discover the batsman to be weak on the leg side, aim at the leg stump.

N.B.—It goes without saying that the bowling must be *length* bowling.

2. Learn to bowl a *yorker*, the most deadly of all balls, whenever you please. This will require practice, and is difficult, but not impossible.

3. The *occasional* slow ball must be bowled without altering the action or run.

4. An eight-yard run is ample. Use your dorsals.

5. If you have started bowling long-hops on the off side with four or five slips, *give* it up at once. These tactics will never make you a bowler.

January 1898

ATTITUDE IN BOWLING

SIR,—In the article 'Bowling and Throwing', in your issue of the 25th inst., appear some remarks upon the position of the bowler's foot. 'It has been asserted that this foot can be raised, or, at any rate, drawn along the ground, just before the ball is delivered.' 'Whether it is possible to bowl effectively off one foot alone in this manner, and whether in ordinary cases, both feet are actually on the ground when the ball is leaving the hand, is a problem of some little importance, which mere human vision can hardly be expected to solve, but photography would make light of.' In connection with this point, allow me to relate the following circumstance: Some thirty years ago, the Butterflies were playing the Gentlemen of Dartford, on Dartford Brent, and the visiting eleven were not a little annoyed at our best bowler, W. L. S., now a well known County Court judge, being, after the first few overs, persistently no-balled by the Dartford umpire. On our asking the reason of this, we were informed that the bowler lifted his back foot from the ground before the ball left his hand; he was a slow left-hand bowler, and leant forward a good deal in the act of delivery. The idea that a bowler could deliver a ball when poised on his foremost foot alone struck us as absurd, until we came to watch our representative's action closely, when we had little difficulty in discerning the correctness of the umpire's contention. I have no hesitation in asserting that in many cases – and especially in those of slow bowlers, human vision can readily solve the problem stated.

ARTHUR G. GUILLEHARD
Eltham, Kent

NO NEED TO REPLY

December 1922

Humorous touches are often to be found in the Sunday papers, and a letter in this week's *Sunday Times* would be hard to beat:

SIR,—The letters which have appeared in the *Sunday Times* concerning the expression, 'It is not Jannock', or 'Jonnock', remind me that there is another, with a similar meaning, the origin of which is generally misunderstood: 'It is not cricket.' Contrary to the common opinion, this has nothing to do with the game of cricket. In the early sixties, in the village of Nether Cornslide, in Norfolk, a Mr Charles Ricketts was, for over forty years, treasurer of the local goose club; and during the whole of that time there was never a penny short at the annual share-out. When regrettable incidents occurred, about Christmastime, in neighbouring villages, people used to say, sadly, 'It is not C. Ricketts'; which in the course of time became, 'It is not cricket'.

B. GRANT
Hampstead

August 1924

Monsieur Alphonse de Perpignan writes: 'You English speak of your wicket in so funny ways and for long time I do not understand him. But I have him now. At the Oval last week the wicket was what you call difficult, and, when a ball from Carter hit him, four of him were down for 137 and the last of him had put on 58 runs. Is it not so?'

CONTENTIOUS ISSUES

October 1888

AUSTRALIAN CRICKETERS

SIR,—In a recent edition of your paper an article devoted to a summary of the matches played by the Australian cricketers contained some very decided opinions as to the great inferiority of a representative Australian eleven at the present time as compared with the full strength of England, and on this assumption a confident hope was expressed that we had seen the last of our Australian friends for several years. I should be glad if you would spare me space for a few words, endeavouring to show that such a summary dismissal of our opponents' claims to equality is at the present time hardly just, and, in fact, so contrary is it to the true statement of the case, that there has perhaps never been a time since these contests commenced in 1878, when the Australians properly represented would have been more likely to beat the old country on her merits than they would be this year.

In the first place, we may take it for granted that this year's eleven is far from representing the full strength of Australia, and indeed it is probable that the moderate amount of success which they have attained is not a little owing to an exceptionally wet season, which enabled their two bowlers to often dispose of their opponents for a smaller score than their own weak batting side were able to reach.

What would be the actual representative eleven is, of course, a matter open to a considerable variety of opinion, but I think the eleven I am about to name would be near enough the mark to illustrate my contention that they would hold their own against all comers: McDonnell, Moses, Giffen, Jones, Scott, Horan, Bonnor, Blackham, Turner, Ferris, Spofforth, with Trott, Jarvis, and Bruce as reserves.

In this eleven those who have been with us this summer are reinforced by Moses, probably one of the four best batsmen now playing cricket; Giffen, a batsman and bowler of the very highest class; Horan, still one of the not too numerous Australian batsmen who are likely to make a really long score against our best bowling; Scott, a first-class batsman; and Spofforth, whose bowling needs no special advertisement. When we remember, in addition to these, that Jones, when in good health, is a really first-class batsman, what a formidable eleven it is! Incomparably stronger in bowling than any eleven that ever entered the field, with Spofforth, Turner, Giffen and Ferris; with Moses, Giffen, Jones, Horan, and Scott for scientific play; with McDonnell and Bonnor to force the game, as only they can; and with the wicket-keeping in the hands of the still unrivalled Blackham. I am inclined to think that such an eleven, could they have been got together, would have proved equal, if not superior, to our full strength; and, moreover, that, in spite of the seven runs victory at the Oval in 1882, this is the first year that the best Australian eleven have been well able to tackle us on any wicket, wet or dry.

Ivo Bligh

November 1888

THE AUSTRALIAN CRICKETERS

Sir,—I read with great astonishment the letter of the Hon. Ivo Bligh, inserted in your issue of Oct. 6, and cannot believe that his view of Australian cricket is indorsed by the majority of those competent to form an opinion. He very prudently states that the team which has just left our shores was not the full strength of Australia, and I think a few of the following facts will be obvious to anyone who follows cricket:

I. Previous to this year the various Australian teams had played 60 county matches, winning 35, losing seven, and drawing 18 games. The sixth team comes, and they get beaten in county matches by five sides, viz., by Lancashire, Notts (twice), Gloucester (twice), Sussex, and Leicester.

II. When a good fast wicket was prepared, their score was seldom much greater than on a sodden wicket, where their runs were all obtained by slogging.

III. If beaten by their opponents on the first innings, they appeared to consider the game hopeless, and played for a draw.

The Hon. Ivo Bligh considers the following men a model team: McDonnell, Moses, Giffen, Jones, Scott, Horan, Bonnor, Blackham, Turner, Ferris, Spofforth. Now Turner was fortunate to come here in an exceptionally wet summer, and hence his performance is certainly a record; yet we have bowlers who are as dangerous on a slow wicket, viz., Briggs and Peel, and many who have better analyses in dry weather. Turner took 314 wickets for 11.38; Ferris took 220 wickets for 14.24; yet Briggs took 61 Australian for 7.57, and Attewell took 41 Australian for 10.

In a phenomenally dry summer like last year, our bowlers' averages would have ousted Turner's easily. I append a few of 1887 averages: Attewell, 89 wickets for 13.81; Watson, 100 wickets for 14.82; Lohmann, 154 wickets for 15.94; Richardson, 45 wickets for 13; Beaumont, 64 wickets for 16; Peel, 114 wickets for 17.80; Wootton, 100 wickets for 18.92.

Spofforth, too, will never be the same man since his accident, therefore, their bowling does not appear to me nearly so dangerous as in 1880, 1882, and 1884. Palmer, by many Australian judges, was considered superior to Spofforth. In addition, considering the marked superiority of our batting over our Australian cousins, I consider they would court defeat by challenging England on a good dry wicket.

A. T. MURRAY

August 1888

REFORM IN CRICKET

SIR,—Although no longer wearing a tall hat and high trousers with short cotton-jointed braces, I retain an interest in the terrestrial sphere of the national game in which I was reputed *facile princeps* forty-five years ago. Your mundane discussions interest me much, and more particularly the last clever volume by Messrs A. G. Steel and R. H.

Lyttelton on cricket. May I be permitted to say a word or two from my point of view?

Now, in my own day the bowler had a superiority over the batsman, but by no means equal to the superiority of the latter now. Why was this? The grounds were uneven, as a rule, and the wickets uncertain. There were not half a dozen first-class grounds in England where a batsman could calculate that the ball would not bump or shoot, or accidentally break at some undefinable angle. If a batsman let alone a ball within fair hitting reach, he could not be sure that he would get another; more likely he would receive notice to quit. Again, if a ball would fairly have hit the wicket, the batsman was liable to be out, and was frequently out, l.b.w. The batsman, moreover, had to run out all hits but 'boothers', and the circular rope inclosing the ground was hardly known.

The game of cricket under such circumstances generally occupied only two days for first-class matches, and the four innings might be put roughly at as many hundreds. Sporting newspapers could not record five individual innings in a day of one hundred each, and one over two hundred (as was the case on Saturday, Aug. 18, 1888), and such scores were, in fact, impossible.

The question arises, therefore, whether cricket is altogether the same game now that it used to be (I am vain enough to think it was never better, or more interesting, than in the old days of Kent v. All England); and if not, whether something ought not now to be done to diminish the superiority which modern batsmen have acquired from grounds like billiard tables for smoothness; from roped inclosures, which so completely save their wind; from the l.b.w. law, which so heavily handicaps present bowlers; from the unrestrained custom of batsmen to let go by as many balls as are not thought perfectly safe to play at.

My ghostly advice is this: (1) Carry out without delay the new l.b.w. law proposed last spring. If the batsman is between the two wickets, and the ball hits him which, in the opinion of the umpire, would have hit the wicket, let him be out. (2) Let some device be found—such as the Hon. R. H. Lyttelton suggests in his book—of a net two yards in front of the ring of spectators, and let all hits which are not over the net be run out. (3) Make a new law to the effect that, if a batsman lets go by two balls running (which, in the opinion of the umpire, were within fair playing distance of the wicket, say 18 in. or 2 ft.), he shall be out if he wilfully abstained from playing at them.

These three simple alterations will probably suffice for all present purposes. The ghosts of old cricketers here above; of Box and C. G. Taylor and Lillywhite, of Hillyer and Redgate, of Mynn and Wenman— all join with me in kind regards and in wishing for those needful changes which may serve best to restore the equality between the bat and the ball as we remember it, and which may best preserve the glorious uncertainty of cricket from degenerating into the more calculable sphere of a game like billiards.

THE MARK + OF THE GHOST OF FULLER PILCH

September 1888

CRICKET REFORM

SIR,—Now that the county matches are often so keenly contested, and results eagerly scanned by thousands of readers of the daily papers, it is a pity that there should be any element of chance in our noble game which might be avoided. I never could understand why there should be any toss for choice of innings in the return match. Surely it would be fairer if the side winning the toss on the first occasion were either to take innings or place their opponents in; or, indeed, they might offer their opponents the choice on the first match, reserving to themselves the right of choice for the return. A good many of the matches have been won during the season through the luck of the side going in first; but in the case of a summer like 1887 it is obviously unfair that a county with great batting strength should have the chance of taking first innings in both of their encounters with another county. Besides the difficulty of hitting off runs on the third day of the match, the side going in second is frequently placed at a great disadvantage through the state of the ground after a long innings on the part of their opponents, as but very few of our grounds still stand the wear and tear of a score of over 250 without showing the effects of the innings in a more or less degree; and there is a third disadvantage, the light. No one will hold that the light between five and seven o'clock in any summer evening (about the time when frequently one side is out and the other side has to commence their innings) is nearly as good as the light prevailing during the rest of the day. The toss for choice of innings in all matches is a custom that has been handed down to us from old cricketing days, and we are all anxious as far as possible to be linked with the past; but as the love for the science of cricket becomes greater every year, surely we ought wherever possible to eliminate from our game the element of chance.

SOUTH WALES

July 1893

CRICKET: A PROPOSED CHANGE

SIR,—Will you allow me to propose a change in the present plan of conducting a cricket match? My object is to make the most interesting game that exists more interesting still, if that is possible, and to lessen the effect of 'luck' in the toss, by equalising the conditions as much as possible. My proposition is this: that when five wickets of the first side are down the other side should go in, and when they in their turn have lost five wickets, the remaining men of the first side should then go in and complete the innings for that side; when they are all out the second side then completing their innings in the same way. The advantages are as follows: The effect of winning the toss is lessened, as the pitch will be less worn before the second side begins to bat, and the effect of rain and of bad light will be more equalised. The long and often tedious fielding by one side for several hours is broken, and the still more tedious waiting to go in by the second half of the first side is pleasantly broken by a spell of fielding in getting the first half of the second side out. It would give the bowlers a rest; and I do not, from any player's point of view, see any possible objection.

From the spectator's point of view I think there is even more to be said for it. It often happens that men have only one day to spare to see, say, the Australians play. They naturally wish to see them (or at least some of them) batting as well as in the field, and by dividing the innings in the way I suggest, the chances of seeing some of each side in are doubled. I trust that the glorious uncertainty of cricket will never disappear; but there can be no harm in lessening the effect of ill luck due to having to play on a bad wicket, which was in good order for one's opponents. I think, too, that it might help to abolish the follow on and all its obvious disadvantages. But even if the follow on is retained, the proposed plan would at least tend to lessen the temptation to try to win a match by not playing cricket, a temptation that some people seem unable to resist. I wish anyone who may read this would organise a game on this plan as an experiment, and in the meantime I should be glad to see what objections there may be, either on the part of players or spectators, to the proposed change.

J. E. E.

July 1960

THE TOSS IN CRICKET

SIR,—Surely there is no sense in tossing in order to see which side has first choice of innings.

It is definitely an advantage in having the choice, likewise it is an advantage playing on one's own ground, therefore in order to make the position more even for the teams it is only right and proper for the visitors in all, other than Test matches, to have choice of innings, and for Tests, for the visitors to have this choice in the first match. Thereafter it should be given alternately between hosts and visitors, which would give the visitors three choices to their hosts' two in a series of five Tests.

J. LANYON
Stebbing Park, Dunmow, Essex

I SAW IT MYSELF

July 1922

An old contributor writes: 'My boy recently egged me on to buy him a new pair of pads. Since he got them he has played seven innings, with the following results: 0, 0, 0, 0, 0, 0, 0. He has decided to use the school pads for the present.' A famous old cricketer once said: 'I am not in the least superstitious, but if I find that in certain circumstances I cannot make runs, I do my best to alter those circumstances.' So that the youngster is in good company.

We are glad to say that the youngster to whose seven duck's eggs in succession we referred last week is himself again. His father writes: 'My boy Ronald has broken his run of bad luck at cricket. He followed up his seven "ducks" by an innings of eight and took six wickets for 32 in the same match. He played in another match last Saturday and made 38, which was top score on his side. He did not bowl in that game, but tells me he virtually got a wicket – their best man. It appears that in trying to throw the wicket down he hit the batsman in the back, and to such good effect that he got out next ball. This strikes one as a rather primitive method of disposing of one's opponents, but apparently it is effective.'

The same writer says: 'A youngster in my office – C. J. Culver – who plays for Highgate and is a promising fast bowler, played a remarkable innings the other day. He went in tenth and made 70 in 20 minutes, incidentally winning the match. He hit two sixes and 12 fours, scoring over 50 without his partner making a run. If he would confine his attention to cricket instead of messing about with lawn tennis he might play for the county some day.'

A correspondent writes: 'The other day on my way north by train I passed five games of children's cricket and saw one ball bowled in each. The first ball was nearly wide to the off, and the batsman, who tried it for six, did not get within a yard of it. The second ball, in a girls' school game, was very much of the same kind, and the batswoman, whom I took to be about ten years old, struck out in the manner of a Parkin, and again did not get within a yard, although she looked very pleased at not being out. The third ball, to a small boy, was much on the leg side, but the batsman's attempt to hit it out of the ground was made after it had gone by. Another leg ball was badly missed by the fourth batsman, and the fifth was completely beaten by a straight ball, which, however, rose about a yard above the wicket. If I did not know from observation and experience that youthful cricketers do sometimes manage to hit a ball, I should think cricket is a funny game.'

August 1910

A correspondent writes: 'In a note in last week's *Field* on an incident in the recent match between Sussex and Lancashire at Brighton it is stated that "under the old order it seems to have been the custom to give a six if the ball went out of the ground, even though it struck the top of a building or a fence on its way." In support of this statement of the old customary interpretation of the law, the case of a hit by Albert Trott at Lord's is quoted. Trott was given six, though the ball "struck a chimney or part of the roof before going out of the ground." This precedent is doubtless of weight, but umpires as a rule did not give sixes in any class of cricket save for hits clean out of the ground. Thus a six was never given at the Oval when the ball hit the top of the concrete stand and bounced out of the ground, while on most grounds if a ball bounced off the top of a shed and over the outer fence of the field it counted four only. It is, of course, obvious that a ball hitting the top of the screen and rebounding into the playing area (as happened at Brighton, where only four was given for the stroke) must have cleared the ropes if the direction of the hit had been a little to the left or right of its actual course. It seems equitable to give six for such a hit.'

DOWN MEMORY LANE

July 1939

A CRICKET CRISIS

Sir,—The following extract from a letter received quite recently from the Lawrence Royal Military School at Sanawar in the Simla Hills, is sent, as I think you may like to publish an account of so unusual a cricketing incident:

'One of the first storms accompanied by tremendous wind created an amazing and rather amusing diversion down on the boys' cricket ground. The pitch matting suddenly blew up, lifting the batsman with it and hurling him down, knocked him senseless. Then the matting proceeded to roll itself up, lifting two or three of the fielders right off their feet, and pitching them bodily several yards across the ground.'

J. K. Tod
Round Windows
Headley Down, Bordon, Hants.

May 1953

CRICKET ON THE GREEN

Sir,—Mr Clarke's article in your issue of April 16th reminds me of the annual match between the Coachmen and the Gardeners that used to be played on the Upper Caterham Cricket Ground some 70 years ago. This was one of the most popular fixtures of the season.

The Coachmen's team was captained by our coachman, by name Munday, who had an enormous bat nearly 1 ft. wide, painted bright scarlet, with a picture of saddlery, stirrups, etc., on the back.

The other team was captained by a neighbour's gardener, who had the suitable name of Garlic. He had an equally large bat, painted green, with a picture of vegetables, spades, hoes, etc., on the back.

I suppose he wished to give his opponents a chance, so he had a large hole in the middle of the bat through which he was to be bowled.

I do not remember either of them scoring.

J. B. Hoare
Meole Brace Hall, Shrewsbury

FAMOUS CRICKETERS

Sir,—I am the daughter of the late E. J. Davies, who held the world's record for the long jump (22ft. 10½in.) until he was beaten by C. B. Fry (birthday April 23rd). I am 67 years of age. When I was about four years old W. G. Grace (birthday July 18th, 1848) who was a great friend of my father used to take me round collecting signatures of first-class county cricketers *only* in a Shakespearean birthday book given me by my father. I have signatures such as that of A. N. Hornby (birthday February 10th, 1847), R. G. Barlow (birthday May 28th) (immortalised by Francis Thompson), Bobbie Abel (birthday November 30th, 1850) and many well known other cricketers.

But what I think is of interest now is that Sir Jack Hobbs (December 16th) now joins the other well known titled cricketers: Lord Harris (birthday February 3rd, 1851), Lord Hawke (August 16th, 1860), and A. O. Jones (same date), Sir Don Bradman (birthday August 27th), K. S. Ranjitsinhji (September 10th), Sir Pelham Warner (October 2nd), Sir Timothy O'Brien (November 5th), Lord Tennyson (November 7th), Sir F. S. Jackson (November 21st), and J. Darling (same date), captain of Australian XI.

The quotation of Shakespeare opposite the signature J. B. Hobbs is as follows:

> O good old man, how well in thee appears
> The constant service of the antique world,
> When service sweat for duty, not for meed!
> Thou art not for the fashion of these times,
> Where none will sweat but for promotion,
> And having that do choke their service up
> Even with the having. It is not so with thee.
> (*As You Like It*, Act II).

Which I think perhaps is applicable, except that he might not like the start.

KATHLEEN FETHERSTON-GODLEY
Hal's Croft, Monxton, near Andover

TITLED CRICKETERS

In her list of titled cricketers Kathleen, Lady Fetherston-Godley (June 18th) omitted the name of that grand sportsman the late Sir C.

Aubrey Smith (England, Sussex and Cambridge), who did so much for cricket and good fellowship in Hollywood.

G. G. BAISS
Duncan, British Columbia

AUTOGRAPHED CRICKET BAT

SIR,—In 1902 my father bought me a bat and asked the makers, Alfred Shaw & Arthur Shrewsbury to autograph it before sending it home. Both were Nottinghamshire players. This gave me the idea to keep it as an autograph bat. I took it to Trent Bridge. A. O. Jones, Notts captain and a friend of mine, introduced me to the County team and to the visitors (Gentlemen of Philadelphia). They all signed the bat, as did members of other visiting teams of 1903–6.

I found players more willing to autograph a bat than to sign an autograph book. Names include Australia and South Africa Test teams; unfortunately I never saw W. G. Grace play. However, the bat was reasonably full of well-known names in cricket by 1906 and I had it varnished.

Between the wars I showed it to a friend who took the bat away to exhibit in a sports shop in London. When I retrieved the bat, I discovered that he had taken it to the England XI v. Australia match at Canterbury. He had scratched the varnish and obtained the names (on the side of the bat) of some of the players in that match. I have read of other autographed bats but have not heard of one containing so many as 168 names. I intend to give the bat to the M.C.C. for their Museum at Lord's.

A. C. BURROWS
Shalford, Guildford

September 1953

THE 'YORKER'

SIR,—Not so long ago I heard a commentator on a Test match remark that he found it difficult to define a yorker. He added that he had no idea how the name came into being.

When I was in the Rugby XI in 1895/6/7 our professional was the great Tom Emmett, who told me that in the early days, when he played for Yorkshire, he was very keen on bowling this kind of ball, and with great success, so much so that another famous Yorkshire cricketer,

George Ulyett, said: 'See 'the, Tom lad, if thou goes on bowling them sort of balls, aa'll have to call them yorkers.' (Pertaining exclusively to Yorkshire.)

A yorker is a ball which will pitch in the block and has a nasty habit, sometimes, of getting under the bat as the stroke is played, generally with dire results.

Tom was a great character and a fine coach of his left-arm bowling. He could almost pitch a ball on a sixpence, and, having scattered your wickets at a net, he would prance up to the crease to demonstrate how the shot should have been played, and he would shout: 'Na, na, Sir, thou's ten minutes laate, cricket time.'

Tom would have been very much against what he called this stay-at-home batting. He used to ask: 'What are you given a pair of feet for?'

Hugh V. Spencer
Manor Lodge, Shanklin, Isle of Wight

NEGATIVE CRICKET

Sir,—To show that clergymen and scratch teams are not the only ones who can hit the ball hard when necessary, the following—for which I make no apology for quoting in full—appears in the late Frank Chester's book *How's That?*:

'At Dover, in 1937, Kent were set to get 218 in 90 minutes, by Gloucester. And they won with 19 minutes to spare, averaging 9 runs an over! There was no wild recklessness about the batting; it was clean, controlled, consistent, scientific hitting, and sharp running between the wickets. Before the innings Valentine, Kent's skipper, asked me if I thought Kent had a chance. "If Frank Woolley knocks 50 in the first two overs, there's slight hope," I replied, though I was not very serious. "Very well, I'm going for them," he declared.

'Charlie Barnett and the Cambridge amateur, G. W. Parker, who had scored a double century in the match, opened the bowling. In less than two overs Woolley had hit 44. And then the off-spinners, Tom Goddard and Reg Sinfield, came on. It is to their credit that during the onslaught which followed they kept attacking the stumps; there was no attempt to curb the run riot with defensive bowling. When Woolley went Ashdown joined Ames; even the dispatch of most of Gloucester's fielders to the boundary could not quell the Kentish fury. Ames hit 70 out of 100 in 36 minutes. Alan Watt, who in his day was one of the biggest hitters in England, took Ames's place and collected 39 in 10 minutes. His winning hit soared like a bird out of the ground. This game was a

wonderful example of what a team can do under fearless leadership. . . .
We need more of the daring and imaginative brilliance of the Valentine
school.'

M. BOYSE
Slaney Lodge, Enniscorthy, Co. Wexford

POINTS OF VIEW

THE ENGLAND ELEVEN – A PLEA FOR YOUTH

SIR,—In reflecting on the disastrous display given by English
batsmen in the last two Test matches, one factor suggests itself most
strongly as contributing to our defeat.

In my opinion – and I write as a medical man who has had practical
experience of athletics and sport in various directions – the failure of
our team, to a considerable extent, must be attributed to the advanced
age of several of the members composing it.

When a man is well over thirty, and approaching forty, what are the
inevitable penalties nature imposes on him?

I would class them under four heads:

1. Loss of Nerve. A man's nerve is best between twenty and thirty.
After thirty, as a general rule, it deteriorates. I believe I am right in
saying this is the view held by most big game shooters. The failure of
English batsmen on good wickets most certainly points, in my opinion,
to failure of nerve at a critical point in the game. A Test match involves
considerable nervous strain, and towards the end of it this strain makes
itself manifest, more markedly, in men approaching the age of forty,
than it does in younger players.

2. Impaired Sight. As a man approaches forty his eye is not so good.
There is undoubted scientific basis for this statement. Most people who
have enjoyed the best of sight show some deterioration as they approach
forty, and many have to wear glasses. Even if for all ordinary purposes
the sight remains normal, the slightest impairment in the accuracy and
rapidity of the visual apparatus must make a lot of difference to the
first-class cricketer.

3. Loss of Activity. After thirty there is a loss of elasticity, a loss of
activity, joints tend to become stiff, and in a game like cricket, where
the movements have to be made with almost lightning rapidity, this
must tell. Our fielding has been considerably below the standard of the
Australians.

4. Mental. After thirty – certainly after thirty-five – there is a loss of enthusiasm, a loss of dash, a loss of the capacity for a supreme effort at a critical juncture which a younger man is capable of exhibiting.

These are all points which suggest themselves to me. Age, and ripe experience in a purely intellectual sphere undoubtedly score; and I am altogether against those who have no use for a man after he is forty. Intellectually, a man is in his prime between forty and sixty. Athletically, between twenty and thirty-five.

It would be supreme conceit, on my part, to criticise the selections of the body of experts chosen for the purpose by the M.C.C., and I have no intention of doing so. I would only urge them, wherever possible, wherever the choice lies between two men, to choose the younger. Hitherto the tendency seems to have been just the opposite.

I do not think we are a decadent community. I firmly believe we produce as fine a race of young men as we have ever done, but I do think we are rather too conservative in our methods, and certainly in matters athletic we are too prone to play on their past reputations, and to ignore their advancing years.

S. HILLIARD

September 1905

LOB BOWLING

SIR,—Now that the cricket season is practically over, may an old cricketer (Rugby XI., *temp*. Crimean War) venture to inquire what has become of the lob bowler? He was ever a *rara avis*, but now he seems to have actually shared the fate of the dodo. Really, to the onlooker the universal sling of different shades, from fast to medium, seems only to possess variety in the several styles of hop, skip, and jump, and contortions of leg, arm, and wrist, which each bowler deems necessary to get the most out of himself. The lob bowler dare not show his face at the wicket. The reply you will get to the question why lobs are left so severely out in the cold is that they are no good on a present-day batsman's wicket. True enough it is that the worst wicket prepared, say, for a county match nowadays is better than the best we ever met forty years ago, but for all that, considering the wonderful way in which the finger action on the ball has been developed by professionals, one feels persuaded that a great deal might yet be done with lobs that has never even been attempted. To begin with, look at the question from the moral funk side. Probably, on an average, there are at least three

in every eleven who are absolute victims to lobs. When they see lobs
go on they are out before they are in. Again, the old mechanical placing
of the field has gone. Now the men are placed with a view to every
stroke; red tape is torn to shreds. One had only to notice seven of
the field to Brearley's bowling at the last test match at the Oval to see
this; they stood in crescent form about 12 or 15 yards from the
wicket, and a 30-yard rope would have joined the two end men of
the seven.

Of course, the eternal l.b.w. question is the real bar. As long as the
batsman is entitled to present a barndoor of pads to every breaking or
twisting ball, so long will cricket continue to be the tedious thing it in
too many cases has become. Every change in cricket seems to result in
making the bowler's handicap heavier and the batsman's, as a consequence, lighter; result, the high rate of scoring which all are agreed
tends to spoil cricket. In every other game, whatever ball it may be
played with, the rules are most stringent as to any member of the body
touching the ball which is not authorised to do so. Why should cricket
have a monopoly (though nothing but a quibble) of allowing a player
to play a ball with his legs when by its rules he can only play it with
his bat?

OLD CRICKETER

LOB BOWLING

SIR,—Some weeks ago you were good enough to insert a letter from
me on the above subject. I feel sure there is a large section of your
readers who would be glad to hear an expression of opinion on this
matter from some of those cricketers who are distinguished with the
pen no less than with the bat. Meanwhile may a mere onlooker, perhaps
somewhat antiquated in his ideas, ask why this form of bowling is so
severely let alone? The first answer that suggests itself is that lobs at
present have no market value. The chief, you may say the only, com-
modity a man taking up cricket as a profession has to offer is bowling.
And what is modern bowling? So-called round, but really overhand, the
lowest delivery of which is higher than that for which Willsher, the
famous left hander, was no-balled about fifty years ago. There is little
variety in the style of it; this, when sought, is only found in pace and
the idiosyncrasy of each bowler. Cannot, then, lobs be worked up into
an asset of value in the bowling department? No bowling becomes
marketable without a great deal of hard work to produce it; are lobs or
are they not worth the expenditure of work upon them to produce them
at their best? Have they ever been seen at their best? Have they really,

within the past generation, ever been taken seriously? Some of our experts could answer these questions in a way worth attending to, even if it was only to call us idiots for asking them.

OLD CRICKETER

[There is difficulty about the practice of lob-bowling at the nets because — at any rate unless the lobs are very good—batsmen will not co-operate. Further, lob-bowling is useless without great knowledge of the game, and, accordingly, does not commend itself at the age when young bowlers are forming their style.—ED.]

LOB BOWLING

SIR,—This class of bowling is as dead as is Queen Anne, the reasons being quite plain. In the present fashionable over-arm bowling the ball leaves the bowler's hand at about the same height from the ground as is the batsman's eye; hence during the first half of the ball's flight, the ball is but little affected by the energy of gravitation, and goes so straight to the batsman's eye that the latter knows but little of the pace of the ball, and therefore cannot form an early judgment of its length, that is, where it will pitch on the ground. Anyone accustomed to shooting young driven grouse from behind a wall will grasp my meaning. The grouse come skimming along, very low and straight at the gun, and the size or perspective of the bird is the only evidence of the speed and distance. If you fire when it is looking as big as a blackbird, you may kill nearly every shot, but miss that moment, and you kill none.

The round-arm slow ball goes through the air almost like the grouse, so far as deception goes, but the lob starts knee high, and it must at first go upwards, crossing the line of sight. This elevation enables the batsman to judge its length and pace, and accordingly he either plays back for the hook stroke or jumps out of his ground and drives. I have seen Mr Grace hit lobs repeatedly almost out of the parish at Lord's, but I never saw a batsman safer and better at lobs than the late George Parr. He hit every ball except a shooter, but all went along the carpet. There never was a better lob bowler than Walter Humphreys, who played for Sussex and went to Australia in Grace's team. Yet when one of my clubs played the Brighton Brunswick Club on the county ground Brighton, the first amateur we sent in knocked nearly 100 runs off Humphreys. I went in late, and carried my bat, finding him quite easy to play, as I always have found all lobs. Knowing how expensive they are, the captain never puts them on until he has exhausted all else; in fact, until he has lost the game. Lobs often pay splendidly against men who cannot bat enough to keep themselves warm; but against good batsmen they are the forlorn hope of their side, and they lose more matches than they win.

Charles Armstrong

July 1958

WHEN A CRICKETER ASKS FOR 'CENTRE'

Sir,—Time having brought my cricket-playing ability to an end, I have umpired matches regularly for some years and note certain changes in the batsman's requests.

When taking guard of the middle stump they ask for 'centre, please', yet they use the word 'middle' when asking for 'middle-and-leg'. There being no circle, centre cannot be the correct request for a guard covering the middle of three stumps. The expression is very common even from players in school teams. I often wonder what the county players ask for when requiring guard covering the middle.

In addition to the term 'centre, please', another request is becoming quite common: 'Centre, please, from where he bowls', so you give guard from one side of the stumps and not from over the top of them.

Owen P. Attewell
Shefford Woodlands, Newbury, Berkshire

January 1977

NOT CRICKET

Sir,—A lap of honour in a Test Match! How degrading. It is bad enough seeing them leaping for joy at the loss of an opposing wicket, and no doubt they will soon be hugging and piling on each other's backs as in soccer.

Mrs Pleasaunce Cardew
Westhanger, Cleeve, Near Bristol

QUESTIONS AND ANSWERS

September 1865

FORMATION OF A CRICKET GROUND

WE have received, by the last mail from the Cape, the following interesting letter:

Cape Town, August 10, 1865.

SIR,—*Can you give us, or put us in the way of getting, a few good practical hints about making a cricket ground?*

In this part of the colony the soil on all sides is very loose and sandy, also much infested by moles, and in summer the grass is completely dried up by the extreme heat of the sun and want of moisture. These, I know, are great impediments in the way of the noble game, but I trust they are not insurmountable.

I am informed that there is no scarcity of funds; but, no one here seems to understand that a real game of cricket cannot be played, neither can the game be practised, upon a ground covered with mole-hills, and on a sandy soil that rises in dust between wickets after half an hour's play, and is covered with tufts of grass that stop the force of a good hit, and annoy a good batsman as well as completely puzzle a good fieldsman.

There are the makings of some excellent cricketers out here; they only want a decent ground to play on. They naturally know very little how to set about making a good ground, particularly with such material as they have, and this is not peculiar. Even on the ground usually played on here, such a thing as a heavy horse roller and a fence to keep cattle off are not thought at all essential.

It is a splendid climate for cricket all the year round, if the sun in a few months in summer is not found too hot; in winter nothing could be better. We all want stirring up about it, and something to put our livers in order.

ONE WHO HAS PLAYED FOR ALL-ENGLAND

N.B. It is my own opinion that some good cricketer should be offered a situation here, as Caffyn was in Australia, but I fear the people are not game for it.

A very uncomfortable state of things for a cricket enthusiast, and especially to one who has played on some of the excellent grounds at home with an All-England Eleven. It appears (and must be a subject of rejoicing) that there is no lack of funds. Would that every club, both at home and abroad, were in the same happy condition. Now let us see what we can suggest; and, first of all, there are certain requisites which must be obtained, for the best workmen in the world cannot work without tools. The needfuls are: A mowing machine, or two if they could be afforded—a large one to go over all the piece, and a small one to go over the wickets with, immediately prior to a match. A water-cart somewhat after the fashion of the carts used for watering the streets of London and other large towns, only lighter. It need not be made either so large, or so strong and heavy. A horse roller is indispensable, a real *sine quá non*—spades, fork, shovel, brooms, &c. The land must, at least ought to be fenced, to keep off cattle, for one strong reason; when the ground is properly managed the herbage on it will be so sweet and rich that the cattle will scarcely ever be off the ground. The moles must all be caught, and the 'tussocks', as we call them (*i.e.* the large tufts of grass), must be pared off, and fresh turves put in their places; after that is done, the whole surface of the ground must be covered over one inch thick, if possible, or half an inch at least, with good firm marl or marly clay; this to be brush-harrowed in, then rolled, then watered and rolled, and rolled and watered, until the face of the ground is as firm as a dining-table; keep up this routine, and the ground will be a delight to every true cricketer. We had the pleasure of submitting these ideas to the highest cricket authority here, the secretary of the All-England Eleven, who confirmed all that we have suggested, and said that with such treatment the ground soon would be A 1. It would, perhaps, be the best and most economical thing in the end to get some good working gardener to superintend the job. Could not the Curator of the Botanic Garden recommend such a one? If so, and the man was what he ought to be, we could guarantee our correspondent a ground that would satisfy the most fastidious. It would doubtless be for the welfare of cricket at the Cape if some good cricketer could be induced to emigrate there and try his luck, or one might be engaged here and sent out, if the Cape Town club thought well. However, we shall be delighted if what we have suggested is of service.

November 1865

RE-LAYING A CRICKET-GROUND

WE are re-laying the cricket-ground in Kendal. The soil is a loam upon a gravelly subsoil, liable to get too hard in dry weather. We have at hand bog-earth, street-scrapings, road-scrapings, both from limestone and bluestone, and bark from the tan-yards. Query 1. Would any of the above do the ground any good before laying down the sod, and which is the best? [No.—ED.] 2. The contractor wishes to mix the soil with sawdust (the committee are opposed to this). Would sawdust do any good? [The very highest point of absurdity.—ED.] 3. What will be the best for a top-dressing, and the proper time for laying it on?—X. [The third query asks for all the information our correspondent really needs. Why relay the ground at all? What better will it be, if the sward is only close and level? None at all. A good firm loam, and a gravelly subsoil are the primest conditions which can possibly fall to the lot of any cricket committee: it is only the face of the ground which requires management and attention, and if the ground does get over hard in a long, dry, hot season, why the obvious remedy of watering will easily set all to rights. Leave the turf as it is, and procure at once as much good clay or marl as will give the turf a dressing of half an inch thick all over the ground; brush-harrow this well into the grass, and then roll the ground with a heavy horse-roller, and keep at this rolling periodically, but especially after rain, until next season, and the club will have as good a ground as it is possible to have. If, as we said, in a hot season the wicket gets too hard and dry for good play, have it well watered with one of the town water-carts the night before a match, and rolled early the next morning. This treatment will, we think, make the ground A 1—at least this is our treatment, the result of large and long practice.—ED.]

August 1896

DRY ROT IN CRICKET BATS

CAN any of your readers inform me of any means of preventing dry rot attacking the handles of cricket bats? The climate here is warm and usually very dry, and I have had more than one bat rendered useless from this cause. There is no outward sign whatever; the handle simply goes.

DOO, *Ceylon*

We have received the following query from 'Myddelton': 'Would you kindly let me know whether in your opinion the umpires gave the correct decision in the following circumstances which occurred recently: A ball from a fast bowler hit the bat and went up about 10 ft. or 15 ft. It was dropping (apparently) so that it would hit the bails when the batsman hit it to point. It would have been a perfectly easy catch for the wicket-keeper. On being appealed to, the bowler's umpire consulted the other one, and the batsman was given out for obstructing the field. Was this correct? I maintain that the batsman was not out, being perfectly justified in defending his wicket.' Law 27 distinctly implies that a batsman is entitled to strike the ball again 'for the purpose of defending his wicket, which he may do with his bat, or any part of his person, except his hands.' On the other hand, he must not wilfully prevent a ball from being caught. It must therefore be left to the umpire to decide. Whatever his decision may be, the batsman and the wicket-keeper cannot both be happy.

November 1924

W. S. writes: 'Can any reader give the complete rendering of "A Ballad of Bad Wickets", being one of the cleverest parodies of Fitzgerald's "Rubaiyat", of which I am aware. Clever in retaining the rhythm of the original and inspiring it with the true O'Marian touch. Who wrote it, and when? A torn fragment of the ballad has recently come to hand, containing four verses which are given below:—

> The pitch heeds not what form the batsman shows,
> But yields a spot alike to fasts and slows;
>   And he who bowls to suit his hungry field,
> HE knows about it all—He knows—HE knows.

> Swipe while you may each drive or pull for four;
>   'T'will help to swell the dilatory score,
>   Swipe, for who knows how short may be your stay,
> And once departed you return no more.

> The scorer's pencil writes, and having writ,
> The thing is done; and though you've made no hit—
>   If you are bowled, you're bowled,
> And there's an end of it.

When shower and shine the wicket do impair,
The rise and hang shall baffle skill and care;
  Swipe, for you know not why they shoot nor how:
Swipe, for you know not whence they break, nor where.'

July 1935

I have received a conundrum from a reader of *The Field* which I venture to give in full in the faint hope that some distinguished mathematician will offer a satisfatory explanation.

'I am a keen cricketer and a rotten bad mathematician. A combination of these attributes has landed me in a quandary, and I am writing to crave your assistance and a decision on the point at issue.

'Discussion regarding the relative merits of two bowlers had ended in acrimony. A perusal of statistics showed that both men, whom I will call A (my man) and B, had, up to date, the same somewhat astonishing figures of 28 wickets for 60 runs, and the upshot of the business was that I backed my man to be ahead at the end of the next match.

'On seeing that in that match my man had taken 4 for 36 while B had achieved a mere 1 for 27, I joyfully claimed my stake. My opponent (whom I do not trust) not only refused to pay, but actually counter claimed, saying that I had backed my man to be *ahead*, whereas, in actual fact, both men were still level. There's something fishy somewhere, and I should be indeed grateful if you could produce the answer which would enable me to claim the half-crown I'm sure I've won.'

The thing works out like this. A—28 wickets for 60 runs and 4 for 36. Total: 32 for 96, which gives an average of 3 runs per wicket taken. B—28 wickets for 60 runs and 1 for 27. Total: 29 for 87, which also gives an average of 3 runs per wicket. I have come to the conclusion that these figures lie, because if you eliminate the 28 wickets for 60 runs which each bowler took, A, with 4 for 36 shows an average of 9 runs per wicket taken, and B, who obtained only 1 wicket for 27 runs, shows an average of 27 runs per wicket taken. Therefore A is three times better than B.

Supposing you have two things A and B to weigh against two things C and D, and you weigh them separately against each other, and you find A is the same weight as C, and you then weigh B against D and find B is three times heavier than D, do you mean to tell me that if you then put A and B on the scales against C and D, that they will be of equal weight, because if you do, I do not believe you. I am sorry about it, but I do not. Such a statement is intolerable and an insult to the intellect, and I have settled *not* to send the proposition to those famous Rushbrooke twins, Messieurs G. S. and J. Y., of Cambridge, for elucidation, partly for that reason and partly on account of the extreme heat. They must be grateful for a rest after their labours and would naturally not welcome a thing like that.

10

HASTY DEPARTURES

Anouilh's observation that 'man dies when he wants, as he wants, of what he chooses' should not be taken too seriously. Certainly most, if not all of the following cases provide an immediate contradiction.

SHOCKING DEATH OF THOMAS HUNT, ONE OF THE UNITED ALL ENGLAND ELEVEN

AT the close of the Rochdale match, in which Hunt officiated as wicket-keeper for the Rochdale Club, he engaged a man named John Wild to carry his luggage to the railway station, which abuts the cricket-ground. The distance is about four minutes' walk; but in order to shorten this, a habit has been contracted by many going to and from the ground of crossing the rails against good advice and positive order. The short cut saves about two minutes. Hunt had adopted this plan during the three days of the match in going to and coming from the Manchester trains. Wild was a short distance ahead of Hunt, and had got nearly to the station when he heard the screaming whistle of an engine, and turned round to look for it. This was the 6.50 train, due at Rochdale from Manchester. At the same time a goods train came in the opposite direction. Wild saw the danger in which Hunt was placed but was unable to render him the slightest assistance, for the next moment he was prostrated across the rails, with both his legs cut off across the calves and all the fingers of his left hand smashed. It appears that the poor fellow was so bewildered at his position between the up-rails that he could discover no place of safety. The shock to his system by the accident produced almost instant delirium, which continued till within a few minutes of his death. During his short interval of reason his voice was extremely feeble. He called for his friend Mr James Clegg, who resides on the 'Freehold' and who never left him from the time the accident occurred. Hunt was born at Chesterfield in the year 1819. By trade he was a coachmaker, but for the last fourteen years has adopted cricket as a profession, and has been a great portion of the time in the service of the Manchester Club, by whom he was much respected. The accident spread a gloom over the evening's proceedings at the Wellington Hotel, to which Hunt had been invited, but preferred going home. The moment his death was announced, the Mayor, R. T. Heape, Esq., who presided, suggested the propriety of terminating the proceedings, and of commencing a subscription for his wife and four children. This course was immediately adopted, and £33 18s. were put down in a few minutes. The Eleven aided liberally, and expressed a hope that all their brethren of the bat would follow their example. A coroner's inquest was held next day, when a verdict of accidental death was returned, with a suggestion that in future the company should strictly prohibit any person from walking on the line. The grief of the widow, who arrived a few minutes after the sufferer expired, was poignant in the extreme.

221

DEATH OF HUNT, THE CRICKETER

SIR,—The melancholy death of Hunt, the cricketer, will, I feel sure, have been reported to you. I write these few lines at the request of a committee formed to obtain subscriptions for his widow and three children [*the previous article credited Hunt with four children*], whom he has left entirely unprovided for. I can assure you that not only have the cricketers of this neighbourhood, but the public, most nobly responded to the call in aid of this poor widow and family. There are many, however, who are beyond the reach of a personal canvass who may be willing to contribute to so good a cause. On behalf of the committee, I shall be glad to receive sums, however small, to be applied to this good work.

I may state that it is intended to invest the money subscribed in the names of three trustees, for the benefit of Mrs Hunt and her children. I especially appeal to Hunt's brother professional cricketers to assist in this good work, as I can from experience say that no one was more than ready than he to assist a brother cricketer in need. I may mention that in collecting subscriptions for an old and deserving cricketer this season, the first sum I received was ten shillings from the poor fellow whose wife and family I now plead for.

GEORGE F. COOKE
Oxford-road Mills, Manchester

July 1865

FATAL ACCIDENT TO A CRICKETER

ON Monday evening, a young man named Barker, who was employed in a broker's office in Liverpool, was playing at cricket at New Brighton, when he was struck on the temple by a cricket ball, and so severely injured that he died almost immediately.

July 1872

DEATH FROM THE BLOW OF A CRICKET BALL

A YOUTH named Hamilton Plumptree Lighton, attached to Repton Hall School, was bowling in the afternoon of the 5th inst. to a fellow-pupil, viz., Richard Sale, on the ground adjoining the hall. In playing the ball back it got up and struck the bowler on the side of the head immediately above the right ear. He was stunned for a few minutes, but on recovering resumed play. He, however, soon desisted, and returned to the hall. A medical gentleman was sent for, who, upon examining the head of the sufferer, discovered a slight bruise on the right ear, but no other apparent external injury. No immediate danger was anticipated, and later in the evening he was considered better. At half-past twelve, however, he became insensible, sank rapidly, and died in about an hour afterwards. Deceased was the son of the Rev. Sir Christopher Lighton of Ellaston Hall, and was seventeen years of age.

September 1875

ACCIDENT TO A CLOWN CRICKETER

THE clown cricketers, on a visit to Maidstone last week, played a scratch match with an eleven of the town and on two nights gave performances at the Concert Hall. On Friday night one of their number, named Edward Wilson, a trapezist, fell from a height of about 25 feet, while endeavouring to catch another athlete's hands, and alighted heavily on his shoulder and the side of his head. He was removed to the hospital, where he lay for many hours unconscious.

December 1877

A shockingly sudden death took place in the early part of June, on the Bramall-lane Ground, Sheffield. In a kind of scratch match, one Samuel Parkin had made two runs, when he threw up his arms and fell dead. The cause was attributed at the time to extreme heat.

September 1893

DEATH OF MR W. D. LLEWELYN

NEWS of the sad death of Mr W. D. Llewelyn, accidentally shot in Penllergaer Woods on Friday, Aug. 25, has been received with profound feeling of regret by all cricketers, to whom he was well known as an enthusiastic follower of the game. Born in April, 1868, the deceased first came into prominence as a member of the Eton College eleven. Proceeding to Oxford, Mr Llewelyn's abilities at once claimed attention, and he played for his University both in 1890 and 1891, occupying the position of hon. sec. in the latter year. The deceased accompanied

Lord Hawke to India last winter, and this season he closely associated himself with the cricket of Glamorganshire, for which county he was a J. P. Mr Llewelyn's brother Charles was married only the day previous to the lamentable occurrence, and he himself was shortly to be married to the eldest daughter of Lord Dynevor.

September 1880

DEATH OF MR G. F. GRACE

THE close of an unusually bright cricket season has been darkened by the sudden death of one whose face has been familiar for years past to the frequenters of most English cricket grounds. It is only a few days since we saw the youngest of the three Graces playing at the Oval for England in the great match against the Australians, and constantly evoking rounds of applause by his splendid fielding. In the same week he played at Stroud for the United South of England against twenty-two of the district; and there caught a violent cold which, augmented, we believe, by sleeping in a damp bed at an hotel, produced inflammation of the lungs. He felt well enough a few days afterwards to travel to London, but, becoming worse while on the journey, stopped at Basingstoke, when he was visited by his eldest brother, Dr Henry Grace. Early in the present week he seemed to be progressing favourably towards recovery, but the disease took a sudden turn for the worse, and he died on Wednesday last, at the early age of twenty-nine. Following in the steps of his brothers, Mr G. F. Grace when almost a boy took his place among the leading cricketers of England, and his career since he first made his appearance at Canterbury is too well known to need recapitulation. He all along kept up his reputation as a correct and safe batsman with fine hitting powers, and at the same time was a most successful fast bowler, while of late years he was deservedly considered one of the finest long fielders in England. Apart from his merits as a cricketer, his genial manners and invariable kindness and good humour made him as popular in the cricket field as he was among his private friends; so that his untimely death will be mourned not only by a large circle of relatives and friends, but by hundreds in every county in England.

DEATH OF MR HENRY GRACE

MR HENRY GRACE, surgeon, of Kingswood Hill, near Bristol, eldest brother of Mr E. M. and Mr W. G. Grace, died suddenly on Wednesday. He left home on Monday to spend a few days at the shooting box of his friend, Mr J. B. Brain (father of the Oxford and Gloucestershire cricketer, Mr J. H. Brain), near Honiton, Devon. While there he had a seizure, from which he never recovered, and death took place before any of his friends, who were telegraphed for, could arrive. Although not so widely known as his younger brothers, he was a cricketer of great ability, and, with better opportunities, would have been in quite the front rank. Between 1855–65 he was one of the best all-round men in the West of England, and on several occasions he played against the All-England Eleven. By the time the Gloucestershire County Cricket Club was formed in 1870 he had married, and could not afford time for three-day matches, with the result that he never represented his county. He was proficient in other branches of sport, and was particularly successful as an angler. Indeed, up to the time of his death, he usually devoted one day a week, or at least, the portion of a day, to this pastime. His was a familiar figure on most of the leading cricket grounds in the kingdom, and he never missed a home match, whether it was played at Clifton, Bristol, Gloucester, or Cheltenham. His popularity was widespread, for he was most generous and kind hearted.

THE LATE V. F. S. CRAWFORD

THE eldest of the three sons of the Rev. J. C. ('Parson') Crawford, Vivian Frank Crawford, whose death has occurred at the age of forty-three, will always be remembered for the phenomenal hitting powers which he showed as a boy at Whitgift Grammar School. In 1897 he scored 1340 runs for the School and had an average of 74, and a great future seemed to be before him, but unfortunately when he began to play for Surrey in the following year it was most unwisely impressed on him that he must play himself in before he began to hit. The result was simply fatal, for his defence was attack, and he was never meant by nature to potter about. If he had been allowed to follow his bent he would most likely have been one of the greatest players of all time. As it was he was naturally inconsistent. In his first season for Surrey he scored only 206 in 16 innings. He was doing much better in the next season when he received a great setback. He was batting at Chesterfield, and when he had started for a run he was suddenly sent back. The result was that, in turning, his spikes caught in the turf and he wrenched his knee very badly. He remained with Surrey, being brilliant and disappointing by turns, until 1903, when he became secretary of Leicestershire, and having a birth qualification for the county he played regularly until 1910, when he went to Ceylon. Two of his innings which stand out in the memory are his 101 out of 133 in an hour and a quarter for Surrey against Lancashire at the Oval in 1900, when five of the best batsmen had been dismissed for 110; and his 172 out of 226 in just over three hours for Leicestershire against his old county, Surrey, at the Oval in 1909. He was a brilliant field as well as a dashing bat, and had great pace in the long field. His health was unfortunately much undermined by service during the war, and when pneumonia attacked him he was unable to withstand it. He was a regular visitor to Lord's and the Oval up to a few days before his death.

September 1924

THE LATE WALTER LEES

BY the death of Walter Lees of pneumonia, at West Hartlepool last week, cricket has lost, not the best, but one of the most useful bowlers Surrey ever had. He was a pronounced swerver, like Rawlin and so many others, but in his day the swerve was merely described as a bias. Again, in his day Lees was described as a medium paced bowler, but he was as fast as most of the fast bowlers of the present day. He was a Yorkshireman, born on Christmas Day, 1876, but, after playing for Halifax, he answered an advertisement which brought him to the Oval. In September, 1892, he played in the Surrey colts match and was at once engaged by the Surrey club, although it was not until 1896 that he played for the eleven. For several seasons he maintained excellent form, but in 1911 he lost some of his skill for no apparent reason. His best year was 1905, when he took 193 wickets in first-class matches, all but a few of them for Surrey. He never played in a Test match, although most players thought he was good enough, but in 1905 he was reserve man at Nottingham. In 1898 he went to the Argentine to coach. At that time the Argentine had had some very good men, including Mr James Gifford, who, in 1898, played in several first-class matches in England, and Mr W. E. Leach, who had played for Lancashire. Lees once did the hat-trick under curious circumstances, when he was playing for High Wycombe against a very strong M.C.C. team. In an interview in *Cricket*, in 1899, he said, 'Braund and I were batting on a bad wicket against Mr Spofforth, whom I had never met before. A ball from him got up and hit me on the elbow, with the result that my hand was closed so tightly that I could not open it for some time. When our turn came to bowl I did not feel able to go on, but when four wickets were down and the M.C.C. wanted only 14 runs to win, I had a go. In the very first over I got rid of young Mr Grace, Russell, and G. G. Hearne with successive balls, and we won the match by four or five runs.'

March 1965

CRUSOE, THE WRITER NOT THE BOOK

BY LEONARD CRAWLEY

AMONG the most brilliant characters of his generation, Raymond Charles Robertson-Glasgow died suddenly on March 4 at the age of 63. After the First World War they talked of him at Oxford, where he went as a scholar from Charterhouse, as the best classic since the days of F. E. Smith, John Simon and Charles Fry. Like them, he was a splendid player of games. He was awarded his cricket Blue as a freshman and represented Oxford against Cambridge at Lord's for four years.

He was a first-class seam bowler of above medium pace and, though both for Somerset and Oxford he often occupied the most humble place in the batting order, he could bat as well as many when it was demanded of him. For instance, at Knowle, near Bristol, when Tom Young fell off his motor-cycle on the way to the ground and could not open for Somerset against Essex, to my great surprise Robertson-Glasgow came in first. He played a grand innings of 88 and with such authority that it was hard to believe he was not a regular opener.

Surprisingly, in four years in the University match he took only one wicket for just under 500 runs and I was the victim. But, in his all-too-brief cricket career, he took nearly 500 first-class wickets, and his scalps included some of the finest in the land in those days, so rich in stroke players.

He was chosen for the Gentlemen against the Players before he left Oxford, and it was a wise man who insisted on his selection for this match for several years after he went down. He was then a schoolmaster and he used to come up to Lord's for this great occasion without having bowled a ball, except to the preparatory schoolboys, who enjoyed his kindly instruction at nets in the summer term. And yet he bowled with all the fire and dash of a fit, hard-boiled professional playing for his living. On one such occasion, I remember Hobbs and Sutcliffe, who survived an ordeal for the best part of two hours, saying that his bowling that morning was the most savage performance with a new ball they had seen for years.

From the time he entered first-class cricket until his death he was known as 'Crusoe,' and as Crusoe he will be remembered. My old friend, Charlie McGahey, of Essex, a fine cricketer and a remarkable character, nicknamed him when he was out first ball to a tall, handsome youth of whom he had never previously heard. Asked by the incoming batsman how he was out, he replied. 'Bowled, middle stump by a fellow called Robinson Crusoe.' Many another suffered the same fate.

He was much the nicest man I have ever met. He loved life and he loved people, and he loved meeting everybody above everything else. In him there was a deeply Christian trait which insisted that he made the humblest minds of the humblest people intensely happy in his brilliant company. Everybody loved meeting him and everybody loved hearing from him. The humorous postcards, which used to appear in our house from his spaniel to our spaniel with suitably kind messages, should have been preserved.

Poor Crusoe was never blessed with robust health. His brilliant mind demanded too much from him and he was frequently ordered to take a rest. Schoolmastering gave him his greatest pleasure just as it did the boys who heard him, but it proved too much for him. In the early thirties he took to journalism and cricket journalism in particular. He was at once an irresistible success, but again and alas he lacked the stamina for day to day work, and latterly he had to content himself with weekly pieces.

His sense of humour was at once captivating since, unlike so many witty people, his fun was never at the expense of others. He always elevated the subjects of his best stories. With a mind like his he was happy in any company and could write upon any subject.

Two years ago he went to Worlington for the Newmarket Sales. I do not think he was ever interested in horses, and I am sure he had no idea what he was going to write about when he arrived. But a few days later his country notes in a Sunday paper showed he had wasted no time in finding out.

A lovable character without an evil thought in his great mind, he has gone all too soon. But thank heaven many will remember him.

July 1965

HAMMOND, THE MAN AND THE ENIGMA

BY LEONARD CRAWLEY

A SINGULAR complexity pervades the life and career of Walter Hammond, the England and Gloucestershire cricketer who died suddenly at his home in Durban, South Africa, at the beginning of the month. He was 62. Several years ago he was involved in a shattering motor accident from which his wonderful constitution alone enabled him to recover. He recently took part in a one-day match with members of M.C.C. in South Africa, and they returned home with the news of his complete recovery. His death, therefore, comes as a shock.

Twenty-two centuries, an aggregate of 7,249 runs at an average of 58 per innings, and 110 catches are against his name in _Wisden_ as his Test record. These figures should be set in the overall picture of 167 centuries, 50,493 runs and 819 catches. He was also a useful bowler of above-medium pace who, when called upon from time to time, enjoyed considerable success. In all, his performances leave him with few superiors in the record book, and the memory of his batting and fielding in the slips should never be allowed to fade.

He was a splendid figure of a man, just under 6 ft. tall and immensely strong; and, clad in white flannels, he suggested the ideal build for an athlete and a cricketer of the front rank. He was a beautiful mover, so beautiful in fact that it was impossible to imagine that there was anything he could not do better than everyone else. He had a passion for bathing—he was a grand diver and swimmer—but, stripped for swimming, he disclosed a pair of knock-knees, the one flaw in an otherwise perfect physique.

I knew him well for 25 years, during which I played in the same M.C.C. side in the West Indies and many times against him in county cricket. Further, I served with him in the same unit for a year in the R.A.F.

As a boy, he admired the batting of Hobbs and Woolley and, watching them from time to time, he evolved his batting technique. He stood at the crease quite naturally, poised and ready for action. And it was immediate action. It had to be, for he raised his bat with a cock of the wrists and drew himself up to his full height with the oil-hole of the bat pointing at the sky appreciably before the bowler delivered the ball. With the exception of Tom Graveney, who by many is considered to lift his bat too high, there is no-one today who plays the same way as Hammond did.

The purpose of Hammond's batting was always to attack the bowler, and oddly enough he attacked him mostly off the back foot. He scored thousands of runs in this manner between mid-off and cover point, and it was no use chasing, for, once the ball had passed the fieldsman, it was four every time. If the bowler pitched the ball up, Hammond would be drawn on to his front foot and would drive majestically.

Because of his wonderful forcing shot off the back foot which so disconcerted all bowlers, he seldom cut in the manner of his mentors, Hobbs and Woolley. He made his runs mostly in front of the wicket. Nor was he ever a great on-side player. When he missed the ball on the on-side, as he did from time to time, he did so with such fluency that it was at once forgotten. He was nimble on his feet and, with the exception of W. J. O'Reilly, the Australian, he gave very few slow bowlers a chance.

He scored runs all over the world against fast bowlers, but he was vulnerable against hostile ones on the fastest wickets since he could not hook. Here was his Achilles' heel. It has always struck me that the basis of supreme batsmanship is a devastating hook shot. I like the story of young Jack Hobbs out hooking again at the Oval. 'Well, Jack,' said a disappointed member of the county committee, 'you will have to cut out that hook shot.' 'No, sir, I won't. I shall have to perfect it,' replied the young man. And anyone who had the impertinence to try to intimidate Woolley was duly thrashed. Walter Hammond was not so armed, but he was a master on sticky dogs wherever he played the game.

He became an amateur in 1938 and the rôle of captain came his way. Whilst he knew all about cricket, he never understood Sir Pelham Warner's dictum on captaincy, namely, that a captain's first duty is to look after his men and make them look up to him as though he were their father. His appointment as captain of M.C.C. in Australia in 1946–7 was not a success. He was often a strange and lonely person, and did not make friends as easily as some more fortunate.

II

AT SCHOOL
AND WITH
CLUB

The Field maintained extensive coverage of
non first-class cricket, particularly with sea-
sonal assessments of talented players at
college and surveys of famous clubs. The
editors, also, never forgot that boys will be
boys, even when they are grown-up.

FATHERS' MATCH

FATHERS' matches are not what they were, if a recent experience at a preparatory school is typical. The game was a frolic, and the qualifications for playing for the Fathers were not so much skill with bat or ball as an ability to clown and keep the spectators amused.

By tradition at this school the Fathers, without appearing to give anything away, must provide the right mixture of lobs, fumbling in the field, and slow returns to the wicket-keeper to enable every one of the 11 boys opposing them to shine. This is not so easy as it sounds. One of the greatest lapses of which a father can be guilty is to make a dropped catch seem intentional. It seldom is, but sometimes an embarrassed father has recourse to this age-old trick. His last fate is worse than his first.

It is an equally grave solecism to have a part in getting your son's best friend out, but the embargo does not extend to one's own son. Indeed, every father is so fearful of getting out the wrong boy (for school friendships change rapidly) that it has apparently long been agreed that a boy can be put out only by his father.

This paternal duty frequently necessitates plots of Machiavellian intricacy. If a son is a good cricketer and his father can neither bowl nor hold a catch, however simple (a not uncommon situation), a run-out must be engineered with the father concerned close to the wicket. Even then the effort may need to be repeated to achieve the desired end.

The Fathers bat left-handed, and it is a privilege they would not willingly forgo. Cross-batted swipes and similar shots are overlooked when made under this handicap, whereas if the same strokes were made right-handed, as by some they undoubtedly would be, their respective sons would dic of shame.

The result of the game is, we were astounded to learn, determined before the first ball is bowled. Depending on the School XI's success, or lack of it, during the season, the headmaster asks the Fathers to win handsomely and thus prevent the boys from becoming unduly self-satisfied, or to concede a win to encourage them in an unlucky summer.

August 1956

HOLIDAY CRICKET, DO'S AND DON'TS

BY MAJOR-GENERAL VALENTINE BOUCHER

With advice to parents who may be members of the selection committee

PARENTS have for some time completed their study of large-scale maps and located some of the less well-known cricket grounds of their district. The job of chauffeur is now with them; the mission to convey the sons of the house, home from school, to the holiday matches which unsung heroes have been arranging for them since early spring. The main burden, during the middle of the week, will fall on mother, but, provided he has himself passed cricketing age yet is not too senile to drive a car, father will doubtless be pressed into service for Saturday duty.

These matches divide themselves broadly into two groups. The first, for older boys, is, from the parents' point of view, a comparatively straightforward affair presenting few administrative difficulties. A senior cricket club will have a schoolboys' section affiliated to it, and the senior club will have made all the arrangements. The parents' responsibility will extend no farther than to deliver their sons at the right ground at the right time, and to ensure that they have enough money for their lunch, tea and for what they will call 'the odd ice'. At the ground, the boys will be taken charge of by a still-sprightly veteran, whose tie is that of a club of household fame.

'A good chap, Daddy (or Mummy),' you will be told afterwards. 'A bit old, but he kept for Loamshire in 1920.'

If it is decided to stay and watch, there is always the chance that father will be asked to do his stint of umpiring. It is an invitation better declined. 'A prophet is without honour ...' and each minute of father's duty at the bowler's end or at square-leg will be one of intense discomfiture for his son, who knows beyond doubt that any decision Daddy may be required to take is bound to be a bad one.

It is wiser, perhaps, to leave these near grown-up young men from their school 1st XIs and 2nd XIs and from their house sides, at first glaring at each other with thinly veiled hostility, then thawing under the mellowing influence of the game, until finally ...

'You know, Daddy (or Mummy), that type from Cliftbury isn't really at all a bad fellow. Held a couple of beauties in the gully. Actually, I've asked him to lunch on Sunday ... hope you don't mind.'

Indeed, if the male members of your family have been so arranged that their age bracket embraces both public and preparatory school,

234

and if you are a one-car concern, the senior game must be left, for then a nicely planned milk-round of delivery and collection will be required.

The second group of holiday matches, for the younger set, is a far more complicated business. First, there is the question of size. The difference between a gallant ten-year-old, all pads and cap, and a youngster of 14, fresh from recent triumphs in his public school 'junior colts,' is the difference, in terms of bulk, between David and Goliath.

There is, too, the undoubted fact that, engaged in this match, are 22 temperamental cricketers, free at last from the steadying influence of the games master. On the part of the stars there will be a distressing tendency to hog the match by bowling unchanged and by batting high on the list. The coveted position of wicket-keeper, unless controlled, is more likely to be won by force of unarmed combat than by merit. Our ten-year-old will, as like as not, find himself fielding in the deep both ends and batting No. 11. It will inevitably happen, again unless watched, that he will be bowled at by a budding Tyson. It will be a wretched match for him, and it can end, if not in tears, at least in a quivering lower lip.

An essential feature of these junior games is, therefore, a form of discreet, supernumery captaincy, exercised preferably by the two grown-up umpires. Their duties will include a general supervision of the arranging of the field, judicious suggestions as to changes of bowling, the exercise of the required restraint over the speed merchants and, at times, the granting of a second life through the medium of a palpably false decision. For these duties they will require the tact of a diplomat and the inconspicuous cunning of a secret agent.

The result of this match is of less importance than that of the senior contest in the neighbouring village. If, however, by the end of the game 22 boys have batted at least once, or better still twice each, and the majority of them have had a bowl, the unofficial captains will have more than earned the cool whisky-and-soda which has been beckoning to them from the sideboard at home since long before the drawing of stumps.

For the mothers, it is a pleasant occasion. There will have been a momentary pang at the thought of the herbaceous border at home, so urgently in need of weeding, or of the growing pile of unanswered correspondence. But once the game is under way, rugs are spread and backs are comfortably supported by the front bumpers of the cars at the edge of the ground, the mothers will fall into friendly conversation. It will mostly be about schools, of course, for not only are a dozen or more preparatory schools represented here, but, unlike similar functions in term time, there is no risk now of remarks being overheard by some lurking headmaster's wife.

Common ground will be found, though the schools range from Eastbourne to Edinburgh. The fussiness of matrons in the matter of the marking of pyjamas; the unimaginative menus of school housekeepers; these and many other matters of import will be debated in full. More intimate matters are better left until the son of the house is on the field, for it is as easy for a mother to shame her young in the holidays as it is at a half-term visit.

Soon 22 tired and, if the back-seat captaincy has been up to the mark, happy little boys troop from the ground, bursting with personal triumphs. The elder son is collected from his own game and, homeward bound, the matches are played anew in shrill treble and rumbling bass.

The chauffeur, if it is father, will reflect that it does not seem so long ago that he was inflicting the same duty on his own parents, for holiday cricket is an English occasion untouched by time.

August 1973

FOUR SCHOOLS AND FESTIVAL CRICKET

BY JEREMY ALEXANDER

How Ampleforth, Blundell's, Oundle and Uppingham make up for things after exams

WHEN the universities, by the timing and importance of exams, insisted that the summer term should be less carefree for school cricketers, an answer was sought in end-of-term festivals. Blundell's, in the person of Chris Reichwald, were quick to see and set the pattern in 1969. After successive and successful annual visits to Uppingham, Ampleforth and Oundle, the second cycle began at Tiverton, in Devon, last month.

The shape of the occasion is clearly established. In January a circular went forth confirming it. Two matches a day allow each to play all in three days. A 10.30 start on the third, with correspondingly earlier finish, gives hosts justification for dispatching guests that evening. Two years ago at Ampleforth it also gave Twohig, one of the home team, time to reach 50 by 11 o'clock and 100 before noon; that must surely be some kind of a record.

The circular contained also details of arrival and accommodation, discipline and departure. These can be awkward testing days for boys and masters. Term has ended, half the players have become old boys, yet masters are still responsible. Does one, for instance, call them 'Sir' or 'George'?

There must, of course, be rules regarding drinking and smoking, cars and curfews. They must be the right rules, framed by broad minds, recognized with respect, interpreted with discretion. What happens on the field reflects the spirit of what happens off it. What happened at Blundell's last month was thoroughly pleasing.

Since 1969, John Patrick has inherited Blundell's cricket, and with it the festival and administrative headaches. On Sunday, the day before the action, it rained hard enough and long enough to put any organizer of cricket off his stroke. It was a day of distraction and short, restless journeys to check that this and that were in hand. Patrick had forgotten to feed his own team, the only boys there for lunch. It was like Christmas eve, the day before nothing more can be done and the thing runs itself.

By six o'clock sun was melting suspense and rendering a scene that seems unique to schools, when tall red buildings and tall thick trees stretch their shadows towards the wicket across an outfield that is as green as it was in May. It is a scene bearing the almost mystic inspiration of a cathedral. It was a welcome easily understood by boys and masters, now arriving on foot and in cars and wandering to inspect the square.

The square was likewise green, the best of it saved by the groundsman, in the manner of his kind, for a mythical match of great importance that never, of course, takes place. School groundsmen are a loyal, dedicated lot, exemplified by Ernie Steele, a Yorkshireman, at Blundell's. But they are cautious to a degree.

By nightfall Ampleforth had come by coach with victories at Stonyhurst and Denstone *en route*, the links of re-acquaintance had been made and conversation was running on the rails of familiarity that all sportsmen can enjoy—reminiscing, the telling of stories, the pulling of legs, the dropping of cues to see if so-and-so still reacts the same—he does—and the asking after absentees.

John Wilcox, games master at Ampleforth and heroic Rugby full-back for England, was having a cartilage out. Allan Watkins, groundsman and coach at Oundle and former all-rounder with Glamorgan and England, could not make it. Les Berry, Uppingham's coach and once a prolific scorer for Leicestershire, was coming later. But the cricket masters and boys were there, formalities had been dispensed and all was set for Monday in the lap of the weather.

The weather obliged. At 8.30 the bursar rang with the latest forecast from Plymouth—'starting sunny; local storms spreading after noon'— but the hills warded the heavy clouds off Tiverton. The start was prompt, the finish premature. As if for safety's sake, Blundell's and Oundle brought their respective matches to a conclusion by tea. Indeed, by lunch each had remarkably bowled out their opponents and assumed the crease.

Blundell's won first, by eight wickets against Ampleforth. Oundle beat Uppingham by five to avenge defeat only a few weeks previously. The former was the better game. Ampleforth are a spirited, extrovert side. They do not like to draw, so seldom do; and they win more than they lose. This is the philosophy of Father Felix Stephens, their mentor and a recent Amplefordian himself, and they practise it with an abandon that could be mistaken for uncaring. Someone has to 'come off' and now no-one did.

Berendt, an opener, was eighth out with 17, but the team never recovered from losing their first five wickets for five runs after reaching 21 without loss. They were all out for 59. Lloyds bowled well and took 4 for 36 in 12·4 overs. Wright bowled better and took 6 for 14 in 12 overs, five of them maidens. There were two superb slip catches. Such things lift bowlers and breed other brilliances.

Blundell's went easily to their target. They took their time, but they had after all made it. Of the four sides they had the keenest edge. Some of Patrick's abrasion has rubbed off on them, as well as much of his belief that games should be won and enjoyed, and in that order only because losing lessens the enjoyment. Marks, a first-rate captain by example, perception and inspiration, is a splendid and obvious disciple. He took one of those catches.

By comparison, the other match, simultaneously visible across a road and two hedges, was bloodless, which seemed surprising between rivals of long standing. When Uppingham began their innings, their master in charge, Garth Wheatley, was toiling in tracksuit round a distant field, a man trying to resist the passage of time. He is one of the old school, where tradition presumed a generation gap.

Uppingham reached 65 for 3, which was adequate, but Osmond's dolly mixture was not as sweet as it looked, and they fell away to 91 in 36·2 overs with time still for Oundle to bat before lunch after the 10-minute interval (take note, Test players.) Osmond took 6 for 48 in 12 overs. Oundle went to 54 for 1, lost three wickets for one run, then only one more in a plod to victory which did not give them time for a swim before tea. Their master, Jeremy Firth, is a Blundellian, not aloof, indeed one of the boys, but one of the quieter boys.

By their teams shall ye know them.

Someone suggested a beer match. Someone always does. There are those who see such capers as reward for taking cricket seriously as a rule. Others prefer not to parody a game they love. That only two showed interest was testimony to the good sense of the Ampleforth and Blundell's boys, to whom the proposition was put. And, as a half-hearted beer match is even worse than a whole-hearted one, the idea was dropped.

The headmaster, Mr A. C. S. Gimson, an Uppinghamian, gave a buffet supper that evening, drizzle started that night, and the telephone rang at 8.30 sharp next morning. The bursar did not announce himself: 'We're on the edge of an East Devon/Wiltshire rain belt.' Well, to judge by the ground, we might have been in the middle of it all night. The games were called off at 10 o'clock, decisiveness to be appreciated by all who have spent days watching rain from pavilions. It was the first day in five festivals to be conceded thus. Fives was played, films were watched, the evening was another jewel and all was well for Wednesday.

Ampleforth and Oundle won the tosses, Uppingham and Blundell's batted first, Ampleforth and Oundle lost. Uppingham made 140, of which Lumsden contributed 40. Ainscough, Ampleforth's captain, took 6 for 38. Ampleforth started badly, then recovered from 40 for 4 to 100 for 4 as Martin Cooper, one of twins, thrashed 62 in 50 minutes. They edged to 120 for 6, but Ainscough was run out and the innings closed at 127. Lumsden's part, again major, was 5 for 32.

Blundell's were 130 for 3 at lunch, 165 all out. Edwards, with 6 for 39, was Oundle's best bowler, but he still left his batsmen too much to do. They raised a mere 62, as Lloyds took 7 for 22 and Vallance held three catches at short leg. Blundell's had won twice without significant runs from Marks—two days later he made 153 out of 236 for 6 for the public schools against the English Schools Cricket Association—and suddenly farewells were in the air and thoughts of Uppingham next year. The examiners may have been cursed, but they are almost forgiven.

April 1965

THE GREATEST SCHOOL XIs

BY ROY MCKELVIE

Some vintage teams which not only were strong in their year but would have held their own in any season

THE trouble with trying to pick out the greatest school cricket XIs over the years is that authoritative references, such as they are, are largely non-committal. Few people, especially schoolmasters, are prepared to commit themselves to any particular team in the manner born to journalists. Thus what follows is very much my own idea and does not go too far back into history.

Having decided which schools qualified for inclusion in my first XI by virtue of the numbers of first-class and University cricketers they have produced, I had to decide what constituted the best XI; a side that wins all its school matches handsomely in a vintage year, or a side that launches several Blues and county cricketers. I settled for a blend of the two.

The choice of schools was not too difficult. Six, Eton, Winchester, Harrow, Charterhouse, Repton and Malvern in that order, consistently produce Blues and county cricketers. Uppingham, who between the two World Wars were a great source of Rugby footballers, are not far behind. Rugby and Marlborough have cast a light but strong line through the game. Haileybury and I.S.C. achieved considerable glory in the '30s and Dulwich, gaining momentum before the Second World War, have a splendid record since. They have won more Blues than any other school since the War.

The choice of specific teams reads like a catalogue of vintage port, beginning with Eton 1921. This, by the way, was a good port year, and the father of one notable Eton, Cambridge and Norfolk batsman is still drinking it.

Eton have produced a bewildering number of fine players and teams and it is by no means unusual to find sides scattered through their records which sired half a dozen county players often including an England man or two. It is tempting to nominate the 1910 side which beat Harrow at Lord's in what is immortally known as 'Fowler's match'. But R. St L. Fowler did too much off his own bat and with his off-spinners.

I chose the 1921 team because it possessed one great cricketer, G. O. Allen, and five other first-class cricketers and because it began an era in Eton's cricket in which the school was not beaten until 1936, by Charterhouse. Admittedly there were many drawn games during this era. But this side beat Harrow and Winchester each by seven wickets. The XI was the Hon. D. F. Brand, R. Aird, G. O. Allen, M. Llewellyn Hill, the Hon. J. B. Coventry, P. E. Lawrie, G. K. Cox, T. C. Barber, M. R. Bridgeman, H. D. Sheldon and Lord Dunglass.

In players, if not sides, Winchester have been almost as prolific as Eton. In fact in the first 50 years of this century Winchester won 84 Blues at Oxford and Cambridge to Eton's 81 and have since then increased their lead. Opinion differs between the 1904 and 1927 teams as being the best, though to me the 1919 one, captained by D. R. Jardine and containing C. T. Ashton, T. B. Raikes, J. E. Frazer, R. H. Hill and M. Patten, looks pretty strong. Yet the later the vintage the better and, in the 1927 side, Winchester opened with two prolific run-scorers, P. G. T. Kingsley and I. D. K. Fleming (200 for the first wicket against Eton), and some very useful bowling. The XI was P. G. T. Kingsley, I. D. K. Fleming, A. M. Tew, R. S. G. Scott, P. N. Townsend, R. S. Walker, J. E. A. Atkinson, P. J. Brett, P. J. W. Milligan, P. E. Mason and A. G. Manners.

Harrow produced some excellent sides at the beginning of the present century and again in the '30s. A good example is 1934, with J. H. Pawle, B. D. Carris, P. M. Studd and M. A. C. P. Kaye. But in 1922 players like H. J. Enthoven, P. H. Stewart-Brown, H. F. Bagnall and two of the Crawleys, L. G. and C. S., had matured through several years' experience in the school side. For this reason I chose 1922— R. M. Baucher, I. G. Collins (a great lawn tennis player and, more recently, an able point-to-point rider), H. J. Enthoven, P. H. Stewart-Brown, C. S. Crawley, L. G. Crawley, K. E. Crawley, F. O. Griffiths Lloyd, H. F. Bagnall, M. Powell and W. E. Anderson.

Charterhouse beat Harrow by eight wickets, Winchester by four wickets, Westminster by 147 runs and drew with Eton in 1946, which was just after the start of the May era. Four of the side played for counties or the Universities and another, Whitby, a fast bowler, took eight for 16 against Winchester. Like most cricket schools, Charterhouse produced some fine players just after the First World War, but I prefer the latter period of 1946, with A. J. Rimell, P. B. H. May, R. L. Whitby, O. B. Popplewell, S. E. A. Kimmins, J. H. Perry, N. R. Burt, D. J. Sword, R. W. Reiss, P. G. Nathan and G. A. Meyer.

It was partly due to a comment made at the time of H. S. Altham's death that this article was written. Among the many great Reptonian sides it was suggested that 1908, captained by Harry Altham, was better even than the earlier sides containing J. N. Crawford and R. A. Young. In 1908, in what became known as 'Bill Cresswell's match', Repton made 263 for seven and dismissed Malvern for 93 and 80. And Malvern contained M. K. Foster of Worcestershire, R. C. Burton, later captain of Yorkshire, and three future Blues. The XI was H. S. Altham, W. T. Creswell, C. E. Squire, A. E. Cardew, R. Sale, I. P. F. Campbell, J. L. S. Vidler, A. T. Sharp, D. F. Fitzgibbon, D. W. Ellis and W. B. Franklin.

In reply to this one might say that Malvern 1910, including Burton, two Naumann's, D. J. Knight, later an England opening batsman, and A. C. P. Arnold, and who beat Repton by an innings and 46, must be near their best. But I have chosen the 1924 side who, against Repton, needed 37 to win with 12 minutes left. Largely through the bat of E. R. T. Holmes, later an England captain, 39 runs were scored in nine minutes to produce a victory by nine wickets. That XI was E. R. T. Holmes, T. B. G. Welch, J. W. Greenstock, C. G. Toppin, H. C. D. Abrams, E. B. Hoefield, N. J. P. Wadley, H. E. S. Bird,

J. E. Davenport, C. F. Chamberlayne, E. R. T. Wells and L. H. Maxwell.

Uppingham bred the late A. P. F. Chapman, but it was during the First World War that he was at school. Their moment of glory, I feel, came in 1932, when they beat Repton by an innings and 122 runs. Shrewsbury by an innings and 152 runs and Haileybury by an innings and 43 runs, drawing with Rugby. Four of the side won Blues and two of them, D. F. Walker and A. F. T. White, captained Oxford and Cambridge respectively. The team was D. F. Walker, J. V. Gillespie, I. C. Henry, F. H. R. Baraldi, R. H. Williamson, N. S. Knight, T. G. L. Ballance, J. B. Green, C. T. C. Woodall, R. H. Ames and A. F. T. White.

Two years after their own year, Uppingham received a ten-wicket defeat from their leading rivals, Haileybury who that season won all five of their school matches including a handsome victory over Cheltenham. Four of the team played for the Public Schools XI. Chief rival for their best XI was the 1945 team under T. W. Tyrwhitt-Drake. The 1934 XI was B. R. Darewski, B. R. M. Hayles, C. P. Mayhew, P. K. Mayhew, R. J. Purdy, P. W. Gale, R. M. Childs, A. M. Hayfield, D. H. Ridler, S. D. Jones and P. H. Annison.

Marlborough's cricket, like its Rugby football, has found a new lease of life in recent years. It was before the First World War that their cricket flourished most and 1908 was a fine side. But 1961 would take some beating, and no other side managed it that year. That team, captained by M. G. Griffith, won nine out of 14 games and on three successive Saturdays scored between 180 and 200 runs before lunch.

Griffith became the first Marlburian to score 1,000 runs in a season, the record previously being held by R. H. Spooner. The XI was M. G. Griffith, D.A. James, J.Hopper, R.S.Leigh, T.S.Cox, M.M.Mordecai, R.K.Burgess, J. R. Style, M. S. M. Johns, T. Jackson and J. R. Harvey. Harvey, by the way, kicked the historic placed goal from a mark for Cambridge against Oxford at Twickenham last December.

It seems that strong rivalries breed strong teams for, two years after losing heavily to Marlborough, Rugby took their revenge by an innings and seven runs over a side described by Sir Pelham Warner as the strongest school team in the country. A. L. M. Linnington, killed in the First World War, took eight Marlborough wickets in the first innings. P. W. Le Gros, a remarkable all-round games player, took nine in the second and caught the tenth. J. L. Andrews scored a century. The full side was W. R. King, P. S. Fraser, I. F. L. Elliott, F. J. M. Thorne, R. A. Boddington, A. L. M. Linnington, P. W. Le Gros, J. L. Andrews, G. G. Jackson, H. J. T. Neilson, A. de Selincourt and E. W. Mason.

Dulwich had their era of the Gilligans, A. E. R., A. H. H. and F. W., before the First World War, followed by another led by S. C. Griffith and H. T. Bartlett in the '30s. But surely few schools have fielded at one time three such fast bowlers as T. E. Bailey, A. W. H. Mallett and H. P. H. Kiddle, killed in the last war, as Dulwich did in 1941. Moreover Bailey and Mallett scored centuries, too. Dulwich 1941 comprised T. E. Bailey, A. W. H. Mallett, R. G. Hulbert, H. P. H. Kiddle, A. F. Harlow, D. W. Walton, O. F. Jackson, A. R. Langston, J. M. Hitchen, H. R. Woolmer, and D. E. Tunnadine.

Other schools have had their great sides. Tonbridge 1919, for instance, was clearly in the same class as some of those mentioned. But I chose my 11 schools for their consistent strength as school sides and their consistency in producing good players, several of whom are now playing for fee or under contract in county cricket.

August 1935

FROM THE PAVILION AT LORD'S

BY LIEUT.-COL. CYRIL FOLEY

A Gigantic Hit by a Schoolboy

LAST year Clifton beat Tonbridge by about 170 runs, and needed another victory this year to make matches even between the two schools. At the completion of the first day's play they certainly looked like doing this for, after making 255, they nearly forced Tonbridge (160) to follow on. On the day's play there could be no doubt as to which was the strongest batting side. The Clifton batsmen showed confidence and aggression, and scored at the rate of 93 r.p.h., actually making 184 runs before lunch. Tonbridge, on the other hand, were uncomfortable and slow, 46 being made in the first hour, 14 of which were extras. R. G. Hobbs was the only one who played really well, his 30 being the top score. E. K. Scott, who could probably bowl a better ball than anyone on either side, got four wickets for 44. For Clifton, M. H. Anderson, their captain, played a capital innings of 89, full of good strokes. V. H. Brookes, the Tonbridge wicket-keeper, kept wicket splendidly. No one, judging as I was by the day's play only, could have thought that Tonbridge had the faintest hope of winning the match.

Next day, Tuesday, July 30th, Clifton made a poor start in their second innings, losing three wickets for 37, amongst them Anderson and J. L. Eberle, who had made 48 in the first innings. G. B. Rawsthorne (32) and J. Weston (32) added a quick 46, during the course of which the latter made one of the biggest hits I have ever seen made at Lord's. On account of the—no! I have promised the Editor not to mention them again—so I will say, 'for excellent reasons', Mr White had to pitch his wicket either a pitch nearer or a pitch further away from the pavilion than is usual, so Mr Findlay, with his customary kind thought for the members, decided upon the former alternative, so that the occupants of the pavilion should get a better view of the cricket and the boys a better chance of hitting them.

It is possible that Weston may have considered it bad manners to disturb the members (he had probably observed several old gentlemen fast asleep), and so concentrated his efforts on the clock and its environments. Anyhow, he on-drove Cobb straight over the F.G. stand notice-board, which is almost in a line with the clock, the ball striking the third line of seats in that gallery. Mr White said it was one of the biggest hits he had ever seen at Lord's. I paced it from the blockhole and made it 119 yds. carry. The fact of the wickets being placed where they were, made the hit such a big one. The ball went a great height, and had it been hit the other way, taking into consideration that the wickets were some 20 yds. nearer the pavilion than usual, I honestly think it would have carried the whole pavilion. All the same, Weston disappointed me. He played such a glorious innings of 124 last year in this match that I expected great things of him. I am afraid he has developed into a mere slogger. Nevertheless, we must give him full marks for that exceptional hit. After he was out no one, bar E. K. Scott, who made 36, did anything. As he also scored 49 in the first innings and took seven wickets for 106 in the match, he was clearly the best all-rounder on the two-days' play on either side.

Clifton were all out for 165, and I am bound to confess that the chances of Tonbridge getting the 261 required to win appeared to me to be nil. However, they showed an entirely different style in their second innings, Cobb playing especially well for 68, and with invaluable help from H. M. Clark (50) and Hobbs (74) the 200 went up for two wickets, and all seemed over. But at 204 Weston dismissed Hobbs and upset the castles of three other batsmen, leaving Tonbridge 12 to win and two wickets to fall. The score crept up to a tie through some fielding errors due to over keenness, when McGreig was run out. Walker came in, and Brookes made the winning hit at six o'clock. It was a great match. Scores: Clifton, 255 and 165. Tonbridge, 160 and 264 for nine.

The Rugby and Marlborough match, played July 31st, August 1st, was also productive of some quick scoring, Rugby getting 166 by lunch time for one wicket. Out of the 90 made for the first wicket, G. E. Hewan, the Marlborough captain, scored 70, including two remarkable hits, one an understudy of Weston's, but not quite so far, and the other well over the square leg boundary, which was 98 yds. from the wicket, paced by that famous hitter and golf architect, Mr Herbert Fowler. Both hits carried about 110 yds. He was out at 268, having scored the remarkable proportion of 176 runs without a chance. J. D. Dickson (35) was promoted and instructed to hit, which he did, and Marlborough declared at 351 for nine, made at the rate of 78 runs per hour. V. Gillett bowled well, and R. D. Clark kept a fine length. The Rugby fielding was excellent. I wonder why the Rugby and Winchester fielding is, as a rule, better than that of any other school. Rugby made a gallant response to this big score, making 126 for one, D. E. C. Steel, the captain (58 not out), and R. D. Clark (38) both playing particularly well.

On the second day, August 1st, Rugby began by losing three wickets for no runs, and with 126 for four looked a beaten side. All the more credit is, therefore, due to D. P. Elliot (88) and P. C. Reynell (100) for adding 168, ably assisted later on by J. R. Bridger (62), who played particularly well, Walford (47) and Dagnall (24 not out). Total, 480. Thanks entirely to Hewan (98), Marlborough saved the match, being 37 runs on and five wickets in hand at the close of play. Of Hewan's display it is difficult to speak too highly. He made 274 runs in the match without giving a chance, and is already a first-class batsman. He reminds me, in many ways, of Hammond. Every one was sincerely sorry that he was stumped off the third ball of the last over when within two of his double century. After him I thought Steel the best player on either side. Score: Rugby 480. Marlborough, 351 for nine, declared, and 166 for five.

July 1934

CAPTAINING A SCHOOL CRICKET ELEVEN

BY D. R. JARDINE

Confidence and Courage a Leader Needs

Sound advice for young cricketers in an article specially written for the 'Field' by a great captain who has led England's teams against Australia, India, New Zealand and the West Indies

IN *The Lonsdale Library Book of Cricket* Mr P. G. H. Fender has laid it down that 'A captain must have confidence in every man on his side, and every man on his side must have confidence in him.'

Now, Mr Fender was undoubtedly the greatest captain of the post-war era. No one would be so short-sighted as to attribute this to one instead of a variety of qualities and talents. For all that, those who know him best, would, in all probability, place in the forefront of these qualities, his amazing capacity to see his sides individually and collectively as swans, and not as the geese we frequently were.

245

It may sound banal to say that mutual confidence between a leader and his followers is a *sine qua non*. Many, however, forget that people seldom have confidence in anyone who has not a fair modicum of confidence in himself, and the uncharitable are not unwilling to confuse confidence with over-confidence in the individual. Such confidence, when not misplaced, is no more, and no less, than sound judgment.

'Possunt Quia Posse Videntur.' To mutual confidence must be added mutual service—it may well be the outcome of such confidence. But the service, which a captain gives to and receives from his side, is the fairest criterion by which anyone may judge or be judged. No man or men can command success—they can only give of their best—but, like a classic crew, those have the best chance of successful service who 'can, because they think they can.'

The head of our Government is the Crown's and Realm's Prime Minister, or First Servant. A captain should occupy precisely this position in relation to his side. None demand his service as much as his bowlers. All of us like to have other people interested in our efforts. Half an hour spent with a bowler and a piece of paper concocting experimental fields will work wonders. No captain can dictate to his bowlers. He can only suggest. The power of suggestion is vastly enhanced, if the bowler feels that the captain is with him in spirit each time he delivers the ball.

Responsibility may weigh heavily, and young eyes quail when faced with youth's inevitable inexperience. Yet with the the realisation of this inexperience, half the battle will be won. A school captain may take heart of grace from the certain knowledge that there is no club or county captain, who would not barter with him his greater experience, for the keenness which is the schoolboy's to command, together with the autocracy he may employ in wielding it.

A deal may be learned from books, and from old school magazines, but, most of all, from the appreciation of one's mistakes. For a change of diet in reading, a budding captain might well digest J. M. Barrie's speech on 'Courage'.

Any captain worthy of the name occupies a large or a small pinnacle. Not only at schools are such pinnacles best set in lonely places, if the bugbear of favouritism is to be avoided. Let him take his courage in his hands—let him accept advice before or during the intervals of a game, in the spirit in which it is given, weighing it in his own mind. But, once the game is on, let him shun advice from a master or a professional standing umpire, and let him see that his bowlers are not similarly embarrassed. No professional or master worth his salt will cavil at this—for the captain is preparing for the big day when such advice will not be forthcoming, save from any of his side whom he may care to consult. In other words, he must not only have the courage of his convictions, but he must practise them. It is too late to begin practising on the big day.

A disciplined side—one that runs with machine-like precision within its limits—is a pride, a joy and an achievement. Yet every side is composed of human, and therefore fallible, elements. In minimising this fallibility lies many an individual and collective triumph, but it is this humanity, and frequently its very fallibility, which furnishes many with the crowning pleasure of retrospect and recollection in the days to be.

A captain need not always disguise his annoyance. This depends entirely upon the individual with whom he is dealing. But he must not lose his temper, if for no better reason than that he cannot permit others to do so. There is, too, one unforgivable sin—sarcasm on the field. I shall not forget hearing and laughing as a certain captain cried 'Save seven' at a slow retrieving fieldsman's back. The fieldsman neither laughed nor forgave.

If the duties have been made to appear onerous, at least the privileges and opportunities are many, as are the temptations. A captain is automatically spared some dirty work. He can very easily spare himself more, but he is not playing for any coveted cap or colours. His reward rather to win service and admiration if he changes the order and goes in ten minutes before an interval, to save some nervous wretch whose colours hang in the balance.

Nerves are a subject apart, and they are study for a volume. That great student of human nature, Rudyard Kipling, was not far wrong when he said that no ordinary Briton cares to have his name shouted out-loud in public. A captain must sometimes call for a catch. 'Budge' or 'Bill' is a better cry than 'Brown' or 'Jones'. The use of a christian or nickname means much to a sixteen-year-old, if it comes from his skipper, and not from his younger sister.

Some mentalities thrive on a scramble for colours. In these days it is generally considered politic to put the aspirant out of his misery as soon as possible. This is not a matter upon which it is possible to lay down any general rule, but the gracious giving of colours should be almost as much a pleasure to the giver as to the receiver. If I may be pardoned, a personal reminiscence of one who, among 'Varsity captains, received service and affection second to none—F. W. Gilligan. One does not easily forget the glow raised upon receiving 'a blue'. Words spoken on such an occasion are often as exaggerated as they are ephemeral, but few, if any, captains would have thought of committing those exaggerated words to paper, to rekindle the recipient's glow on his return to his rooms.

A word on the organisation of school cricket. As great a man as the

247

late Lord Curzon found it well-nigh impossible to delegate authority. Happy the man who can do so. It may well be that there are several old colours of equal standing in a school, and the delegation of a game or part of the school's cricket may prove no small balm to such, as well as enabling the captain to concentrate on the eleven. It is no use half delegating; it must be all or nothing. Mutual trust again.

The larger the number of thirteen or fourteen-year-olds known to the captain by name, the greater his influence on the school's cricket as a whole, and the ordinarily high standard of fielding expected from the school, might be materially improved by a system which allows any member of the eleven to excuse a fag from further duty at the nets for any feat of courageous fielding. The compliment will ring all the truer if accompanied by recognition and the use of the fag's right name.

After the big School match of the year, there is frequently a sense of hiatus—something accomplished or the reverse. Here lies the chance to concentrate on the next year's eleven, and the promising sixteen-year-olds' International and County Cricket may fail and wither away—it will be a sad day if such a fate ever overtakes School or Village Cricket 'forty' or any number of years on.

July 1963

I ZINGARI *v.* LORD PORCHESTER'S XI

BY SIDNEY ROGERSON

And a brief outline of IZ's history and customs before a report on the game

THE oldest of the Wandering Clubs proper are I Zingari. They were formed after a supper at a hotel in Bond Street in 1845. The founders were four undergraduates who, while up at Cambridge, had been interested in acting as well as in playing cricket. So their club was formed with the two objects of 'cricket and acting', the acting side of the activities being carried out by the Old Stagers.

IZ is in almost complete contrast to the Free Foresters. Whereas the latter are characterised by a near rustic absence of rules and formalities, IZ bears evidence of an undergraduate tendency to try to elevate a cricket club into a species of mystery. This impression is increased by the paradox that while the inner workings of the club are shrouded in secrecy, it takes a curious pride in parading its rules, officers and members in its Year Book. They sound rather odd by modern standards. The secretary's name is given as A. Secret. The Perpetual President is the man originally elected in 1845, referred to as 'The late Bolland,

W. P.' He died in 1865. The Founder and Annual Vice-President in perpetuity is the late Baldwin, J. L. Both of the Governors are also 'late', and not till the position of Governor Emeritus is reached is the occupant of the office a living person.

The rules merit the adjective quaint, though one captioned 'Irritation' might be copied into the rules of cricket clubs the world over— county and below: 'Zingaric bowlers are requested not to become rubbers of heads, hats, caps, etc. when a ball acccidentally passes near a wicket.' So might the last rule, labelled 'Reiteration': 'Keep your promise—Keep your temper—Keep your wicket up.'

One of the stricter rules of the club is that no Zingaro, except with the permission of the Governor in very special circumstances, must on any account turn out to play against the club.

From its earliest days IZ associated itself with the county of Kent, and Canterbury in particular. It is doubtful whether the club played any part in establishing Canterbury Week, though as early as 1848 an IZ team took the field during the week. On the other hand, the Old Stagers have probably been more active at the Canterbury Festival than the cricketers.

The club has always been a notably exclusive coterie—it was recently described as a cricket club with a social qualification—and perhaps for this reason it is no coincidence that the days of its greatness were in the second half of the nineteenth century with matches played on the grounds of the great country houses, the highlight of the season's activities being an Irish tour, when the team was entertained and put up by the Viceroy of the day at Viceregal Lodge. *Autres temps*, indeed, though I find it strange that again, unlike the Foresters, there is no confession that 'the morning bat demands the evening ball.'

Today it is only the veteran category of members, described as 'candidates for the asylum of aged and decayed IZ,' who have memories of these golden years. There is no doubt that at that period IZ was a cricket force to be reckoned with and, as late as 1904, beat an amateur England XI, albeit not a fully representative one, by six wickets. Since those days times have changed, and in the current season the fixture list totals only 22 matches, only one of which is dignified as a two-day encounter. Yet IZ still stand out on any cricket field in their black, red and yellow colours—'Out of darkness, through fire, into light'—though why this legend should be applied to a club founded in such happy circumstance is, like so many other things associated with IZ, difficult to understand.

IZ apprenticeship system is well worth noting by other clubs. An invitation to become a candidate for membership, or 'Sibene' (short for the Latin *si bene se gesserint*—if they shall acquit themselves well), comes out of the blue; it is wholly impersonal and in character with the esoteric atmosphere of the club. In view of the foregoing I felt it seemed appropriate to watch their match at Highclere against Lord Porchester's XI.

Here the cricket is fired by the enthusiasm of Lord Porchester himself, who, out of love of the game, runs a team made up from his personal friends, local cricket notables—of whom there are many in this very residential part of England—some regular draftees from the local village XI, and according to the strength of the opposition, occasional importations from the Hampshire ground staff. Thus against IZ, F. G. Mann, ex-captain of England, was representative of dwellers in the district, and M. Burdon, of the county XI. It takes much energy as well as money in these days to keep such a ground and its staff in commission, but Porchester does it in a manner as unselfish as it is public-spirited. May he long continue to raise his standard and the teams he assembles to do battle for him.

IZ won the toss and, though there had been recent rain, chose to bat first on a wicket which could justifiably be described as sporting. As the club XI was led by so distinguished a racquets player as Michael Coulman, it was not surprising that it also included other racquets celebrities such as C. J. Swallow, the present Canadian and U.S. champion, as well as Hugh E. Webb, a former public school champion and Oxford captain; Webb was also an Oxford cricket Blue who made 148 in the 1948 university match, an innings memorable for his cavalier treatment of Trevor Bailey, then Cambridge's fast bowler. It was Webb who opened for IZ with I. McCausland, the latter dark and powerfully built, Webb, for all his 40-odd years, cherubically youthful in countenance.

The score had reached 65 without notable incident before McCausland was well taken in the slips by Burdon off Parker-Bowles, a fastish right-hander who, on this wicket, cut the ball back from the off. He, like Mann, is a local resident. At 18 Burdon came on and Webb drove his first ball for four to reach his 50. Five runs later he was out most unluckily, caught at the wicket off one of the balls which jumped vertically from a length and reached the wicket-keeper via the bat handle and batsman's pad. In my view Webb's 52 made in 65 minutes was the best knock of the match. He scored fluently all round the wicket, and hit an excellent six off J. May, the veteran ex-captain of Wiltshire, and his running between wickets was wholly in keeping with his juvenile appearance.

When his turn came to bat, Mann got an almost identical ball at the very start of his innings, to which he offered no stroke, but could not avoid, and most unluckily had to retire for a duck. C. B. Fry, grandson of the great C. B. was bowled by Burdon at 94, and at the same total J. A. Prodger was brilliantly stumped on the leg side by Nource standing up to Parker-Bowles. Nource is a dark, compactly built young South African who is qualifying for Hampshire. On the evidence of his performance in this match he should be an acquisition for the county because he showed later that he can also bat.

At 118, A. R. B. Burrows was bowled by Parker-Bowles who, at 137, had a hand in another wicket. Burdon bowled a high full toss which J. H. H. Illingworth swept powerfully round to leg where Parker-Bowles was standing 2 yds. from the batsman. He took the catch off his face with entire ease. The rest of the IZ innings was all Parker-Bowles, who ended with eight wickets for 56—a fine piece of fast-medium bowling. The IZ total was 155.

F. A. Underdown, a one-time gentleman-rider and now well known as an actor, opened the innings for Lord Porchester with young Nource, but although they started briskly the total was only 39 when the former was bowled by Charles Black for 13. Nource continued to play attractive forcing cricket, driving well through the covers, but at 83 he was caught there off Burrows, who had relieved Black. Thereafter a minor collapse ensued, three wickets falling rapidly.

The arrival of John Spencer not only stopped the rot but turned it into a breathless race to victory. Big and powerfully built, he is a champion of the local village XI, and from his first arrival at the crease began to punish severely any short or over-pitched balls. Accelerating as he went on, he had made 69 when he scored the run that gave his side victory at 159 for 7—victory by three wickets with time to spare.

Although he hit so hard—his 69 not out included five sixes and only seven singles—it was anything but rustic slogging. Most of his runs came from clean, straight drives and some powerful lofted hooks, with which he dispatched any ball short of a length.

August 1962

THE FREE FORESTER SPIRIT

BY SIDNEY ROGERSON

The largest wandering cricket club play for fun all over the world

THE Free Foresters' membership is larger than any other wandering club—upwards of 2,200. As it includes most amateurs in county cricket, it is also the strongest club. Indeed, it is the only wandering club which today figures in the first-class cricket fixtures with its matches against the Universities of Oxford and Cambridge. It plays far more matches than any other club. Its fixture list this season is 87, including one-, two- and three-day matches, several overseas matches and an extended tour of Holland.

The list begins in February with a game against the Kongonis at Nyeri in Kenya, and ranges through matches played in Singapore, Hong Kong and Germany, until it ends in mid-September with one against Eton Ramblers. Free Foresters' opponents are characterised by a fine catholicity: schools, regiments, other clubs and military formations. Striking evidence of the club's strength is that it occasionally fields up to five or six XIs on the same day. Lastly, it only misses being the oldest club by a few years, and celebrated its centenary in 1956.

It conforms to the character of a normal cricket club having no built-in peculiarities or idiosyncrasies. It exists to promote the playing of cricket as a game, for the sake of the game. It has the unusual distinction, some may think it a virtue, of having neither a president nor a chairman. Its members are not required to have been educated at any particular school, to have been born in any particular country, or to belong to any particular religious denomination. They are not forbidden to play against the Club.

The sole requirement for selection is for a prospective candidate to have, without any soliciting on his part, played for the Club at the invitation of a member and to have taken a satisfactory part in the game. Thereafter his candidature goes forward for consideration by the Committee at the end of the year. The principle of barring any candidates from proposing themselves is common to most of the best of the wandering clubs. Prospective members must be invited, vetted on their performance on the field and off, and approved by the Club's Committee.

Something of the spirit of English village cricket characterised the birth of the Free Foresters. Historically the Club originated in a match organised by a local 'squarson', the Rev. W. K. R. Bedford, on the ground at his rectory at Sutton Coldfield in July 1856. This initial fixture was played between an XI drawn from Cheshire and one composed of players from Needwood in Staffordshire and the Forest of Arden in Warwickshire. The next year the match was repeated and an XI picked from the two teams played four other matches at Rugby, Leamington and Manchester. The result of these matches was the decision to abandon the original idea of forming a club with its home-ground at Sutton Coldfield, and create a wandering club of life members.

I was lucky in seeing the 64-year-old fixture between the Free Foresters and the Gentlemen of Suffolk, played on the beautiful Victory ground at Bury St Edmunds on August 10 and 11, two of the best cricketing days of the summer. The Foresters had first use of a green but easy-paced wicket, but against steady and intelligent bowling by Petrie, who was able to bend back the ball off the seam, and bowled to his field, and took seven wickets for 59, failed to make full use of their opportunities, until rescued by a stand between Sir Charles Mott-Radclyffe and Lieut.-Colonel N. J. Wilson, the latter being top scorer in the innings with an excellent knock of 70. Free Foresters' first innings closed for 227.

The Gentlemen made a poor start against Styles and Callander who took five wickets, and who, be it recorded, had motored alone from Perth just to play in this match, and motored back alone on the Sunday! Eight wickets were down at the close of play, and, despite a fighting knock by John Bridge, last out for 49, the Gentlemen were all out before lunch on Saturday for 155.

With a lead of 72, Free Foresters failed to push the score along as the occasion demanded, but after a happy partnership between P. A. Walker and J. Stuck, were able to declare at 186 for seven, leaving the Gentlemen of Suffolk to make 259 to win in two and a half hours. With the wicket growing increasingly easier, and the Free Foresters' tactics going a little astray, the Gentlemen of Suffolk, by superior forcing tactics, and a brilliant not out 122 by Ridsdill-Smith, backed by 43 from Parsons and some big hitting by Corke, managed to beat the clock by ten minutes and win by six wickets.

June 1963

A SEAMANLIKE GAME OF CRICKET

BY SIDNEY ROGERSON

The Incognitis set the Royal Navy a hard task but the sailors finish only four runs short of victory

LITTLE younger than I Zingari and Free Foresters, the Incogniti were formed in May 1861, the occasion being 'the victory of a scratch XI captained by C. J. Brune, the old Cambridge bowler, over the X.Y.Z. Club' in a match at Lord's. In more than one way the Incogs, as they are known for short (their full title is 'Incogniti incognitis', meaning unknown only to the unknown), are a remarkable club, not least for the keen support they are able to rely upon from their membership. They provide the best possible confirmation of the claim that, whatever may be the state of first-class cricket, cricket at the level of the wandering clubs is now flourishing as seldom before.

The Incogs' membership is restricted to no more than 750 playing members in the British Isles, but they seem to have no difficulty in rallying sufficient players for their long list of fixtures.

In 1961 the Incogs played more than 90 games against the Foresters' 87. Moreover, these included the tours for which the Incogs are justly famous: a week each in Oxford and Cambridge, and tours in Denmark, Holland, the West of England and the Channel Islands to round off the season. Members virtually queue for a place on these tours.

Candidates for membership of Incogniti are required to play three full days' cricket to qualify, but in spite of this candidates are forthcoming in abundant numbers and from them, some 45 new members are elected yearly. Like the Foresters, Incogniti are catholic in their intake. Their members are not drawn from any particular part of the country, or from any particular professions, though there may be a slight bias towards the London area and its environs, and, as will subsequently be shown, a bias within the Services to the Navy.

It should, however, be recorded that in addition to the home membership, Incogs have separate clubs in Kenya and in Western Australia. These are affiliated to the parent club and wear the same colours of black, yellow and purple, but for all practical purposes are fully independent bodies in their own area.

The Incogs' list of fixtures is as varied as it is long. They play public schools, regiments, clubs in and around the London area, besides the tours mentioned. I chose to attend their recent encounter with the Royal Navy.

The annual match between Incogniti and the Royal Navy is one of the more important in the calendar of club cricket. This year the weather gave it a special significance, because the two days of May 25 and 26 were the first which could be called near ideal for cricket. Hot sun, a gentle breeze and a cloudless sky made conditions at the United Services' ground at Portsmouth favourable for large scores and rapid scoring.

Yet Incogs, who batted first, made a slow start, although favoured also by some surprisingly uncertain fielding by the Navy. In spite of several dropped catches the score was still in the nineties at lunch time. Throughout the game one feature was the fluctuation in the rate of scoring. In every two-day game there is always the responsibility for the captain to see that his side maintains a scoring rate and reaches a total which will enable him to declare and ensure a fighting finish and thus prevent the match petering out in a draw.

The occasion produced captaincy at its best. Leading the Incogs was the experienced Mike Ainsworth, big and raw-boned, who was for many years captain of the Navy, but is now a master at a well-known preparatory school. Against him was a young marine lieutenant, John Foster, the reigning captain of the Navy XI.

After lunch the Incogs' rate of scoring accelerated rapidly with some big hitting by David Chapman. At one time over 130 runs were scored in the hour. At this stage the problem was when Ainsworth should declare, and it is possible that by going on batting until tea, when the total was 320 for nine wickets, he made an error. Normally in such conditions 250 or thereabouts would be a reasonable total.

Opening for the Navy, Foster and Tordoff took the score to 125 before being separated, and were level pegging, so that when the former reached his 50 Tordoff was on 47. The rate of scoring was slowed down by some accurate bowling by John Smith, himself a Naval lieutenant. Nevertheless, Foster was able to declare in his turn at noon the next day at the score of 182 for four, to which he himself had contributed 73 and Tordoff 53.

Again Incogs started off at a moderate pace, but speeded up later, so that Ainsworth was able to declare at 2.30 p.m. with the score at 133 for four, leaving the Navy to make 272 to win in just under three hours. Against some admirably tight bowling and fielding the Navy were at first pegged down, and at 4 p.m. had scored only 85. Thereafter, with wickets falling regularly to the slow, left-arm bowling of G. M. Hughes-Games, the batsmen began to open up.

Foster again passed the half-century, but was never wholly at ease. The later batsmen hit out hard, but no attempt was made to bustle the field. Perhaps the Navy knew that Ainsworth was too hardened a campaigner. Nevertheless, the score crept up, and though the proceedings in the final stage were so deliberate that they would probably have evoked a charge of gamesmanship in a different class of cricket, the close came with the Navy wanting only four runs to win with their last two batsmen at the wicket. All in all, a remarkably successful finish—even if it ended in a drawn game!

It was notable that the club paid the Royal Navy the compliment of including six active or retired Naval officers in their XI.

12

BOOKISH CRICKET

More or less at the same time as *The Field* became established, literature on cricket started to expand. Since then, it would seem that the game has attracted a larger bibliography than any other outdoor sport. It may surprise some to know that many devotees have always been reluctant participants and even occasional spectators. Their addiction is confined mainly to heady delights from the printed page.

CRICKET LITERATURE

ROBERT ABEL, the Surrey cricketer, is not unknown as a modest writer on cricket, and he now makes a re-appearance with a handbook on the game, for beginners. Besides the usual instructions for making the various hits and for bowling, positions are illustrated from photographs. We are dubious as to the correctness of the figure 'playing back', but some of the statements in the letter-press are beyond cavil. Take, for instance, this one: 'Many a run is made from a good stroke, especially with fast round-arm bowlers.' None can gainsay it; though good strokes sometimes make runs off slow as well as fast bowling. The volume is published by Dean and Co. at 1s. Also at the price of 1s., Messrs Arrowsmith, of Bristol, publish a complete history, by J. N. Pentelow, of the Test matches that have been played with Australia since 1877. The story of each match is told in its proper place, and other statistics are added, the whole forming a compendium which must recommend itself to the cricketing community.

'GREAT BATSMEN'

SIR,—First, may I thank you for the able and appreciative review which appeared in your issue of Oct. 28 of *Great Batsmen: their Methods at a Glance*, and then take very mild and humble exception to one or two points in it? Your reviewer writes:

There are many examples in this book of a complaisant batsman apparently endeavouring to make the stroke required of him from a ball imperfectly suited to it.

Now, this criticism is not really quite fair. There are 600-odd action photographs used in the book, but Mr Beldam and myself discarded nearly twice as many on the score of the very point mentioned above, and kept only those which show the player playing the stroke exactly as he would in an actual match. Even the best players occasionally play a stroke imperfectly, and of this there are many, I venture to say, instructive examples in the book. I do not think that one per cent. of the pictures show players trying to play a given stroke from an unsuitable ball. Indeed, I can only remember one solitary example of this kind, viz., in the case of Mr L. C. H. Palairet. Mr Beldam's method did not consist merely in asking a player to play a given stroke and then trying to bowl, or have bowled, a suitable ball; in many, if not most cases, the batsman played 'the ball as bowled' quite naturally.

Your reviewer picks out the case where Mr W. G. Grace has missed the ball, and characterises our comment that 'correctness of form is one thing and timing the ball, &c., another,' as somewhat vapid. But in writing that comment I had in mind that, either in his own great book on the game or in his chapter in the Badminton volume on cricket, Dr Grace remarks on the curious fact that there are some players whose 'style' is perfect yet who make few runs, while there are others whose 'style' is bad yet who score freely and copiously. There is, to my mind, nothing at all curious in this, because the human mechanism of a stroke may be perfect and yet the stroke may be absolutely bad from imperfect timing or from injudicious application. And I am quite sure that many batsmen do not recognise the fact that 'form' and 'timing' and 'selection', though all three essential to a perfect stroke, are really three separate and independent factors in a stroke. I see no reason to blush for having suggested this point in commenting on the picture in which 'W. G.' made one of his rare mistakes.

Then again your reviewer writes that 'Mr Fry does not appear to realise this very fully.' 'This' being the fact, that many batsmen discard their faults of 'stance' in their 'secondary positions'. Why, sir, there are pages and pages on this particular point! Then, sir, with all deference, I stand by my opinion that the forward defensive stroke is a bad one. Your reviewer says that 'few strokes are made save on a more or less well founded conjecture.' Certainly—in the case of bad players. But the best players do not play on conjecture of any sort; they watch the ball on to the bat and play the ball as they see it. It is precisely this that constitutes the excellence of such players as Ranjitsinhji, V. Trumper, F. S. Jackson, A. C. MacLaren, J. T. Tyldesley, R. E. Foster (and of the late Arthur Shrewsbury). It is this very 'playing on conjecture' that makes the difference between a good and very good batsman.

Then as regards the 'blind spot'. I do not say it does not exist. I say that it has not a separate objective existence, and that it is made by the batsman himself, either because he judges the ball imperfectly or because he stands or moves his feet wrong. I do not hint at the non-existence of 'good length'; I say that if a batsman judges the length of a ball to perfection and works his feet to perfection, forward or back, the difficulty of a good length ball disappears. I dare say my own want of lucidity of exposition misled your reviewer as to my meaning. But that is what I meant to say.

C. B. FRY

[Our correspondent's statement of the methods adopted in securing the photographs must, of course, be accepted as final. The remark to which he takes exception merely conveys the impression produced by certain photographs on the reviewer, and, if Mr Beldam did not dictate to the batsmen the strokes to be made, but left them to play each ball on its merits, we are glad to have elicited this important detail concerning a most interesting production. The second point may be left as a matter of taste and opinion. With regard to the 'secondary position', there was no intention of implying that an insufficient number of pages was given to its discussion, but rather that the badness of the fashionable first position might have been more emphatically explained, since it is one of the things chiefly imitated by inferior players. It is interesting to learn that Mr Fry uses the expression 'to watch the ball on to the bat' as conveying a literal truth and not merely as a vividly descriptive but slightly hyperbolic expression. His belief must of course take into account the velocity of the ball, the duration of an image on the retina, the time required by the nerves to transmit sensations to the brain and impulses to the muscles, &c. It also suggests an inquiry as to the reason why even the select batsmen are sometimes bowled. As for the 'blind spot', it would hardly occur to anybody who understands the meaning of words that it can have anything but a subjective existence or to any cricketer that it will trouble him in the case of a ball whose length he judges perfectly.—ED.]

July 1917

THE AUCTION SALE AT LORD'S

IN the course of the Army match at Lord's last Saturday, there was, for the first time in the history of Lord's, an auction sale on the ground. The sale was originated and organised by Mr E. A. C. Thomson, on behalf of St Dunstan's Hospital for our blind soldiers, and sailors, and many gifts had been received. Mr George Robey was the auctioneer and the chief prices in a sale which realised £90 were as follows

Love's 'Cricket'—two editions, 1740 and 1770—and many other items, given by Mr J. R. Hoare; £20.

Bat with signatures of all the players in the Triangular Tournament of 1912, given by S. F. Barnes; £7.

Bat with which Wilfred Rhodes made 179 for England against Australia, at Melbourne, in 1912, given by Wilfred Rhodes; £5. 10s.

Two one-year's subscriptions to the *Field*, one for an English address and the other for an Australian address, given by the Directors of *The Field*; 11gs.

Bat with signatures of Sir Douglas Haig and other British generals at the front, given by Mrs Samuel, hostess of the War Chest Club; £5.

Two bats with autographs of Dr W. G. Grace, given by Mrs W. G. Grace; 2gs.

Bat with which Robert Abel scored 2000 runs, given by Robert Abel; £2.

Bat used by Victor Trumper in 1904, given by Messrs Wisden; £2.

Bat with autographs of the teams in the first Test match at Sydney in 1911, given by Capt. P. F. Warner; £2.

Framed copy of a drawing by H. Eldridge, entitled 'An Eton Cricketer of 1805', given by Mr E. R. Portal; 2gs.

Boomerang and woomera used by King Cole, a member of the Australian team of aboriginals, given by Mr W. Shepherd; £2. 10s.

Two cricket balls, with autographs of Sir John Jellicoe and Sir William Robertson, given by Messrs John Piggott; £2.

Bat with autographs of leading variety artists, given by Mr George Robey; 3gs.

It has been said that the auction sale which had been arranged on behalf of St Dunstan's was a great disappointment, because it did not produce as much money as had been expected, but it may be doubted whether many of the purchasers really had bargains as is supposed. In all probability the sale would have been more successful if there had not been several drawbacks. It began so long after the advertised time that many would-be purchasers had become tired of waiting and had gone away, and as almost invariably happens in similar circumstances the proceedings had the appearance of being hurried. It would perhaps have been better if the auctioneer's chair had been placed at the foot of the mound with the spectators rising above him. As it was, those who were not in the front rows could not see what was going on, nor could they hear very plainly. In addition the band was playing not very far off, and the frequent applause of the spectators watching the game was not a little disturbing.

August 1922

A little book entitled *School and College Cricket in India* is written by P. N. Polishwalla and published by K. Ida and Co., Bombay. It contains quite a remarkable record of Indian school cricket, and the difficulties of compiling such a book must have been enormous. It is curious that this year's incident at Oxford, when a player was allowed to continue his innings after being given out l.b.w., was anticipated in India in 1910. 'On an appeal by Medical College against one of St Xavier's batsmen the umpire, M. Dady M. Raja, first declared him out, but on the player explaining that he had played the ball before it hit his leg guards, the umpire changed his decision and allowed him to continue his innings. Whereupon the Medical College raised a protest, the decision of which by the Northcote Shield Committee was that the match be replayed. St Xavier's, on the ground that this decision illegally overruled the decision of the umpire, declared their intention of not trying reissues in the match; hence the Medical College was declared to have won the shield.'

A few notes taken from the book show that some remarkable things have been done in connection with school cricket in India. Thus, in 1907 a player named Aubrey Holloway scored 131, which included 30 boundary hits, for St Joseph's against St Paul's. In the last 19 years the Elphinstone College team has travelled 25,000 miles in its tours. Framroz Ardeshir Major took eight wickets for no runs in 1919 for the New High School against the Goculdas Tejpal High School. Owing to the rain one of the Elphinstone College matches lasted for eight days, 'and H. Gimi (now Dr Hirji Gimi) being not out was present in the tent for eight days.'

The book gives some interesting notes about each of the colleges, and quotes a moving appeal from the *Elphinstonian* of Sept. 1918, as follows: 'Lastly we are much in want of sincere cheering-up by the spectators, which goes a long way in enlivening the spirits of the players. There was very little attendance in our tents, and the absence of ladies in our tents in contrast to the fairly good attendance in the opposite ones was conspicuous.'

April 1923

THE PRICE OF A SET OF *WISDEN*

SO many people are anxious to know the market value of a complete set of *Wisden* that there is evidently a widespread desire either to buy or sell the 60 issues of this famous cricket annual. In trying to estimate the market value many difficulties at once present themselves. Very soon after the cricket library of the late Mr T. Padwick, of Redhill, was offered for sale in the nineties a great and undisguised slump came over old cricket books. It was said at the time that Mr Padwick used to give *carte blanche* to a large number of booksellers, with the result that his library contained an undue number of duplicates, which may indirectly have brought about the slump. A few of the rarest books always held their own, but collectors were often able to pick up real treasures at a very small cost indeed. Since the War signs have been frequent that the old cricket book is coming into its own again, and there is very little doubt that, if the wealthy collectors of rare books knew how exceedingly rare some of the earliest cricket books are they would be very glad to give high prices for them. In the meantime booksellers' catalogues are of very little use, as far as cricket books are concerned. A first edition of *Nyren* may be offered at a guinea or at about five pounds, and a second edition of *Felix on the Bat* may be priced at anything from two guineas to four. Everything seems to depend on whether the bookseller knows something about the rarity of certain books. The differences in prices are truly phenomenal—a man may sometimes buy a good crciket book much more cheaply in the West End than he could buy it in Whitechapel. In estimating the value of a set of *Wisden* it seems to me that before very many years have passed by *Wisden* must suffer the fate of a series of bound volumes of the *Art Journal* or the *Graphic*, the old *Gentlemen's Magazine* or *Harper's Magazine*. That is to say they are rapidly beginning to take up so much space on the bookshelves that only the few will eventually be able to spare them the room. All these magazines are so charming in their contents that vast numbers of people would be only too delighted to have them if it were not for their bulk. This year's *Wisden's* is nearly two inches thick, or about the same thickness as the half-yearly volume of *Harper's*, and I should doubt very much whether in 20 years' time many people will be anxiously inquiring as to the price of a set. My own opinion is that at the present time it might be worth while to give £25 for a set as a speculation. But in order that the question may be considered from several points of view, I have asked several gentlemen, who have been past-masters in the art of collecting cricket books, to give their own opinions. Their replies will be found below.

W. A. BETTESWORTH

Mr A. L. Ford writes: As to a set of *Wisden* I am afraid I am not much of a guide, but the general price named in the old book catalogues was £15 15s. So much must depend on the condition of the volumes. If they have the names of former owners written in, or have torn covers and dirty dog's-eared pages, or ink blots, and matches marked, as is so often the case, from my point of view such numbers are worthless and the value of the set materially diminished. Then, again, some have been bound, and those I should look upon as quite ruined and of very small value. The worth of the publication comes in simply because it is a book of reference, the only one in which can be found the county, university, and public school matches. All newspaper writers want to refer to those, and often discussions arise between individuals as to occurrences in old matches, and *Wisden* is wanted for reference. In itself the books have no intrinsic value, and at the book auction sales they realise a mere nothing, say, 2d. a number, and no bookshop would give more to any owner taking a copy for sale. The dealers buy these for an old song and lose nothing by keeping them; so they stack them on their shelves, and if anyone comes along they sell one or two at 10s. or 5s. each, and thus cover the cost of perhaps a whole shelf full, and will not sell otherwise. And especially as to the year 1895, which is as scarce as the *Fred Lillywhite* 1853 the shop would ask 20s. for it. Up to the end of *Scores and Biographies*, which contains all that *Wisden* does, I should not consider the book of any consequential value. *Scores and Biographies* contain the births and deaths of all known players, which helps it much to retain a value. The dealers know nothing as to what price they should name, and if a person goes to buy and inquires the price, they go to a desk and look at Gaston's or Taylor's *Bibliography of Cricket* and see what values are there suggested.

The late Mr Alfred D. Taylor wrote: You ask the price I set upon a complete set of *Wisden*. I suppose, in bibliographical phraseology, a set of *Wisden* should be worth just as much as it will fetch, though professional dealers, with their prevalent profiteering propensities, might rule otherwise. Broadly speaking, old cricket books, like other securities I wot of, have not advanced in price with the times. (Note. This was written at the end of 1920.) Cricket literature is at a discount at the moment, *Wisden* possibly supplying a solitary exception. Why this should be passes my comprehension, for, except from a collector's point of view— those who pay any price for anything they do not already possess— *Wisden* is not nearly so accurate as it should be. Haygarth's Monument, as *Scores and Biographies* has been most aptly described, is, on the other hand, far more valuable as a work of reference to my way of thinking. It is still possible to pick up sets at a reasonable figure, and the scores bring us down to 1878, from which date one can carry on with the less scarce issues of *Wisden*. On the other hand, the Cricketer's Bible, as *Wisden* has been called, teems with errors and omissions. Did not J. B. Payne some 18 years ago attempt to modify the defect when he issued his *Scores and Analyses*, a book devoted to the particulars of some 60 matches not recorded in *Wisden*? It was not until W. H. Knight took up the editorial reins in 1869 that the bowling analyses were published. All this by way of preface. What is a set of *Wisden* worth? Twenty-five years ago a set went begging for many months at £8. Mr Gaston valued it at £10 when he catalogued Mr Padwick's library. Five years later the same set changed hands at £15 10s. When I penned the *Catalogue of Cricket Literature* I fixed the price at 18 guineas. Taking all this as my data, I should be greatly surprised if a set did not realise 20 guineas under the hammer, this figure being my estimate. A local dealer told me some short time since that he could easily dispose of a few sets for £30. What he would be willing to pay is another matter.

The Rev. R. S. Holmes says: It is not easy to answer your question, for the value of cricket books is constantly changing. E. M. Grace's set of *Wisden* fetched £32 in August, 1911. Since then there has been the scarce 1916 issue (the W. G. Memorial), which has been offered at 25/–. A fair price for a complete set would be £35. The proprietors of *Wisden* have put what seems to me a fancy price on several issues.

Mr A. J. Gaston states that in April, 1920, he sold a set of *Wisden* for £18, but that now he should estimate the value at much more than that.

Mr F. S. Ashley-Cooper writes: You ask me to say what, in my opinion, is the value of a complete set of *Wisden's Cricketers' Almanack*. It is difficult to say because, as a thoughtful man once observed, much depends on whether one is a buyer or a seller. For some reason, which is quite a mystery to me, certain volumes have been given quite a fancy value; in fact, many of these I have seen offered for a shilling or even sixpence apiece, whilst they have been priced in printed lists at 1, 2, or 3 guineas. These high prices I never could understand. A short time before the war a dealer offered a complete set for 12/-, and, naturally, found no difficulty in procuring a purchaser. That, of course, was exceptional, but even at a well-attended auction sale in 1916 I saw another set, in the original covers, knocked down for 2½ guineas. There must have been many present who were interested in cricket literature, for almost immediately afterwards there was some spirited bidding for a copy of *Surrey Triumphant or the Kentishman's Defeat*, which brought in 2 guineas. It is, however, generally at private sales, where the seller (often a lady) is apt to accept the first offer received, that the greatest bargains, from the purchaser's point of view, are made. In such circumstances dealers have often obtained for a few shillings what they well know to be worth pounds. It is fairly safe to say that a set of the *Almanack* is worth what it will fetch. Many years ago I received by the same post offers from two dealers, the prices asked being £12 and £40. Some time later I called on the man who required the latter sum and reminded him of his offer, as I was anxious to learn how he arrived at the figure. 'You must be Mr Ashley-Cooper,' he said. I acknowledged the fact and, upon pressing him for an explanation, was told (whilst he thoughtfully scratched his ear), 'Well, you see, sir, I was told that you would buy anything on cricket that was offered you!' This may have been some-what flattering, but it was not altogether satisfactory. The dealer admit-ted that he had sold the set afterwards for 9 guineas, and he appeared perfectly content when he recalled the transaction. Mr R. E. Bush told me that he bought Dr E. M. Grace's set, complete from the com-mencement, for £32, but this, of course, was a series of unusual personal interest, for each volume, bound in green morocco, contained the auto-graph of 'The Little Doctor.' Mr P. F. Warner, too, informed me that he had insured his complete set—given him as a wedding present by Mr Harry Luff—for £50. The latter fact reminds me that a dealer (a great lover of the game) once declared the value to be 50/- if buying, £50 if selling, and £100 if insuring, but of course he did not intend to be taken quite seriously. Taking everything into consideration, I should say that a complete and perfect set of the *Almanack*, in the original covers, whilst not being so valuable as a run of *Britcher*, would be worth £25. It is, however, no easy matter to assess the value of the 60 volumes, when a set is sold at public auction for $2\frac{1}{2}$ guineas during the War, and another, privately in 1922, for £100. It may interest your readers to know that a set of the *Almanack*, complete from the commencement, weighs $38\frac{1}{2}$ lb. and requires 4ft. $9\frac{1}{2}$ in. of shelving accommodation.

May 1923

FIFTY BEST BOOKS ON CRICKET

COMPILED BY ALFRED J. GASTON, author of *Bibliography of Cricket*.

Boxall, T., *Rules and Instructions for Playing at the Game of Cricket*, 1st edition 1803, 92 pp.; 2nd edition 1804, 50 pp. (The rarest books on the game published.)

Nyren, J., *The Young Cricketers' Tutor*, 1833.

Pycroft, J., Rev., *The Cricket Field*, 1851.

Haygarth, A., *Scores and Biographies*, 1744–1878.

Fry, C. B., *Batsmanship*, 1921.

Fry, C. B. and Beldam, G. W., *Great Batsmen, 1905*; *Great Bowlers*, 1906.

Knight, A. E., *The Complete Cricketer*, 1906.

Badminton *Book on Cricket* (three editions, 1888, 1898, 1920).

Wisden's *Cricketers' Almanack*, 1864 to date.

Lillywhite's *Annuals* (Buff, Green and Red Series).

'Felix', *On the Bat*, 1845.

Grace, W. G., Dr, *Cricket*, 1891.

Bettesworth, W. A., *The Walkers of Southgate, 1900; Chats on the Cricket Field*, 1907.

Lucas, E. V., *The Hambledon Men*, 1907; *Willow and Leather*, 1898.

Gale, F., *The Game of Cricket*, 1887; *Echoes from old Cricket Fields*, 1871.

Box, C., *English Game of Cricket*, 1877.

Daft, R., *Kings of Cricket*, 1893.

Caffyn, W., *'71 Not Out'*, 1899.

Ranjitsinhji, K. S., *Jubilee Book of Cricket*, 1897.

Betham, J. D., *Oxford and Cambridge Scores*, 1905.

Hawke, Lord, *W. G. Grace Official Biography*, 1919.

Harris, Lord, *Lords and the M.C.C.*, 1920; *History of the Kent Cricket Club*, 1907; *A Few Short Runs*, 1921.

Alverstone, Lord, *History of Surrey Cricket*, 1902.

Holmes, R. S., *Yorkshire County Cricket*, 1904.

Ashley-Cooper, F. S., *Eton* v. *Harrow*, 1922; *E. M. Grace*, 1916; *Gentlemen* v. *Players*, 1900.

Taylor, A. D., *Annals of Lords*, 1903.

Norman, P., *Annals West Kent Cricket Club*, 1897.

Bedford, W. R. K., *Annals of the Free Foresters*, 1895.

Davey, W., *Canterbury Cricket Week*, 1865.

Luckin, M. W., *South African Cricket*, 1915.

Warner, P. F., *Imperial Cricket*, 1912; *Book of Cricket*, 1922; *My Cricketing Life*, 1921.

Wilson, F. B., *Sporting Pie*, 1922.

Jessop, G. L., *A Cricketer's Log*, 1922.

Cardus, N., *A Cricketer's Book*, 1922.

Pullin, A. W., *Talks with Old English Cricketers*, 1900.

Fitzgerald, R. A., *Wickets in the West*, 1873; *Jerks in from Short Leg*, 1866.

Denison, W., *Sketches of the Players*, 1846.

Laver, F., *Australian Cricketer on Tour*, 1905.

Giffen, G., *With Bat and Ball*, 1898.

Moody, C., *Australian Cricket and Cricketers*, 1894.

Lilley, A. A., *Twenty-four Years of Cricket*, 1912.

Barlow, R. G., *Forty Years of Cricket*, 1910.

Trevor, Philip, Colonel, *Lighter Side of Cricket*, 1906.

Ford, W. J., *Cambridge University Cricket Club*, 1902; *Middlesex County Cricket Club*, 1901.

Ashley-Cooper, F. S., *Middlesex County Cricket Club*, Vol. 2, 1921.

Cricket, A Weekly Record of the Game, 1882–1913.

The Cricket Field (Newspaper), 1892–5.

American Cricketer, 1877 to date.

Gordon, Home, Sir, *Cricket Form at a Glance*, 1902.

Collins, W. E. W., *Old Country Cricketer's Diary*, 1898.
Lester, J. H., *Bat* v. *Ball*, 1900.
May, P. R., *With M.C.C. in New Zealand*, 1908.
Fender, P. G. H., *Defending the Ashes*, 1921.
Patterson, W. S., *Sixty Years of Uppingham Cricket*, 1909.
Waghorn, H. T., *Dawn of Cricket*, 1902.
Hutchinson, Horace, *Cricket (Country Life)*, 1903.
May, J., *Cricket in North Hants*, 1906.
Hall, J. E., *Sixty Years Canadian Cricket*, 1905.
Polishwalla, *Fifty Years' History Indian Cricket*, 1914.
Bone, D. H., *Fifty Years Scottish Cricket*, 1898.
Lawrence, J., *Handbook of Cricket in Ireland*, 1865–1881.

October 1924

THE LATE MR A. L. FORD

OWING to lameness Mr Ford, who has died at Lynmouth in his 81st year, was never able to play in first-class cricket as he would certainly have done but for his handicap, for he was an unusually good wicket-keeper. As it was he played club cricket all over England for nearly 50 years, and in his earlier days often played for Southgate, being a cousin of the Walkers. But he is best known as a collector of cricket books and prints, and there is hardly a known print or book of which he had not a copy. He began his career as a collector in a curious manner. In his school days he had bought F. Lillywhite's *Guide* yearly as it came out, and had kept all the copies. But in 1861 he thought he would like to have a set from the commencement, as well as a clean copy of the 1853 issue, his own copy being much worn. So he went to John Lillywhite's shop in Seymour Street, off Euston Road. He has told in *Cricket* of 1906 what then happened. 'On learning what I wanted, Lillywhite produced a higgle-de-piggledy collection of the remainder of every kind of cricket publication which had been issued during the period of Lillywhite's tenure of the shop. As Lillywhite's was the leading shop in connection with the game, all cricket publications were naturally sent there for sale as they came out. These remainders were tied up in old handkerchiefs (now called sashes), which were at that time printed with pictures of cricket teams, etc., and distributed among the players in the principal matches. The sight of the books at once suggested to me the idea of collecting. So, after satisfying my wants with regard to the *Guide*, I asked the prices of the other items. Lillywhite said, "Oh, they are of no use, and I shall be glad to get rid of them. You can have the lot for 10/-."

Perhaps I need hardly say that I bought them.' Beginning to collect thus early in life, Mr Ford naturally had opportunities for bargains such as are never found now, and many of his most valuable possessions cost only a shilling or two. All the cricket and other valuable books in his library were most beautifully bound, and it will be extremely interesting if they are now sold, to see what prices they bring. Many of his rarest prints—most of them unknown elsewhere—were published in one of the special numbers of *The Field*, and for many years, more especially during the winter months, he constantly contributed invaluable notes to *The Field*, for his knowledge of cricket lore was profound and entirely unusual. He was an excellent raconteur. One of his best stories was concerned with B. J. T. Bosanquet's father, who, he said, was the real inventor of the 'googlie'. 'Once when I was keeping wicket for Enfield at Stratford, Essex, in a match against the Great Eastern Railway,' he said, 'I had occasion to stump three men from successive balls off the elder Bosanquet's bowling, and the last of the three batsmen, on being given out, turned round and said. "Well, I'm ——. First chap said balls came from leg: second said they come from t'other way; and I'm —— if this one didn't come straight!"' In 1885 Mr Ford published an *Index to Scores and Biographies*, vol. 1–13, and in 1897, under the signature of 'An Old Cricketer', he wrote *Curiosities of Cricket, from the earliest Record to the Present Time*, but only 25 copies were printed.

August 1924

So many matches have been ruined by rain this season that if Longfellow had been alive and visiting England he would probably have written:

> When I look from my window at night,
> And the street down below is all bright,
>   All gleaming and glist'ning with rain,
> I know that the season for cricket,
> The flannelled fools at the wicket,
>   Is come with the summer again.

August 1935

CRICKETER'S AUGUST

With August comes full yield;
    Then Cricket wears a mantle overgrown,
And counties in the field
    Lose gloss, as though they wished the season
      flown.

But August bears a flood
    Of boys that flee dead languages and kings.
Spring still is in their blood,
    And bids them throng to watch heroic things.

The holiday they make
    Should gladden Cricket, quicken its old heart.
And bid its champions wake
    To play, with zest, a memorable part.

Then these, when they are old,
    Shall bless their youth, be glad they were alive.
Make one more 'age of gold,'
    And start their tales: 'In nineteen thirty-
      five....'

G. D. MARTINEAU

July 1945

MY CRICKET SCRAP BOOKS

BY A. S. DIXON

IT was in 1893 that I began my scrap books. The visit of an Australian cricket team aroused my youthful enthusiasm, especially as *Punch* welcomed them with an alphabet. It began something like this:

    A is Australia the land of their birth
    B Bruce and Bannerman, batsmen of worth
    C is for Coningham, more than a learner
    D is the demon, once Spofforth, now Turner.

There were, moreover, in those days two weekly papers throughout the summer wholly devoted to cricket. Of these my favourite was *The Cricket-Field*, because in each issue there was an interview with some famous cricketer together with his portrait, and among the number were such boyhood heroes as Gregor MacGregor, J. J. Ferris and Captain Wynyard. (I hoped that these 'Chats on the Cricket Field' would be published in book form, for certainly they would have been assured of the sale of one copy.) In this way the first album was born, and the first scrap was an oval picture containing the portraits of the players of all the first-class counties—there were then only nine of them—and of the universities; about 130 portraits in all. To give a name to each of these was beyond my powers—some like 'W. G.' and 'Ranji' were obvious—but in course of time I was able to distinguish the majority.

From then onwards the album became my hobby. Any small store of pocket-money, supplemented occasionally by a tip from some kindly relative, was devoted to the purchase of some penny, or even twopenny, paper that gave the photograph of one of the county teams or of some famous cricketer. Like Topsy, the collection of pictures grew; and it was a proud moment when the last picture was pasted in, and I embarked on album No. 2. This contained two special features. In 1897, A. E. Stoddart took his second team to Australia, and Jim Phillips travelled with them. 'Jim' had been commissioned by some sports paper to write weekly letters and to take photographs. Jim Phillips may or may not have been a good umpire—Sir Stanley Jackson and C. B. Fry seem to agree on this point—but he was not an artist with the camera. Nevertheless, I bought the paper and added his pictures to my collection.

At the same time there happened to be in my house at school one of the senior boys who came from Sydney. Every week he received a copy of some Sydney paper, which devoted considerable space to the doings of Stoddart's men and illustrated its accounts of the matches. As I found that these papers found their way to the W.P.B., I nervously asked if I might have them and, permission being graciously granted— he was a very senior boy and a member of the VIII—I rescued them, cut out the pictures and in this way acquired photographs of such men as Victor Trumper and M. A. Noble, then embarking upon their great careers.

About this time the tele-photographic lens made its appearance and at once effected a vast improvement in the cricket pictures of the illustrated papers. At the same time, too, I became less dependent upon the occasional tip, and even a sixpenny paper was not beyond my means. It was actually, I think, in 1899 that the cinematograph was introduced into the cricket field—I well remember it at Sheffield in the one Test Match played there—and one could see a photograph bearing the title 'Clem Hill completes his 50 and celebrates it thus'; and clearly recognise the players therein. In fact, the camera more and more invaded the cricket world, and photographs of teams entering and leaving the field and of batsmen going out to start the innings were frequently to be seen. One of these still lives in my memory. It shows A. C. Maclaren and L. C. H. Palairet leaving the pavilion at Old Trafford to start the last innings of that never-to-be forgotten fourth Test Match in 1902.

By 1914 I had completed my third volume, and the fourth was well on its way. I had, I think, the photographs of every first-class cricketer, English, Australian and South African, together with two or even more photographs of each of the county teams, various 'action' pictures, and what I have heard described by the vendor at Lords, the 'characteriskit' sketches of that clever artist 'Rip'. And then came the war, and for four years there was no first-class cricket, and there were no more pictures.

During those four years my guardian was moved to another 'living', and, when I next arrived at my new 'home', I was told in response to my inquiry that my albums had been thrown away. 'Oh', said my 'aunt', 'we didn't know you wanted those old scrap books, we thought they were just rubbish.' But for some reason, album four had been overlooked, and I have it still. I wish that I could think it had the value of the Sibylline books. This is the story in brief of my scrap books. I should like to have given it a happier ending.

April 1953

CAUGHT OUT

AN anthology should not only consist of the choicest passages written upon the subject with which it deals, it should also include quaint and sometimes challenging statements. These thoughts were inspired by a passage in Mr Gerald Brodribb's anthology of cricket verse. Who, for example, could resist analysis of the following lines:—

> No German, Frenchman, or Fiji, will ever master
> cricket, sir,
> Because they haven't got the pluck to stand before
> the wicket, sir.

Mr Brodribb, let it be said at once, makes prompt apology to the Fijians, who are indeed born cricketers. Particularly is this true of their fielding. A few months ago, the world of bat and ball applauded Warrant Officer Pedro Kubu, of the Fijian Regiment, for catching a swallow when playing in Malaya. The feat was no accident, for the swallow had circled round him three times, and the fieldsman clearly intended to demonstrate that he was no bird's fool.

Fijian cricketing prowess is nothing new. As soon as The Royal Navy introduced the game into the islands, it was taken up with enthusiasm, and tribes would challenge one another for a prize of ten pigs. If, then, the verses are so much at fault over one of the principals, we should test their accuracy regarding the others. Has no German ever excelled at cricket? Apparently not. It seems that only those who had close ties with England, like our early Hanoverian princes, ever took the game up with success. C. B. Fry once asked Hitler why the Germans did not play cricket, and received the strange reply, 'there are too many regulations.'

There have been attempts to introduce cricket into France. The Laws have been translated into French, there is a French cricketing guide (written by a Scot), and, during the sixties, the Empress Eugénie interested herself in the Paris Cricket Club. France, however, has never produced a notable cricketer, even though members of Huguenot families (Bosanquet for example) have given a new twist to the game. A French nobleman could not understand why well-born Englishmen toiled after the ball, instead of deputing menials for the task, and the Emperor Napoleon III, showing less comprehension than his wife, sent his servant to an Englishman who had made a spectacular catch, requesting that the performance should be repeated.

Yet, if the anonymous dogmatist has so far proved correct on two points, we should still be warned not to accept rash generalisations about a game which is truly British in being unpredictable. The spirit of cricket is perhaps more like Puck than King Willow. Make any unguarded pronouncement on the game—in prose or in verse—and you can almost hear the impish laughter as your ideas go somersaulting like an uprooted stump.

September 1967

CLOSE OF PLAY

How shall we live, now that the summer's ended,
And bat and ball (too soon!) are put aside,
And all our cricket deeds and dreams have blended—
The hit for six, the champion bowled for none,
The match we planned to win and never won?
Only in green-winged memory they abide.

How shall we live, who love our loveliest game
With such bright ardour that when stumps are drawn
We talk into the twilight, always the same
Old talk with laughter rounding off each tale,
Laughter of friends across a pint of ale
In the blue shade of the pavilion.

For the last time a batsman's out; the day
Like the drained glass and the dear sundown field
Is empty: what instead of summer's play
Can occupy these darkling months ere spring
Hails Willow once again the crownèd king?
How shall we live so life may not be chilled?

Well, what's a crimson hearth for, and the lamp
Of winter nights, and these plump yellow books
That cherish Wisden's soul and bear his stamp—
Time's ever-changing, unalterable score-board,
Thick-clustered with a thousand names adored:
Half the game's magic in their very looks.

And when we've learnt those almanacks by heart,
And shared with Nyren ... Cardus ... the distant thrill
That cannot fade since they have had their part,
We'll trudge wet streets through fog and mire
And praise our heroes by the club-room fire:
O do not doubt, the game will hold us still.

THOMAS MOULT